SUPERMAN THE MAN OF STEEL

BELIEVE

Collection Cover Art by Kevin Nowlan

SUPERMAN Created by
JERRY SIEGEL and JOE SHUSTER.
By Special Arrangement
with the Jerry Siegel Family.

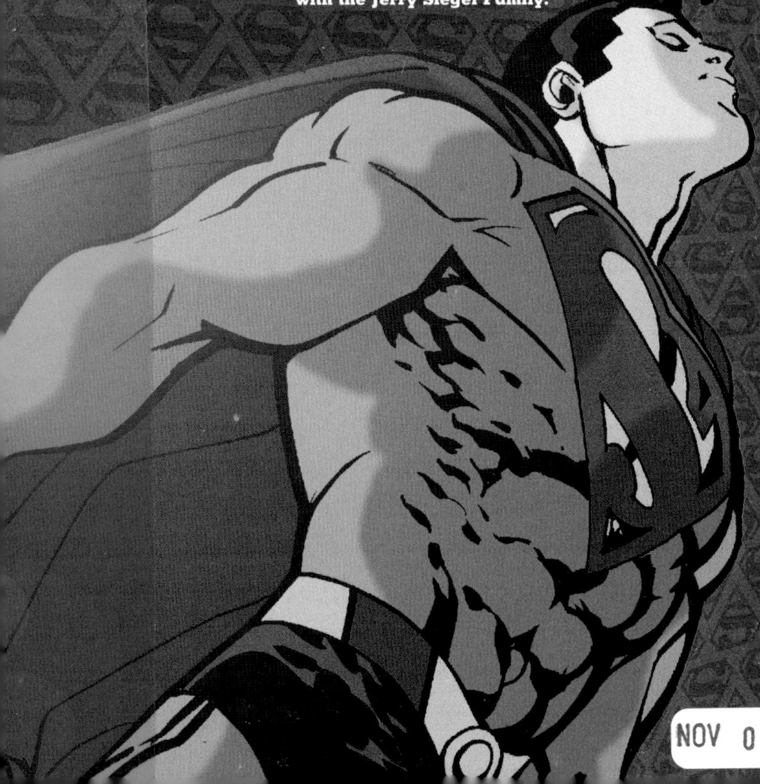

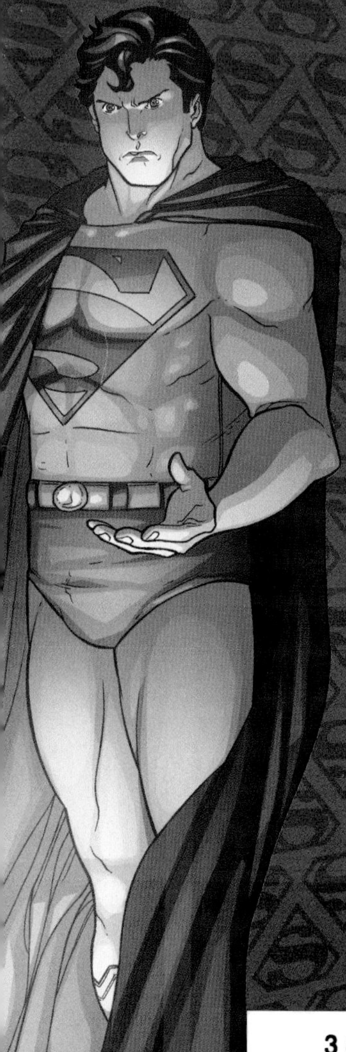

Lysa Hawkins Tom Palmer, Jr. Casey Seijas
Associate Editors – Original Series
Eddie Berganza Will Dennis Maureen McTigue Sean Ryan
Editors – Original Series
Rachel Pinnelas Editor
Robbin Brosterman Design Director – Books
Louis Prandi Publication Design

Bob Harras Senior VP – Editor-in-Chief, DC Comics

Diane Nelson President
Dan DiDio and Jim Lee Co-Publishers
Geoff Johns Chief Creative Officer
John Rood Executive VP – Sales, Marketing & Business Development
Amy Genkins Senior VP – Business & Legal Affairs
Nairi Gardiner Senior VP – Finance
Jeff Boison VP – Publishing Planning
Mark Chiarello VP – Art Direction & Design
John Cunningham VP – Marketing
Terri Cunningham VP – Editorial Administration
Alison Gill Senior VP – Manufacturing & Operations
Hank Kanalz Senior VP – Vertigo & Integrated Publishing
Jay Kogan VP – Business & Legal Affairs, Publishing
Jack Mahan VP – Business Affairs, Talent
Nick Napolitano VP – Manufacturing Administration
Sue Pohja VP – Book Sales
Courtney Simmons Senior VP – Publicity
Bob Wayne Senior VP – Sales

SUPERMAN: THE MAN OF STEEL: BELIEVE

DC Comics, 1700 Broadway, New York, NY 10019
A Warner Bros. Entertainment Company.
Printed by RR Donnelley, Crawfordsville, IN. 9/27/13.
ISBN: 978-1-4012-4705-8

Library of Congress Cataloging-in-Publication Data

Superman, The Man of Steel : Believe.
pages cm.
"Originally published in single magazine form as ADVENTURES OF SUPERMAN DIGITAL CHAPTER 1, ADVENTURES OF SUPERMAN 623, ACTION COMICS 810, 0, SUPERMAN 185, SUPERMAN: FOR TOMORROW, SUPERMAN 80-PAGE GIANT 1, 2."
ISBN 978-1-4012-4705-8
1. Graphic novels. I. Title: Believe.
PN6728.S9S944 2013
741.5'973—dc23
2013027736

SUSTAINABLE FORESTRY INITIATIVE
Certified Chain of Custody
At Least 20% Certified Forest Content
www.sfiprogram.org
SFI-01042
APPLIES TO TEXT STOCK ONLY

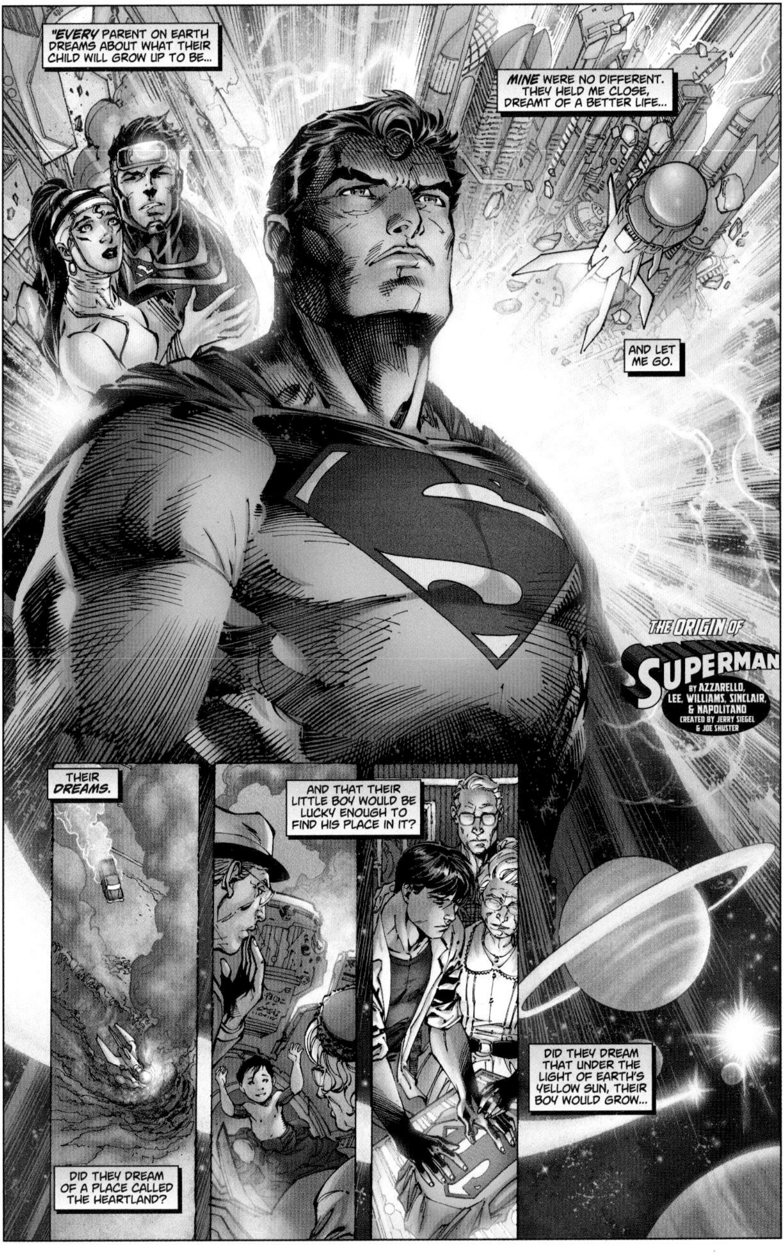
"EVERY PARENT ON EARTH DREAMS ABOUT WHAT THEIR CHILD WILL GROW UP TO BE...
MINE WERE NO DIFFERENT. THEY HELD ME CLOSE, DREAMT OF A BETTER LIFE...
AND LET ME GO.
THE ORIGIN OF
SUPERMAN
BY AZZARELLO, LEE, WILLIAMS, SINCLAIR, & NAPOLITANO
CREATED BY JERRY SIEGEL & JOE SHUSTER
THEIR DREAMS.
DID THEY DREAM OF A PLACE CALLED THE HEARTLAND?
AND THAT THEIR LITTLE BOY WOULD BE LUCKY ENOUGH TO FIND HIS PLACE IN IT?
DID THEY DREAM THAT UNDER THE LIGHT OF EARTH'S YELLOW SUN, THEIR BOY WOULD GROW...

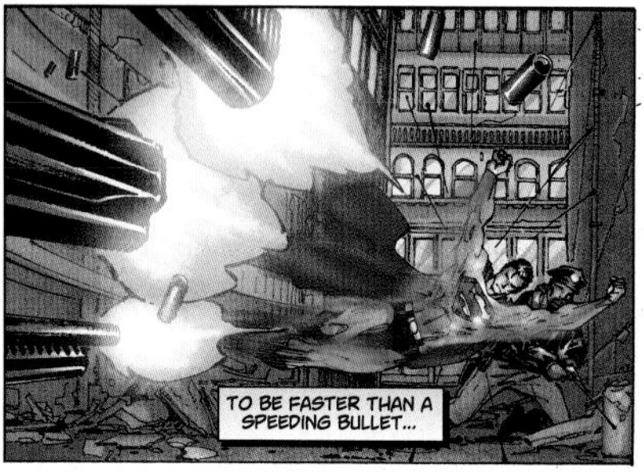

TO BE FASTER THAN A SPEEDING BULLET...

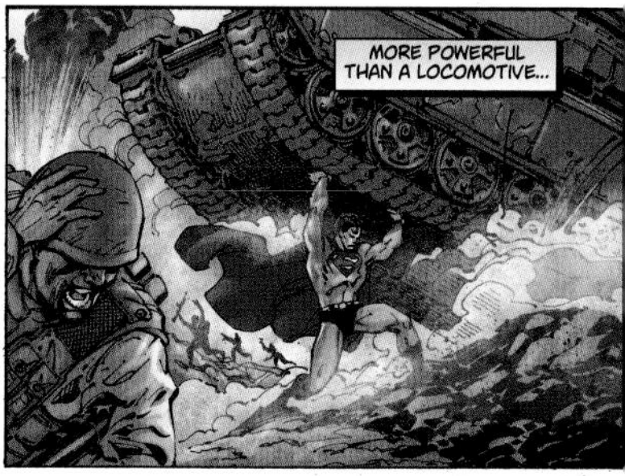

MORE POWERFUL THAN A LOCOMOTIVE...

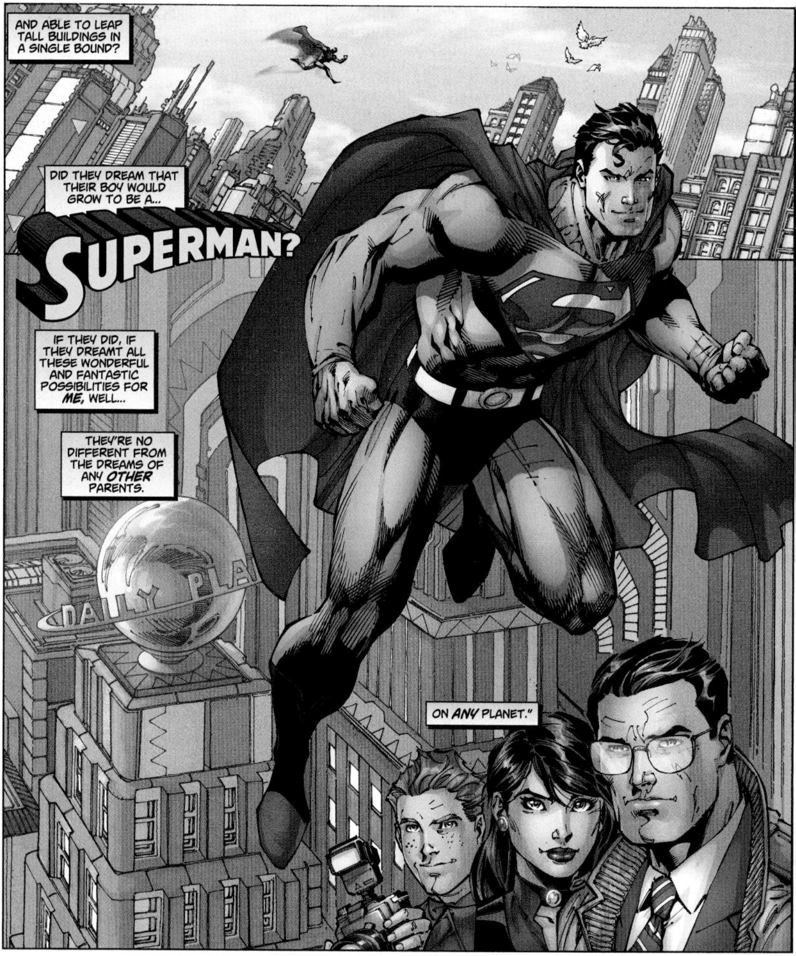

AND ABLE TO LEAP TALL BUILDINGS IN A SINGLE BOUND?
DID THEY DREAM THAT THEIR BOY WOULD GROW TO BE A...
SUPERMAN?
IF THEY DID, IF THEY DREAMT ALL THESE WONDERFUL AND FANTASTIC POSSIBILITIES FOR ME, WELL...
THEY'RE NO DIFFERENT FROM THE DREAMS OF ANY OTHER PARENTS.
ON ANY PLANET."

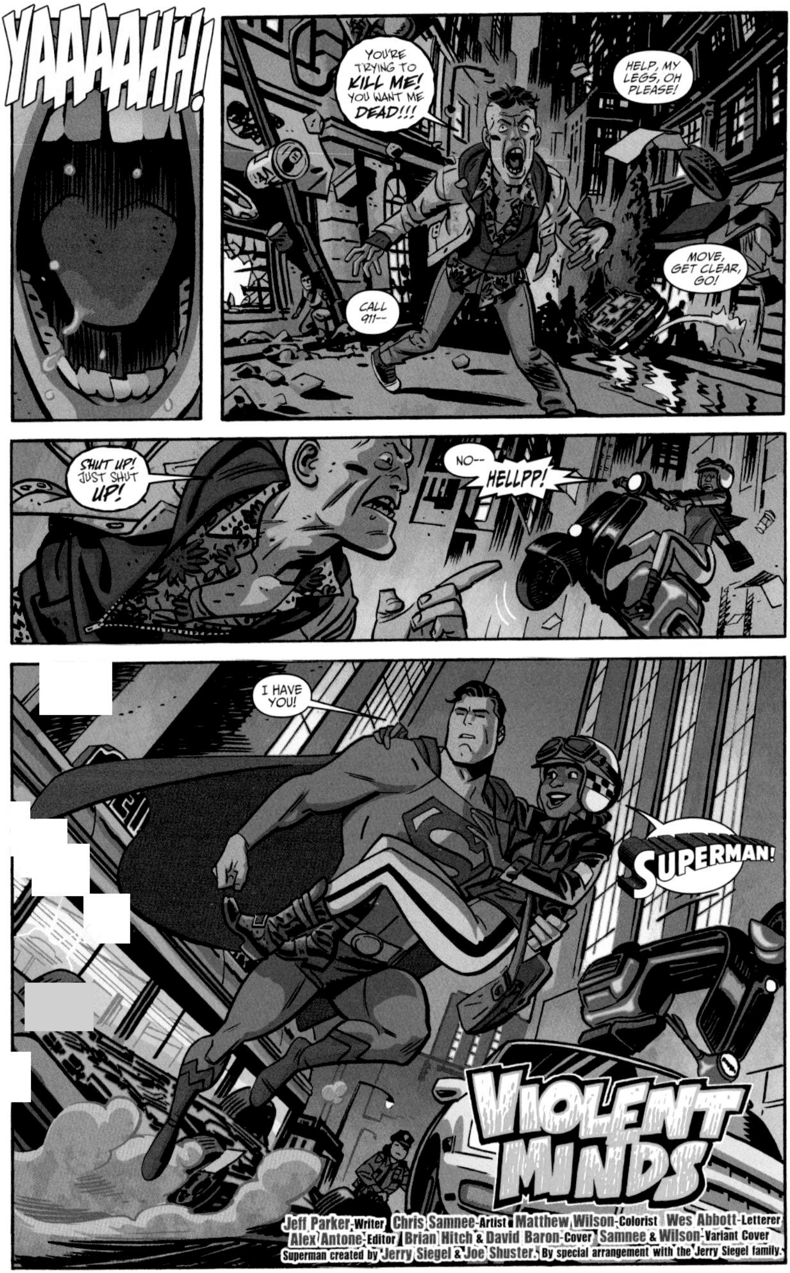
YAAAAHH!
YOU'RE TRYING TO KILL ME! YOU WANT ME DEAD!!!
HELP, MY LEGS, OH PLEASE!
MOVE, GET CLEAR, GO!
CALL 911--
SHUT UP! JUST SHUT UP!
NO-- HELLPP!
I HAVE YOU!
SUPERMAN!
VIOLENT MINDS
Jeff Parker-Writer Chris Samnee-Artist Matthew Wilson-Colorist Wes Abbott-Letterer
Alex Antone-Editor Brian Hitch & David Baron-Cover Samnee & Wilson-Variant Cover
Superman created by Jerry Siegel & Joe Shuster. By special arrangement with the Jerry Siegel family.

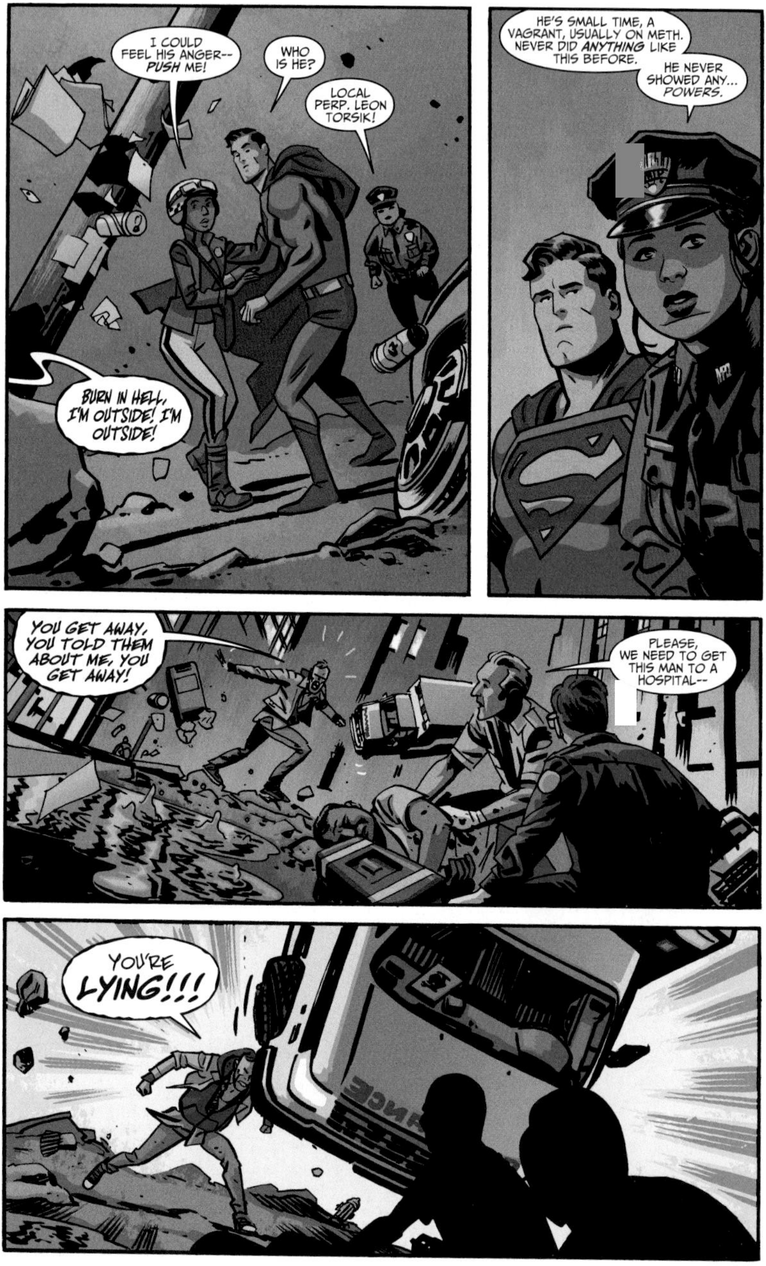
I COULD FEEL HIS ANGER-- PUSH ME!
WHO IS HE?
LOCAL PERP. LEON TORSIK!
BURN IN HELL, I'M OUTSIDE! I'M OUTSIDE!
HE'S SMALL TIME, A VAGRANT, USUALLY ON METH. NEVER DID ANYTHING LIKE THIS BEFORE.
HE NEVER SHOWED ANY... POWERS.
YOU GET AWAY, YOU TOLD THEM ABOUT ME, YOU GET AWAY!
PLEASE, WE NEED TO GET THIS MAN TO A HOSPITAL--
YOU'RE LYING!!!

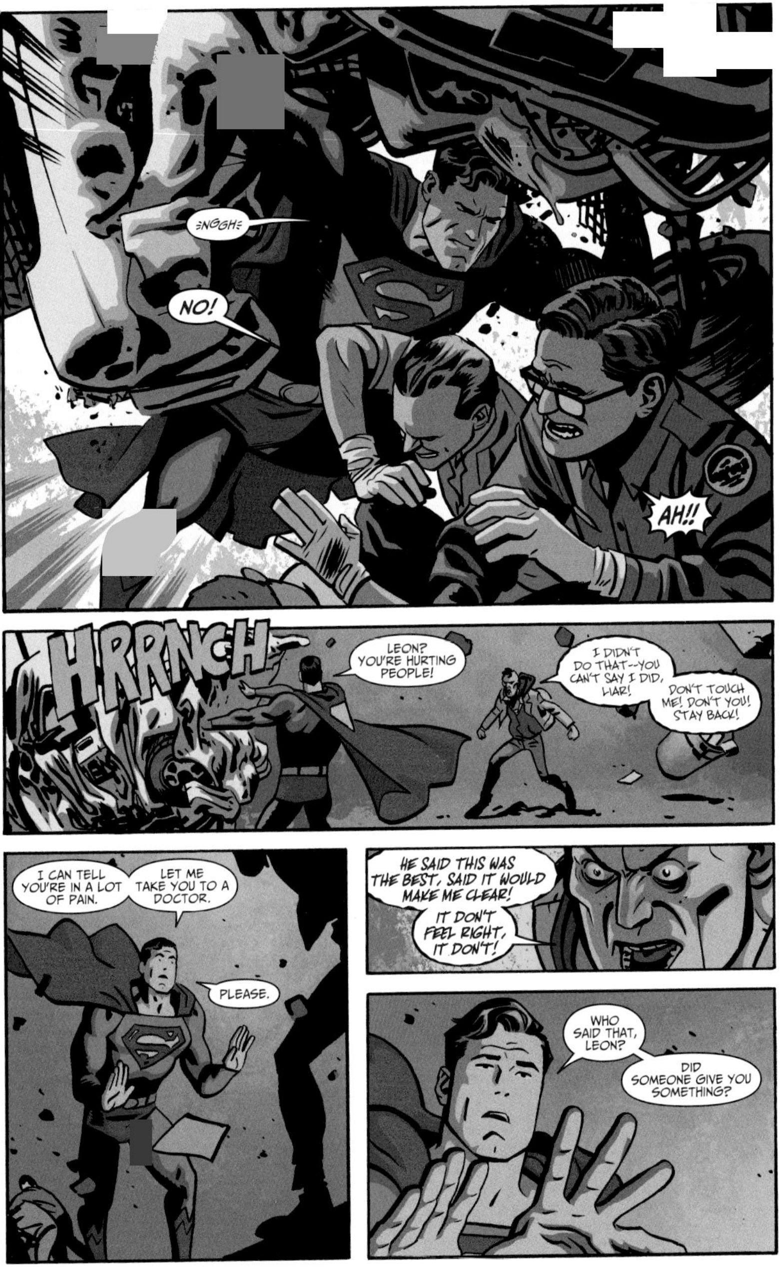
NGGH
NO!
AH!!
HRRNCH
LEON? YOU'RE HURTING PEOPLE!
I DIDN'T DO THAT--YOU CAN'T SAY I DID, LIAR!
DON'T TOUCH ME! DON'T YOU! STAY BACK!
I CAN TELL YOU'RE IN A LOT OF PAIN.
LET ME TAKE YOU TO A DOCTOR.
PLEASE.
HE SAID THIS WAS THE BEST, SAID IT WOULD MAKE ME CLEAR!
IT DON'T FEEL RIGHT, IT DON'T!
WHO SAID THAT, LEON?
DID SOMEONE GIVE YOU SOMETHING?

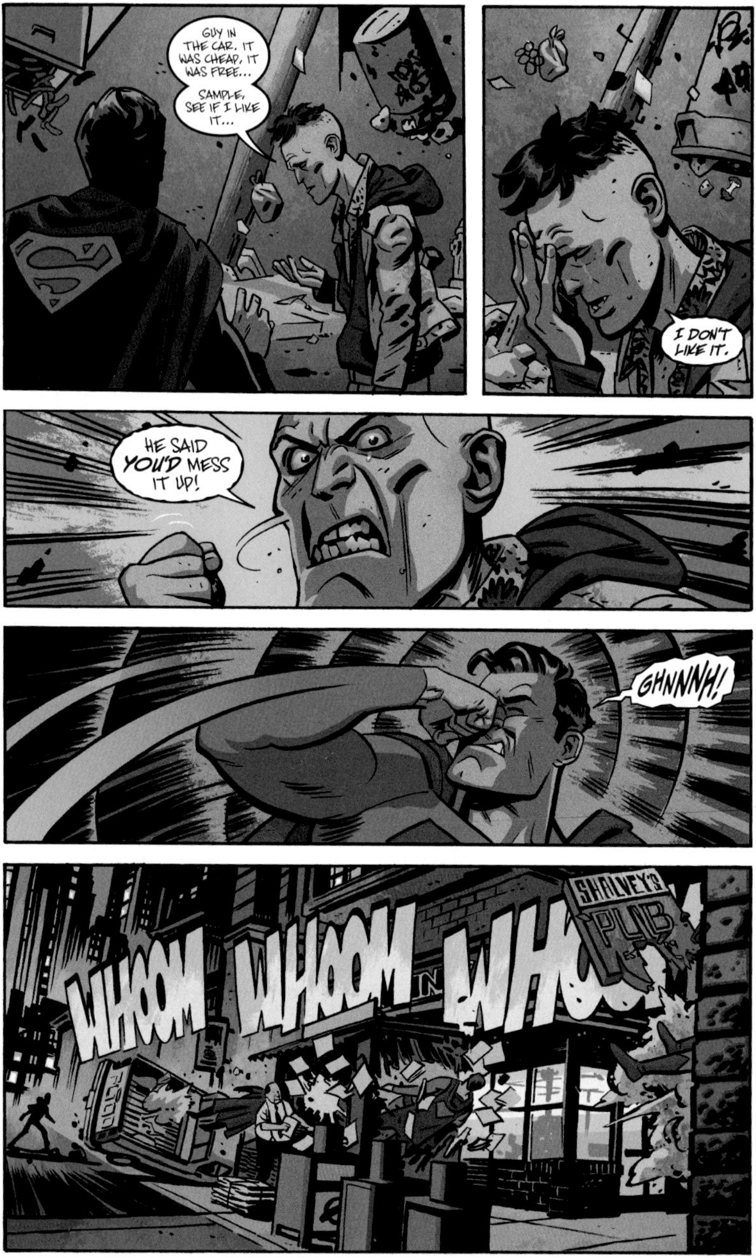
GUY IN THE CAR. IT WAS CHEAP, IT WAS FREE...
SAMPLE, SEE IF I LIKE IT...
I DON'T LIKE IT.
HE SAID YOU'D MESS IT UP!
GHNNNH!
WHOOM WHOOM
SHALVEY'S PUB

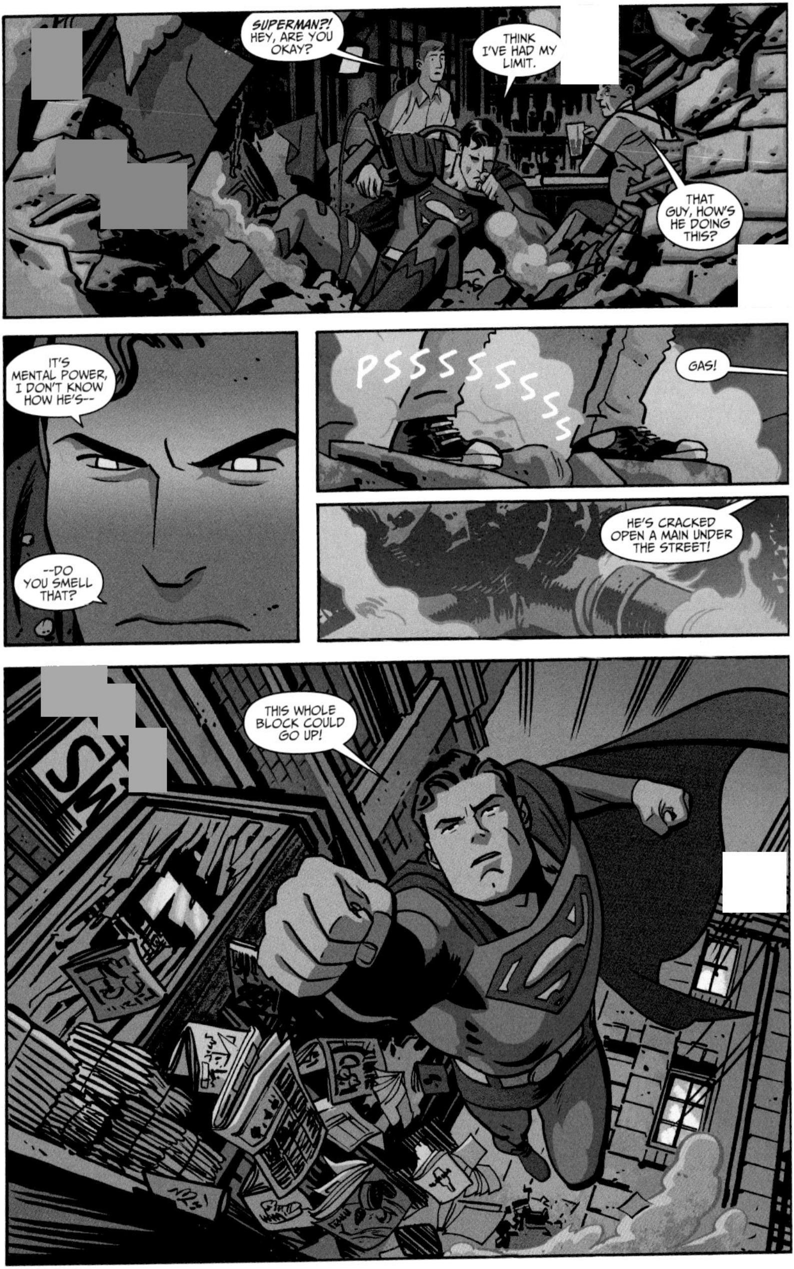
SUPERMAN?! HEY, ARE YOU OKAY?
THINK I'VE HAD MY LIMIT.
THAT GUY, HOW'S HE DOING THIS?
IT'S MENTAL POWER, I DON'T KNOW HOW HE'S--
--DO YOU SMELL THAT?
PSSSSSSSSS
GAS!
HE'S CRACKED OPEN A MAIN UNDER THE STREET!
THIS WHOLE BLOCK COULD GO UP!

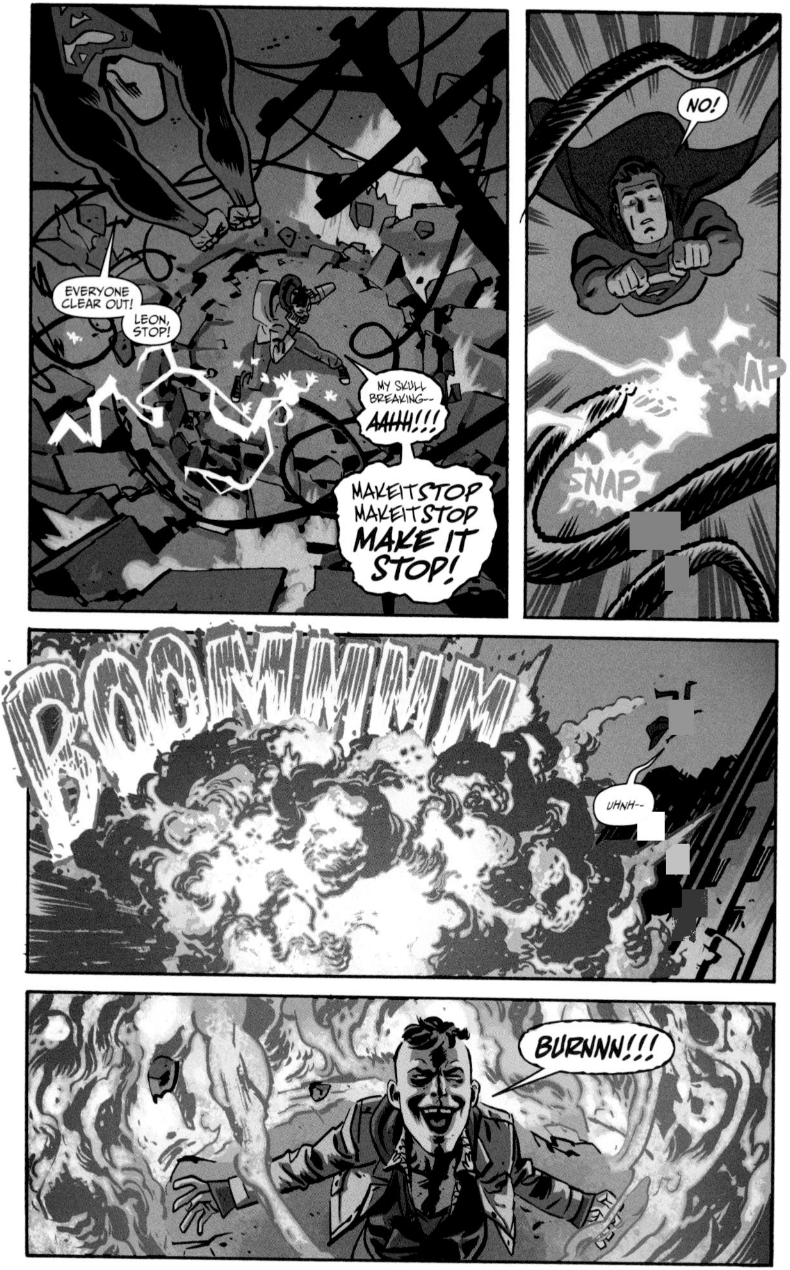
EVERYONE CLEAR OUT!
LEON, STOP!
MY SKULL BREAKING-- AAHH!!!
MAKEITSTOP MAKEITSTOP MAKE IT STOP!
NO!
SNAP
SNAP
BOOMMMM
UHNH--
BURNNN!!!

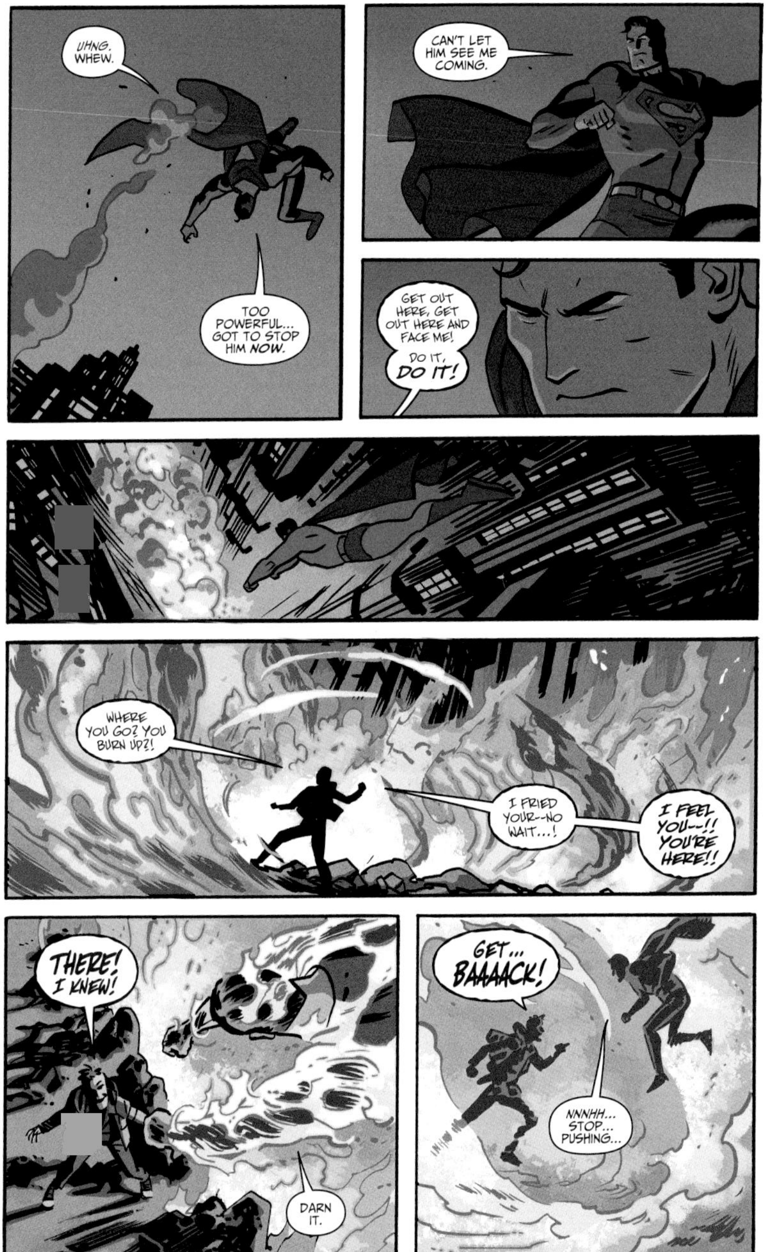
UHNG. WHEW.
TOO POWERFUL... GOT TO STOP HIM NOW.
CAN'T LET HIM SEE ME COMING.
GET OUT HERE, GET OUT HERE AND FACE ME!
DO IT, DO IT!
WHERE YOU GO? YOU BURN UP?!
I FRIED YOUR--NO WAIT...!
I FEEL YOU--!! YOU'RE HERE!!
THERE! I KNEW!
DARN IT.
GET... BAAAACK!
NNNHH... STOP... PUSHING...

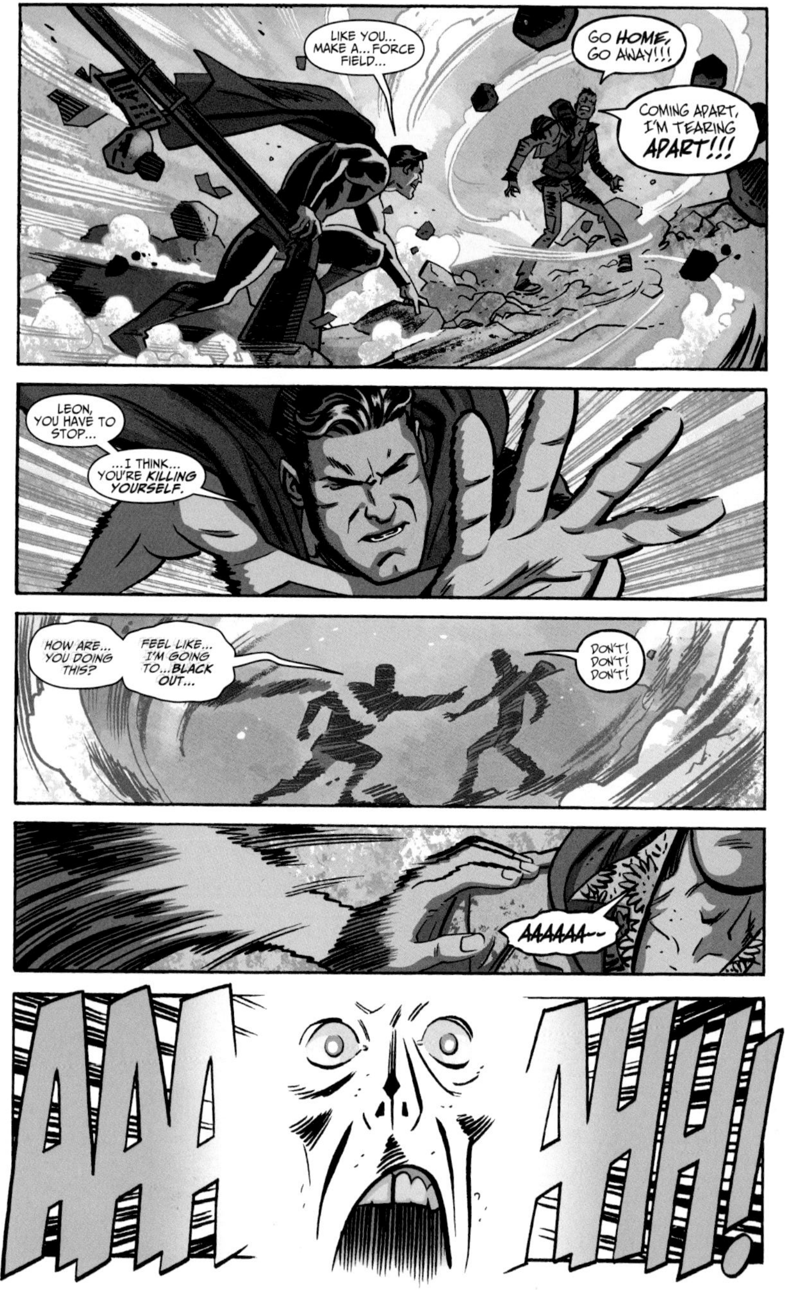
LIKE YOU... MAKE A...FORCE FIELD...
GO HOME, GO AWAY!!!
COMING APART, I'M TEARING APART!!!
LEON, YOU HAVE TO STOP...
...I THINK... YOU'RE KILLING YOURSELF.
HOW ARE... YOU DOING THIS?
FEEL LIKE... I'M GOING TO...BLACK OUT...
DON'T! DON'T! DON'T!
AAAAAA--
AAAHH!

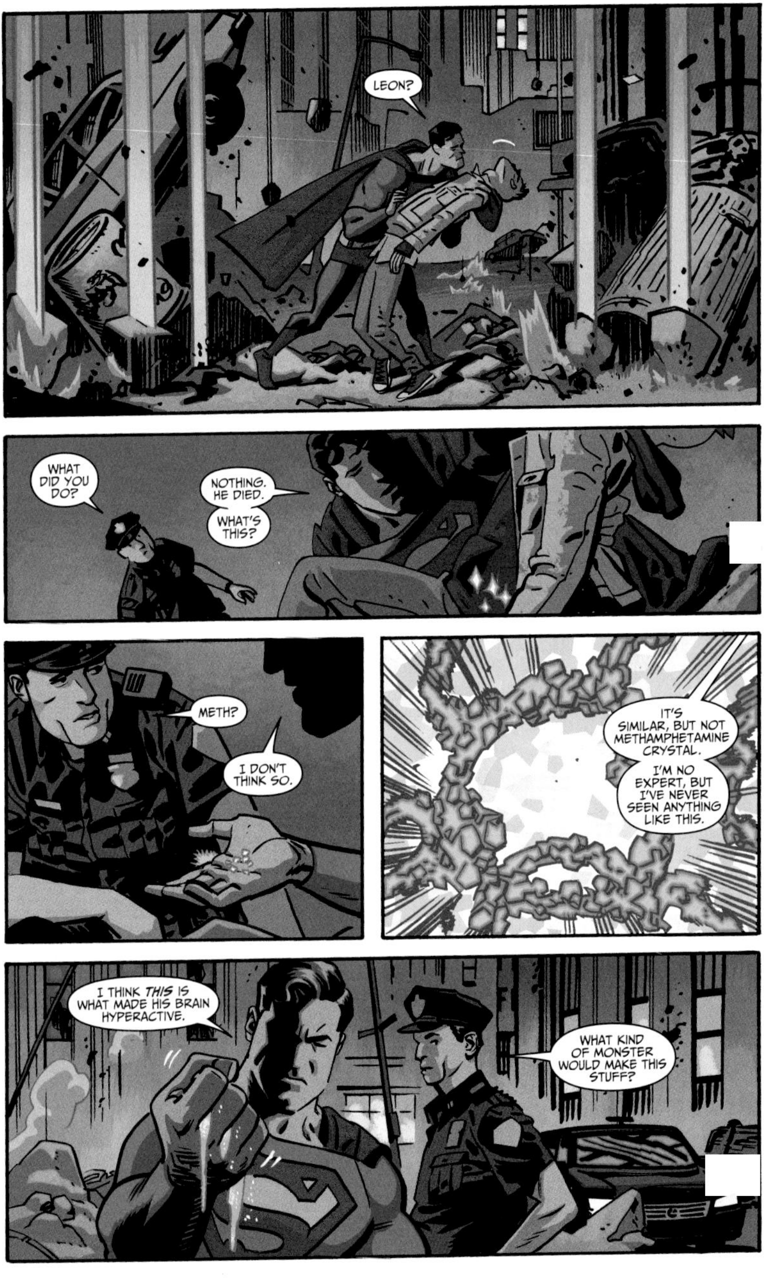

LEON?
WHAT DID YOU DO?
NOTHING. HE DIED.
WHAT'S THIS?
METH?
I DON'T THINK SO.
IT'S SIMILAR, BUT NOT METHAMPHETAMINE CRYSTAL.
I'M NO EXPERT, BUT I'VE NEVER SEEN ANYTHING LIKE THIS.
I THINK *THIS* IS WHAT MADE HIS BRAIN HYPERACTIVE.
WHAT KIND OF MONSTER WOULD MAKE THIS STUFF?

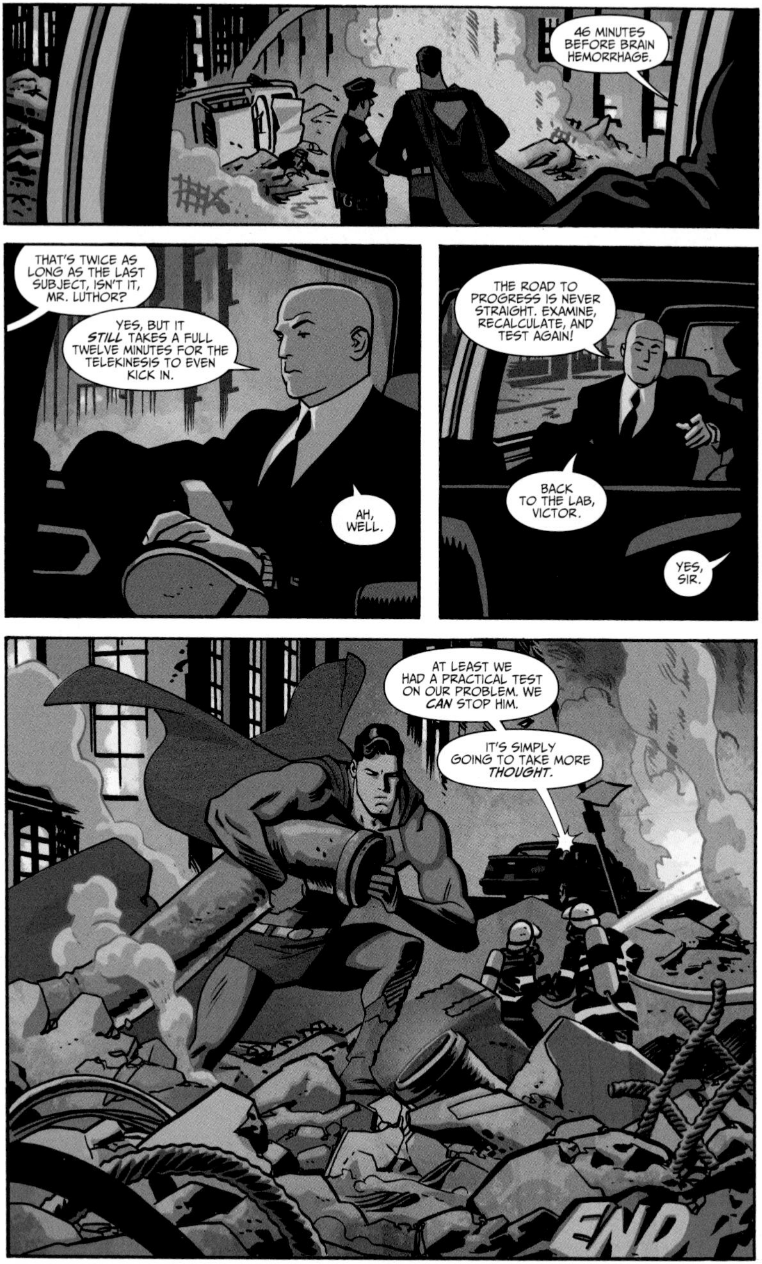
46 MINUTES BEFORE BRAIN HEMORRHAGE.
THAT'S TWICE AS LONG AS THE LAST SUBJECT, ISN'T IT, MR. LUTHOR?
YES, BUT IT *STILL* TAKES A FULL TWELVE MINUTES FOR THE TELEKINESIS TO EVEN KICK IN.
AH, WELL.
THE ROAD TO PROGRESS IS NEVER STRAIGHT. EXAMINE, RECALCULATE, AND TEST AGAIN!
BACK TO THE LAB, VICTOR.
YES, SIR.
AT LEAST WE HAD A PRACTICAL TEST ON OUR PROBLEM. WE *CAN* STOP HIM.
IT'S SIMPLY GOING TO TAKE MORE *THOUGHT.*
END

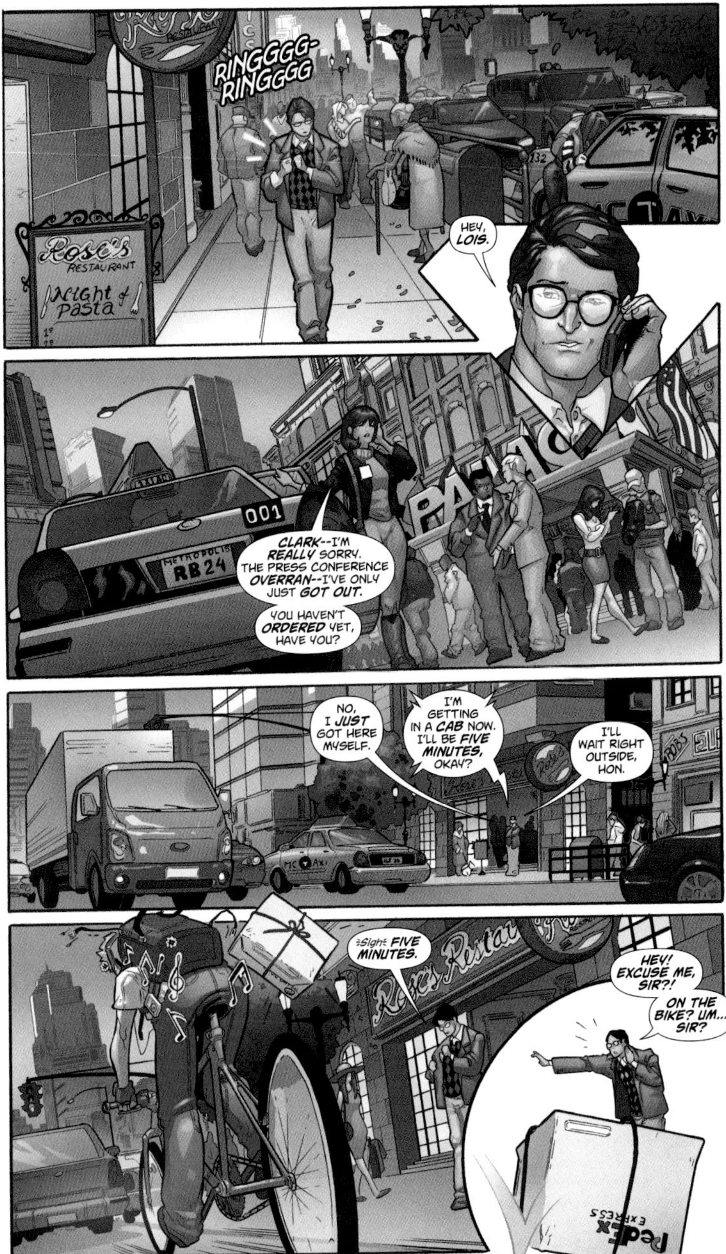
RINGGGG-RINGGGG
Rose's RESTAURANT Night of Pasta
HEY, LOIS.
001
METROPOLIS RB 24
CLARK--I'M REALLY SORRY. THE PRESS CONFERENCE OVERRAN--I'VE ONLY JUST GOT OUT.
YOU HAVEN'T ORDERED YET, HAVE YOU?
NO, I JUST GOT HERE MYSELF.
I'M GETTING IN A CAB NOW. I'LL BE FIVE MINUTES, OKAY?
I'LL WAIT RIGHT OUTSIDE, HON.
Sigh FIVE MINUTES.
Rose's Restau
HEY! EXCUSE ME, SIR?!
ON THE BIKE? UM... SIR?
RedEx EXPRESS

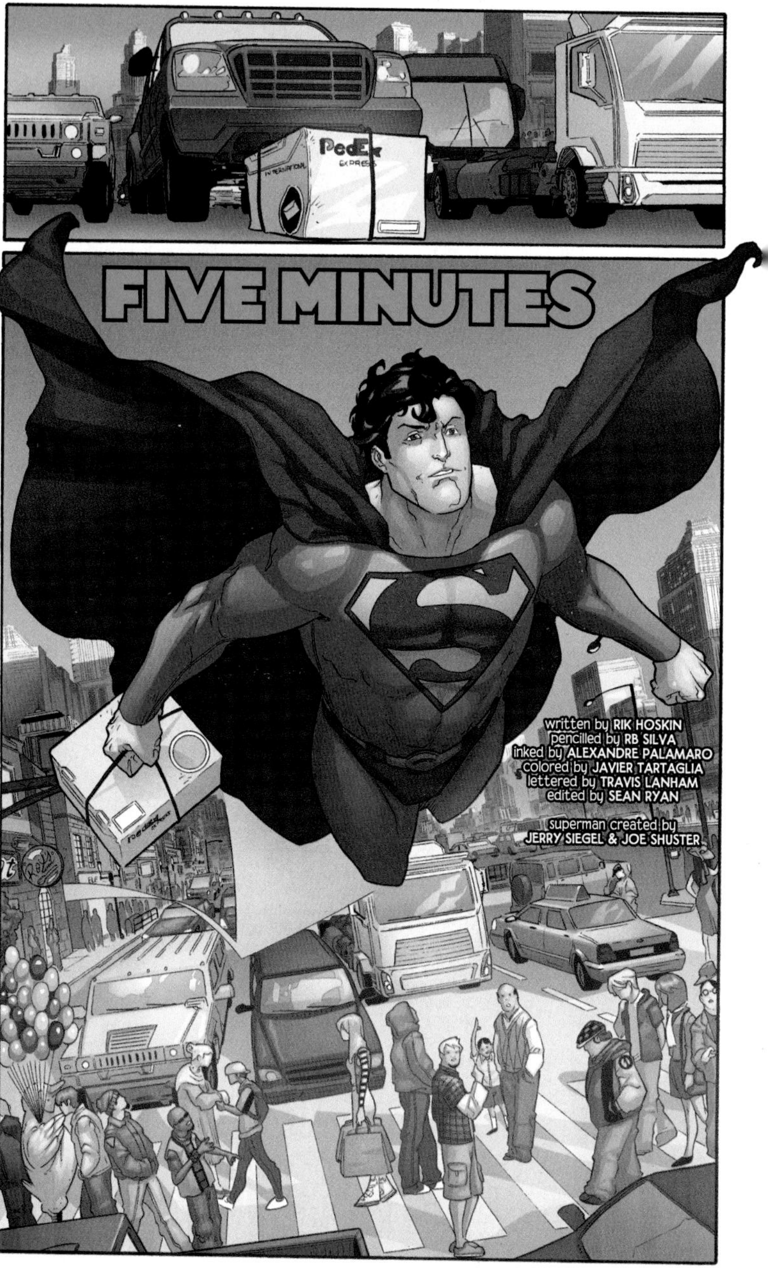
FedEx
EXPRESS
INTERNATIONAL
FIVE MINUTES
written by RIK HOSKIN
pencilled by RB SILVA
inked by ALEXANDRE PALAMARO
colored by JAVIER TARTAGLIA
lettered by TRAVIS LANHAM
edited by SEAN RYAN
superman created by
JERRY SIEGEL & JOE SHUSTER

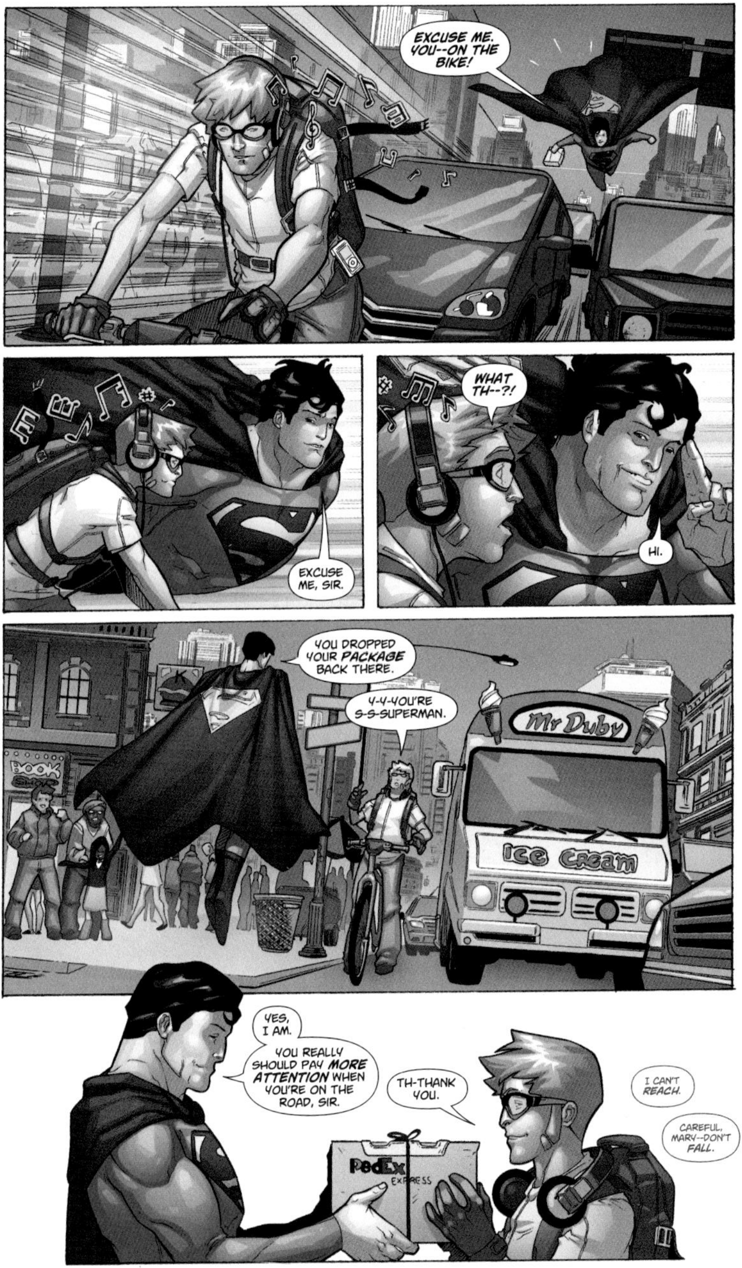
EXCUSE ME. YOU--ON THE BIKE!
EXCUSE ME, SIR.
WHAT TH--?!
HI.
YOU DROPPED YOUR PACKAGE BACK THERE.
Y-Y-YOU'RE S-S-SUPERMAN.
Mr Duby
BOOK SHOP
Ice Cream
YES, I AM.
YOU REALLY SHOULD PAY MORE ATTENTION WHEN YOU'RE ON THE ROAD, SIR.
TH-THANK YOU.
I CAN'T REACH.
CAREFUL, MARY--DON'T FALL.
FedEx EXPRESS

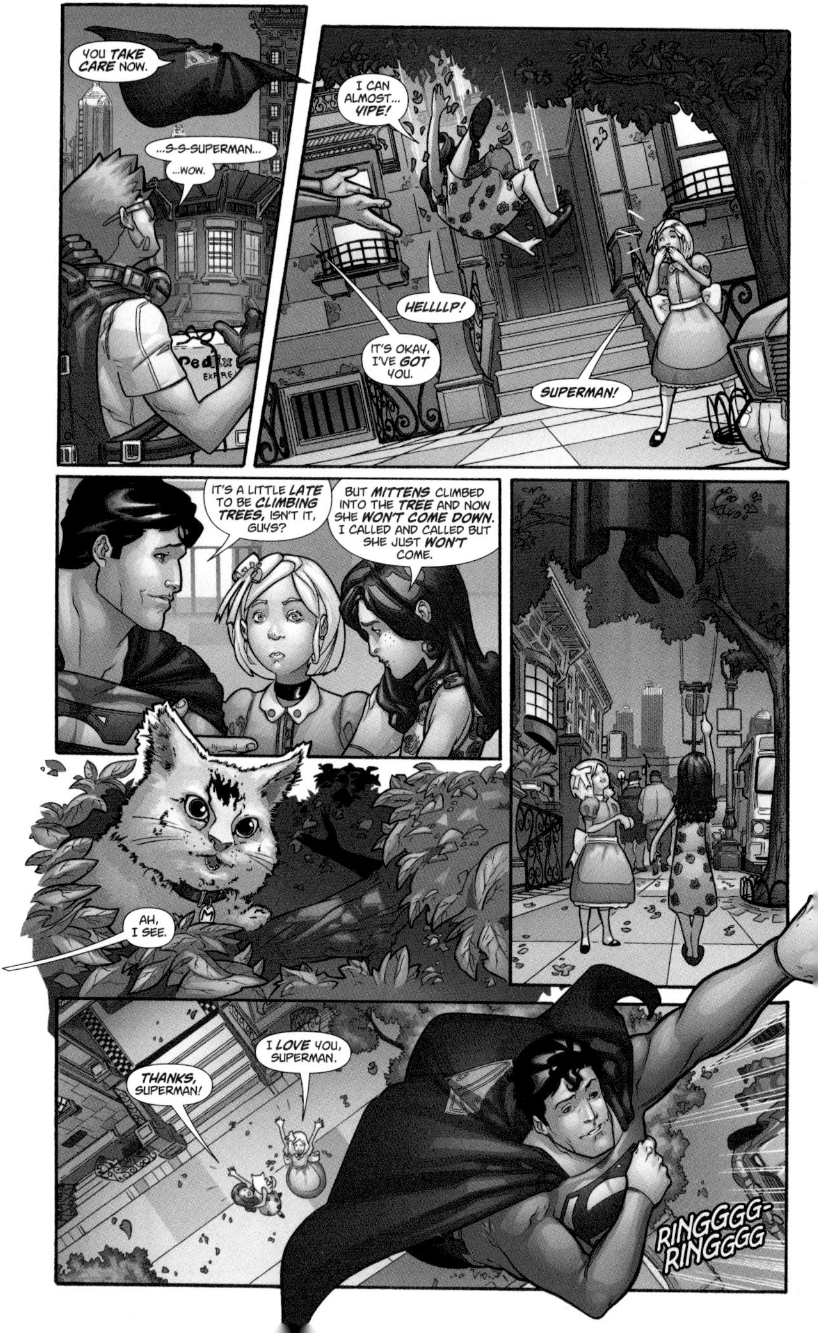
YOU TAKE CARE NOW.
...S-S-SUPERMAN...
...WOW.
I CAN ALMOST... YIPE!
HELLLLP!
IT'S OKAY, I'VE GOT YOU.
SUPERMAN!
IT'S A LITTLE LATE TO BE CLIMBING TREES, ISN'T IT, GUYS?
BUT MITTENS CLIMBED INTO THE TREE AND NOW SHE WON'T COME DOWN. I CALLED AND CALLED BUT SHE JUST WON'T COME.
AH, I SEE.
I LOVE YOU, SUPERMAN.
THANKS, SUPERMAN!
RINGGGG-RINGGGG

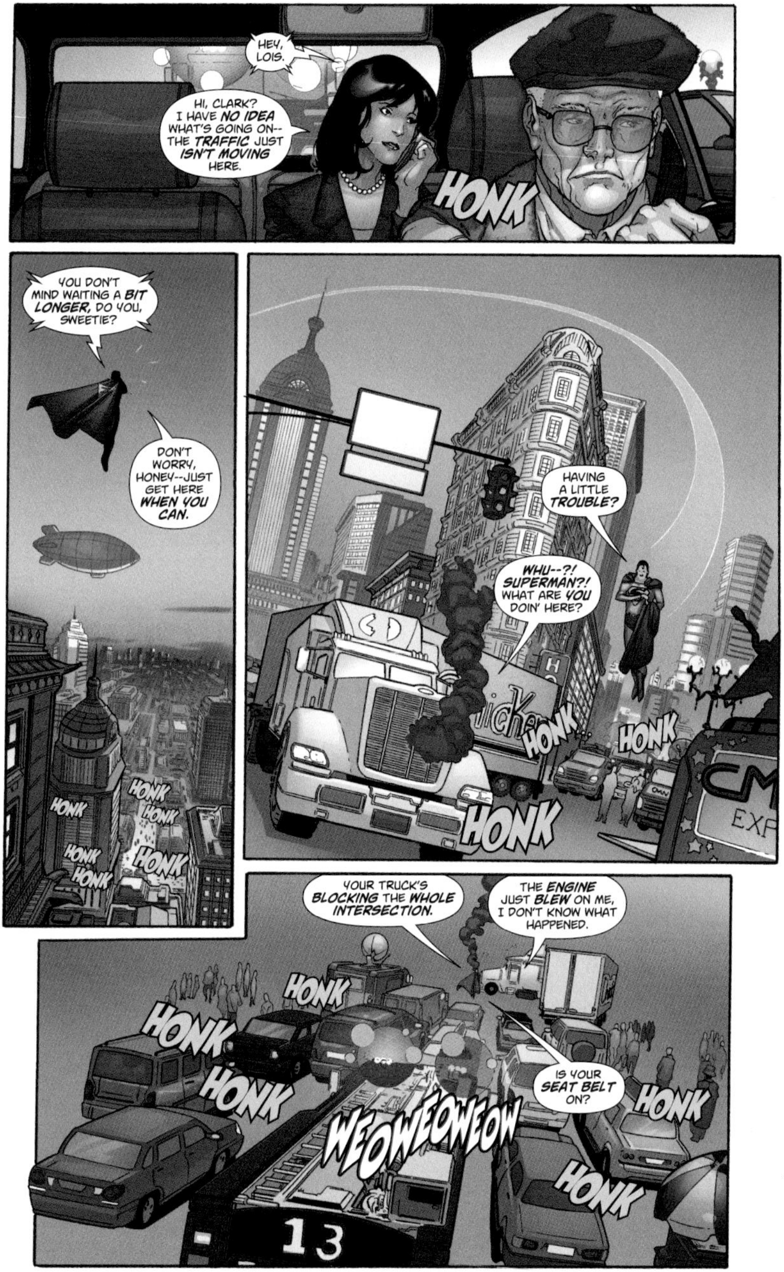
HEY, LOIS.
HI, CLARK? I HAVE NO IDEA WHAT'S GOING ON-- THE TRAFFIC JUST ISN'T MOVING HERE.
HONK
YOU DON'T MIND WAITING A BIT LONGER, DO YOU, SWEETIE?
DON'T WORRY, HONEY--JUST GET HERE WHEN YOU CAN.
HONK
HONK
HONK
HONK
HONK
HONK
HAVING A LITTLE TROUBLE?
WHU--?! SUPERMAN?! WHAT ARE YOU DOIN' HERE?
HONK
HONK
HONK
YOUR TRUCK'S BLOCKING THE WHOLE INTERSECTION.
THE ENGINE JUST BLEW ON ME, I DON'T KNOW WHAT HAPPENED.
HONK
HONK
HONK
IS YOUR SEAT BELT ON?
HONK
WEOWLEOWEOW
HONK
13

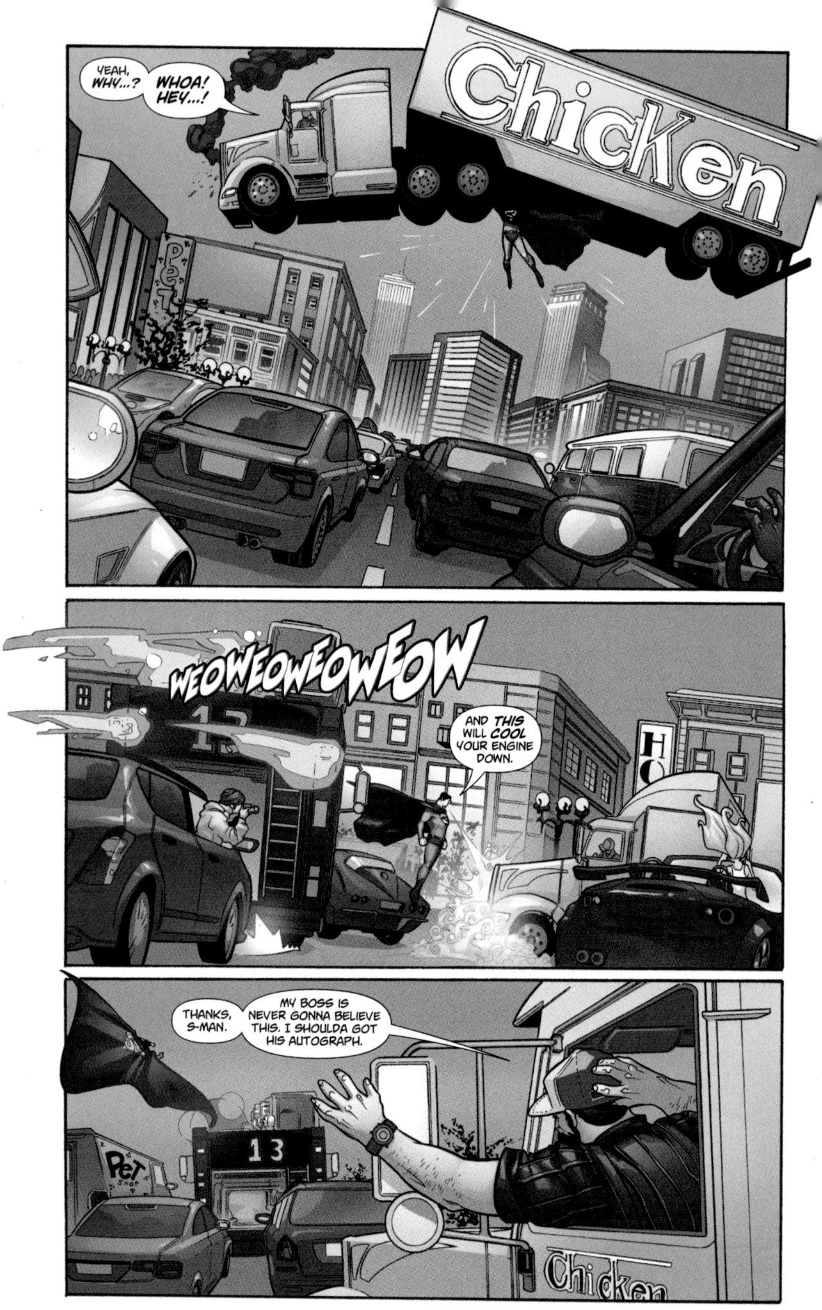
YEAH, WHY...?
WHOA! HEY...!
Chicken
WEOWEOWEOWEOW
AND THIS WILL COOL YOUR ENGINE DOWN.
THANKS, S-MAN.
MY BOSS IS NEVER GONNA BELIEVE THIS. I SHOULDA GOT HIS AUTOGRAPH.
13
PET SHOP
Chicken

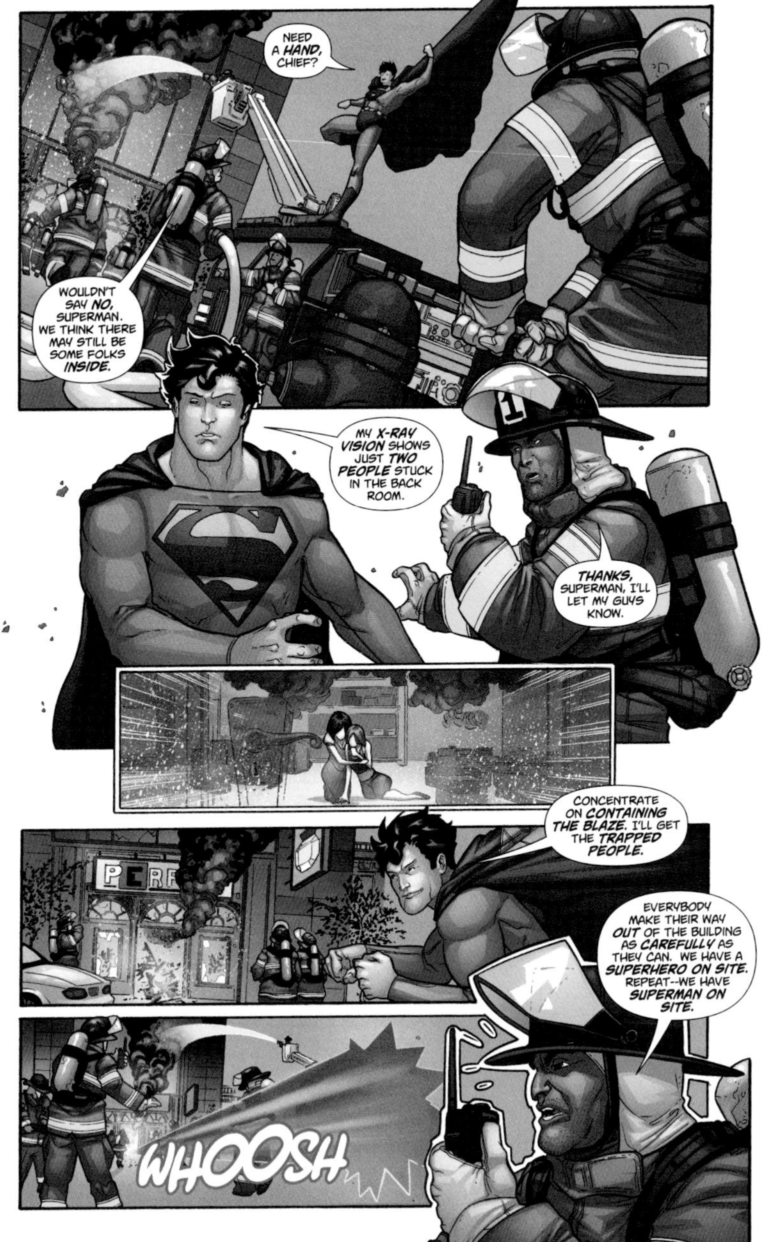
NEED A HAND, CHIEF?
WOULDN'T SAY NO, SUPERMAN. WE THINK THERE MAY STILL BE SOME FOLKS INSIDE.
MY X-RAY VISION SHOWS JUST TWO PEOPLE STUCK IN THE BACK ROOM.
THANKS, SUPERMAN, I'LL LET MY GUYS KNOW.
CONCENTRATE ON CONTAINING THE BLAZE. I'LL GET THE TRAPPED PEOPLE.
EVERYBODY MAKE THEIR WAY OUT OF THE BUILDING AS CAREFULLY AS THEY CAN. WE HAVE A SUPERHERO ON SITE. REPEAT--WE HAVE SUPERMAN ON SITE.
WHOOSH

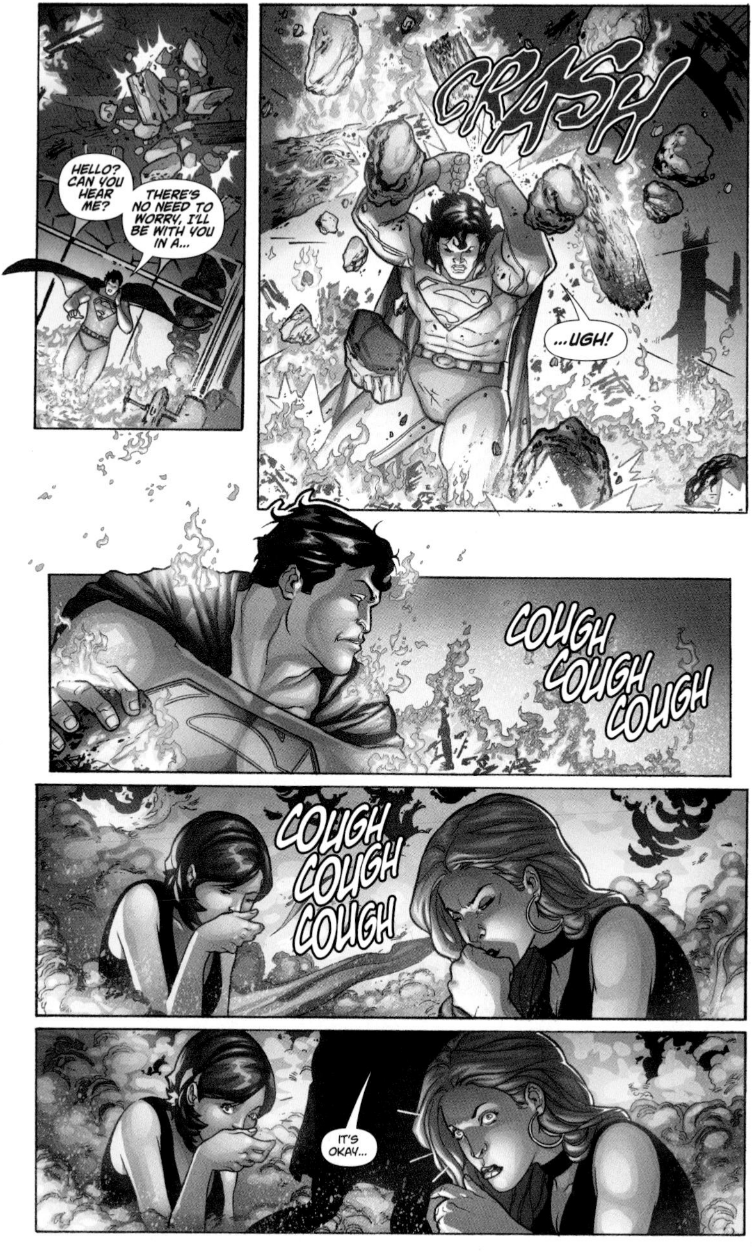
HELLO? CAN YOU HEAR ME?
THERE'S NO NEED TO WORRY, I'LL BE WITH YOU IN A...
CRASH
...UGH!
COUGH COUGH COUGH
COUGH COUGH COUGH
IT'S OKAY...

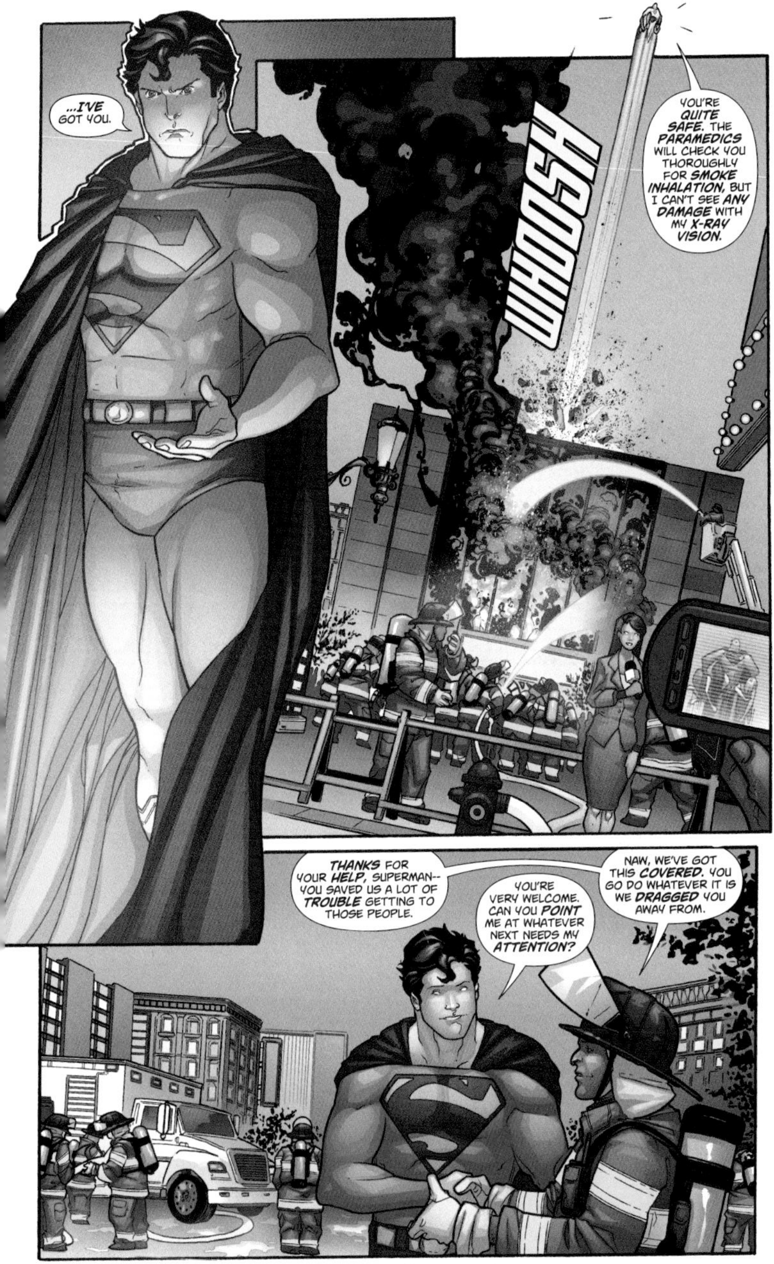
...I'VE GOT YOU.
WHOOSH
YOU'RE QUITE SAFE. THE PARAMEDICS WILL CHECK YOU THOROUGHLY FOR SMOKE INHALATION, BUT I CAN'T SEE ANY DAMAGE WITH MY X-RAY VISION.
THANKS FOR YOUR HELP, SUPERMAN-- YOU SAVED US A LOT OF TROUBLE GETTING TO THOSE PEOPLE.
YOU'RE VERY WELCOME. CAN YOU POINT ME AT WHATEVER NEXT NEEDS MY ATTENTION?
NAW, WE'VE GOT THIS COVERED. YOU GO DO WHATEVER IT IS WE DRAGGED YOU AWAY FROM.

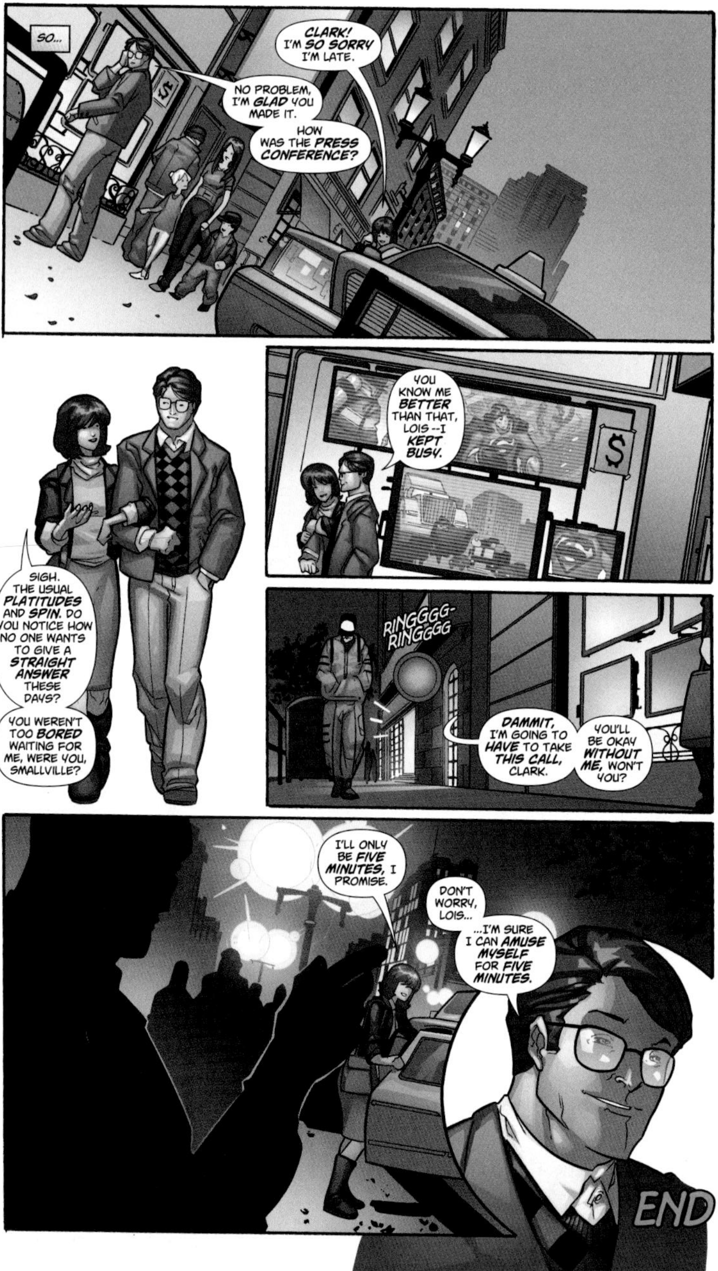

SO...
CLARK! I'M SO SORRY I'M LATE.
NO PROBLEM, I'M GLAD YOU MADE IT.
HOW WAS THE PRESS CONFERENCE?
SIGH. THE USUAL PLATITUDES AND SPIN. DO YOU NOTICE HOW NO ONE WANTS TO GIVE A STRAIGHT ANSWER THESE DAYS?
YOU WEREN'T TOO BORED WAITING FOR ME, WERE YOU, SMALLVILLE?
YOU KNOW ME BETTER THAN THAT, LOIS --I KEPT BUSY.
RINGGGG-RINGGGG
DAMMIT, I'M GOING TO HAVE TO TAKE THIS CALL, CLARK.
YOU'LL BE OKAY WITHOUT ME, WON'T YOU?
I'LL ONLY BE FIVE MINUTES, I PROMISE.
DON'T WORRY, LOIS...
...I'M SURE I CAN AMUSE MYSELF FOR FIVE MINUTES.
END

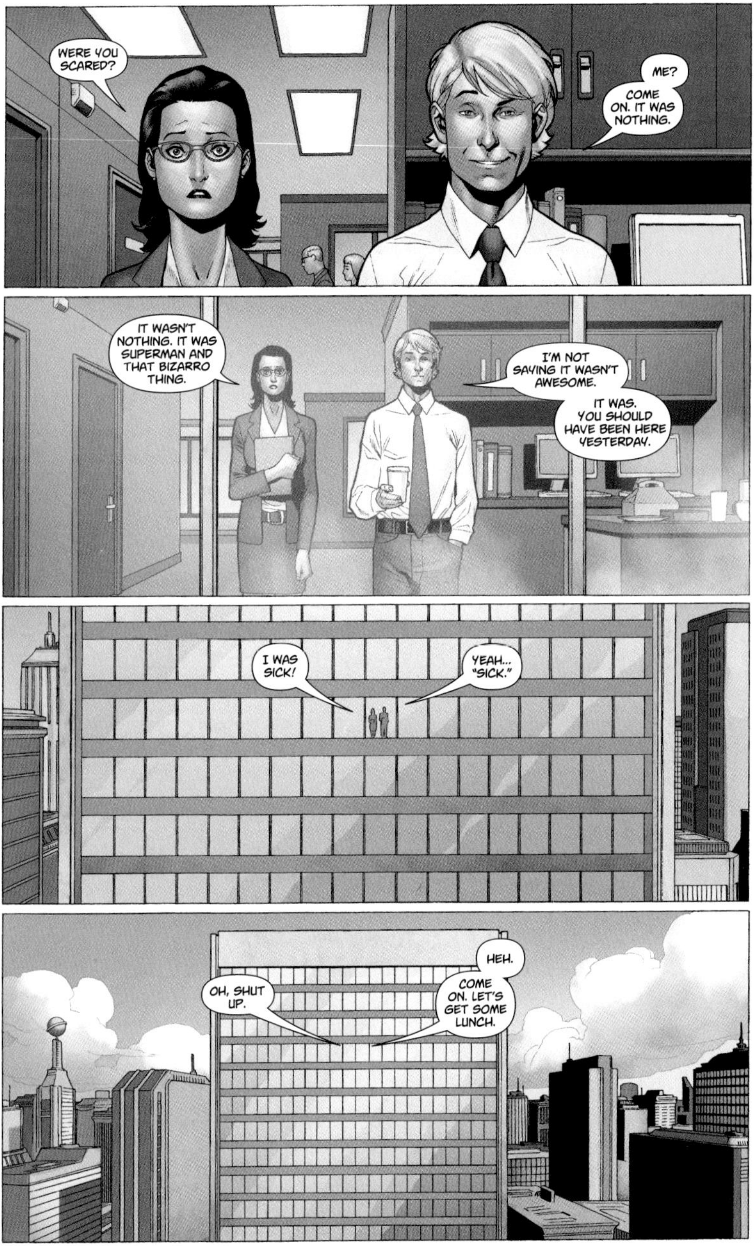
WERE YOU SCARED?
ME?
COME ON. IT WAS NOTHING.
IT WASN'T NOTHING. IT WAS SUPERMAN AND THAT BIZARRO THING.
I'M NOT SAYING IT WASN'T AWESOME.
IT WAS. YOU SHOULD HAVE BEEN HERE YESTERDAY.
I WAS SICK!
YEAH... "SICK."
HEH.
OH, SHUT UP.
COME ON. LET'S GET SOME LUNCH.

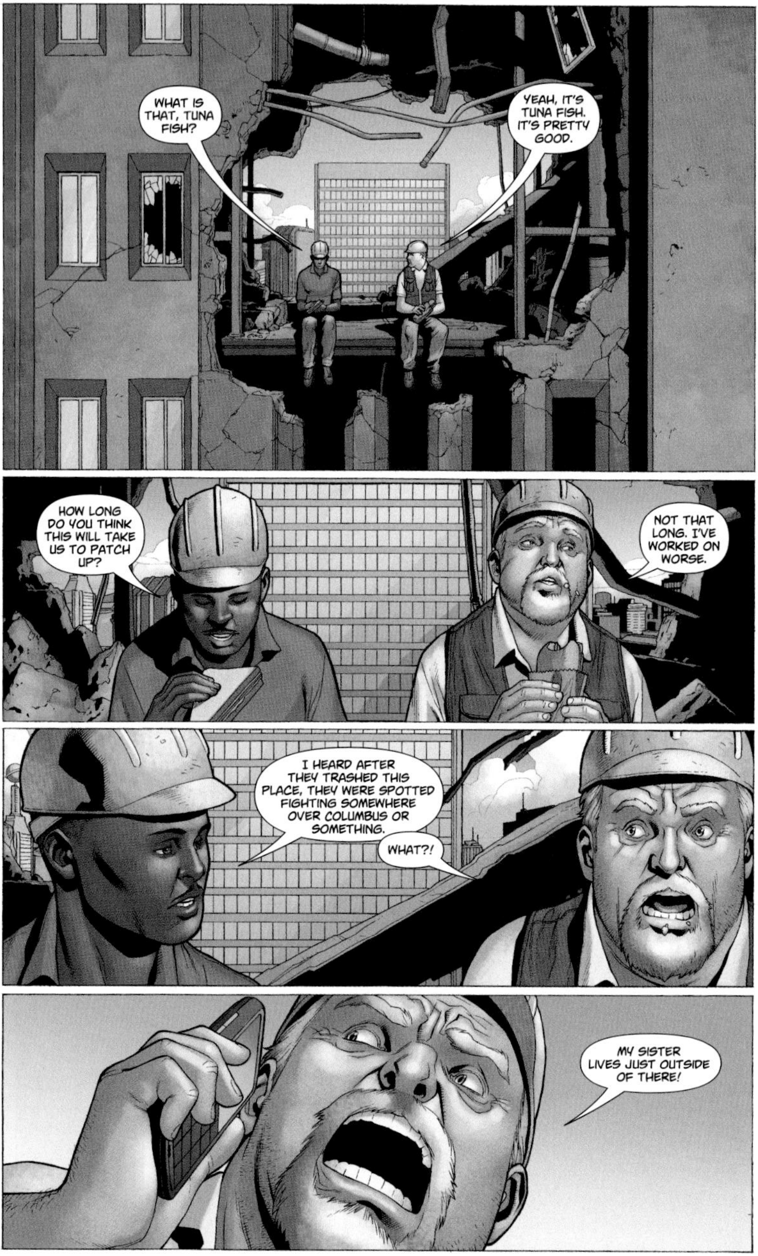
WHAT IS THAT, TUNA FISH?
YEAH, IT'S TUNA FISH. IT'S PRETTY GOOD.
HOW LONG DO YOU THINK THIS WILL TAKE US TO PATCH UP?
NOT THAT LONG. I'VE WORKED ON WORSE.
I HEARD AFTER THEY TRASHED THIS PLACE, THEY WERE SPOTTED FIGHTING SOMEWHERE OVER COLUMBUS OR SOMETHING.
WHAT?!
MY SISTER LIVES JUST OUTSIDE OF THERE!

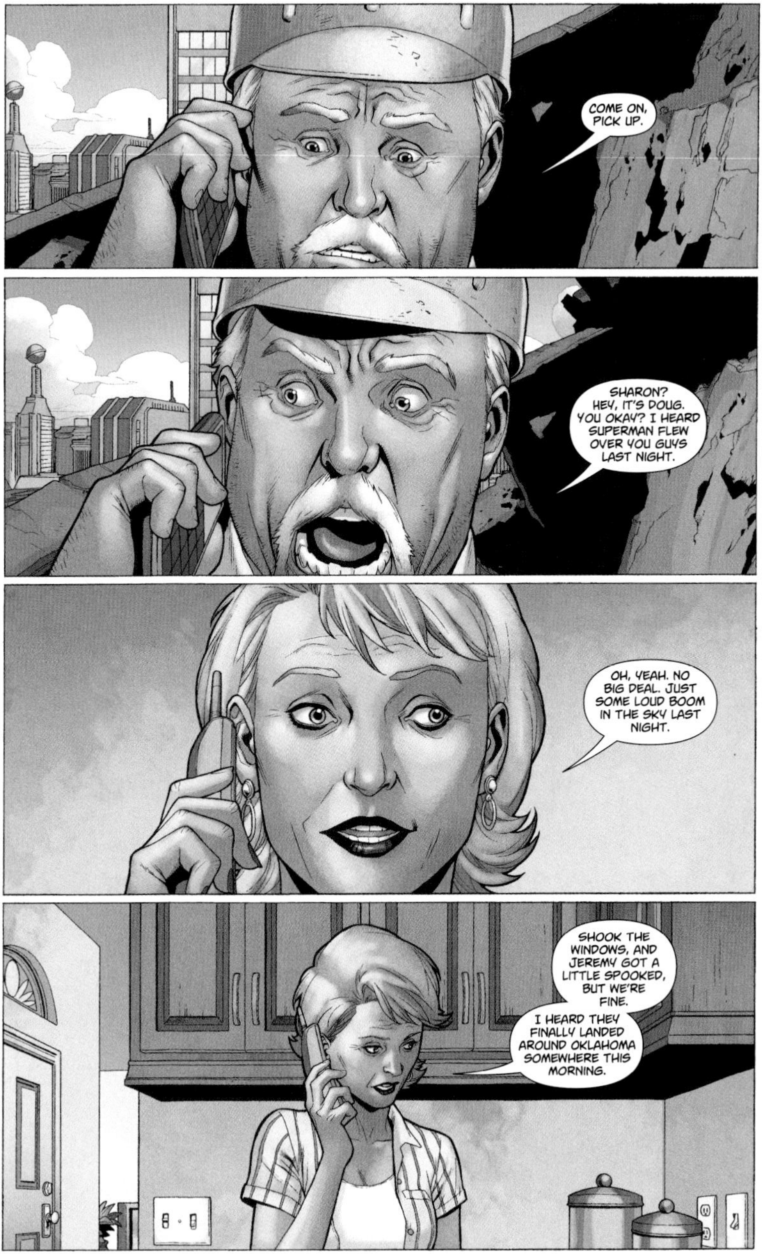
COME ON, PICK UP.
SHARON? HEY, IT'S DOUG. YOU OKAY? I HEARD SUPERMAN FLEW OVER YOU GUYS LAST NIGHT.
OH, YEAH. NO BIG DEAL. JUST SOME LOUD BOOM IN THE SKY LAST NIGHT.
SHOOK THE WINDOWS, AND JEREMY GOT A LITTLE SPOOKED, BUT WE'RE FINE.
I HEARD THEY FINALLY LANDED AROUND OKLAHOMA SOMEWHERE THIS MORNING.

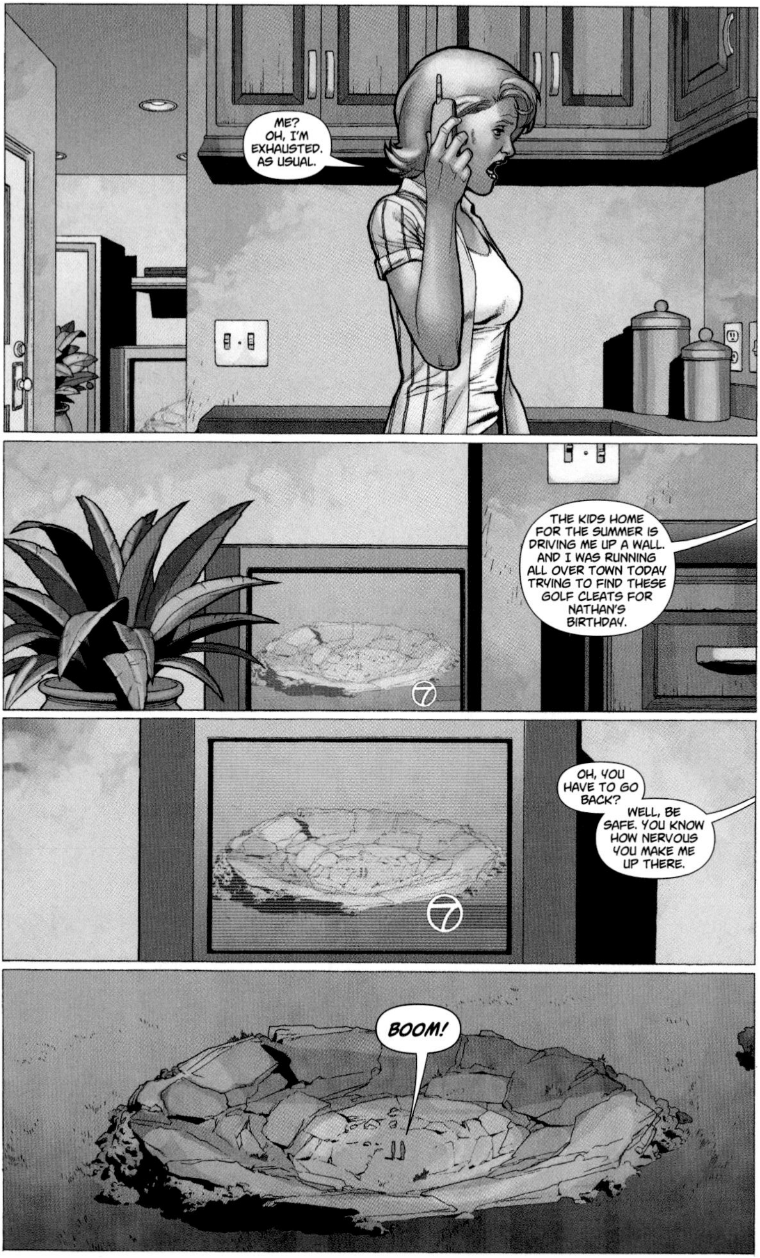
ME? OH, I'M EXHAUSTED. AS USUAL.
THE KIDS HOME FOR THE SUMMER IS DRIVING ME UP A WALL. AND I WAS RUNNING ALL OVER TOWN TODAY TRYING TO FIND THESE GOLF CLEATS FOR NATHAN'S BIRTHDAY.
OH, YOU HAVE TO GO BACK?
WELL, BE SAFE. YOU KNOW HOW NERVOUS YOU MAKE ME UP THERE.
BOOM!

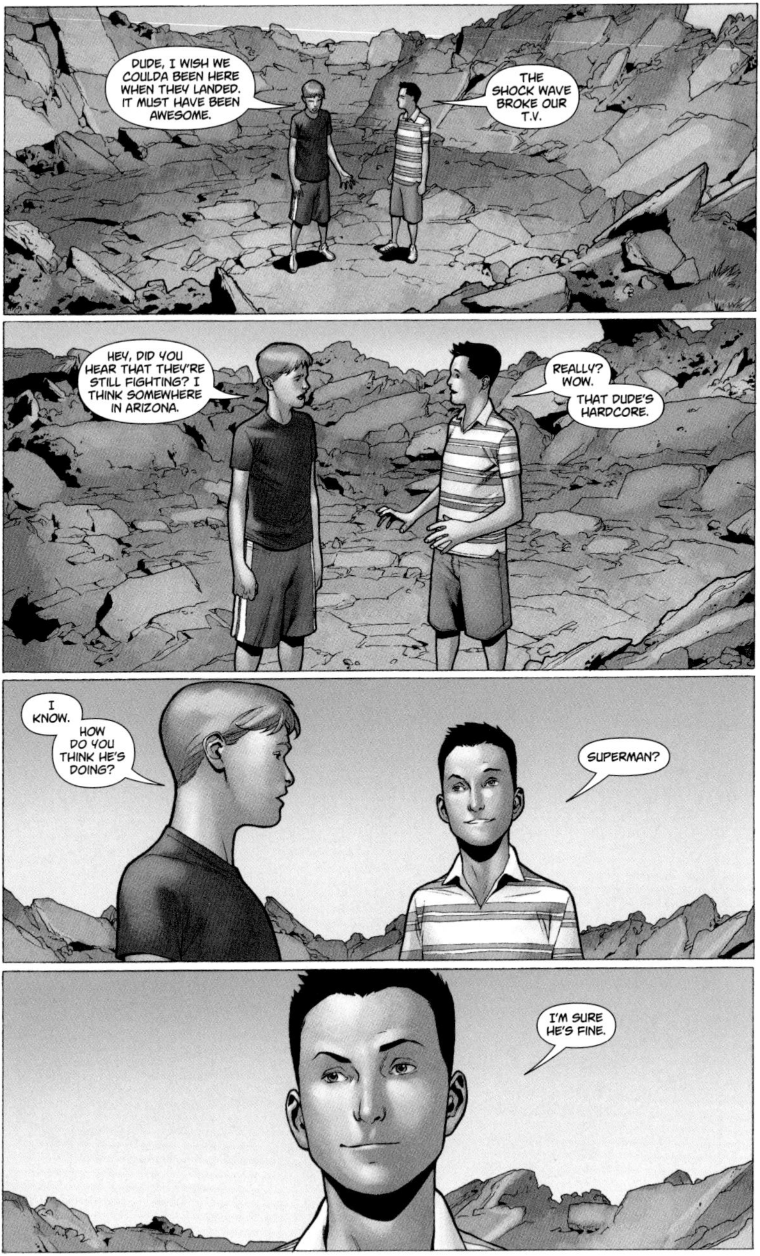
DUDE, I WISH WE COULDA BEEN HERE WHEN THEY LANDED. IT MUST HAVE BEEN AWESOME.
THE SHOCK WAVE BROKE OUR T.V.
HEY, DID YOU HEAR THAT THEY'RE STILL FIGHTING? I THINK SOMEWHERE IN ARIZONA.
REALLY? WOW.
THAT DUDE'S HARDCORE.
I KNOW.
HOW DO YOU THINK HE'S DOING?
SUPERMAN?
I'M SURE HE'S FINE.

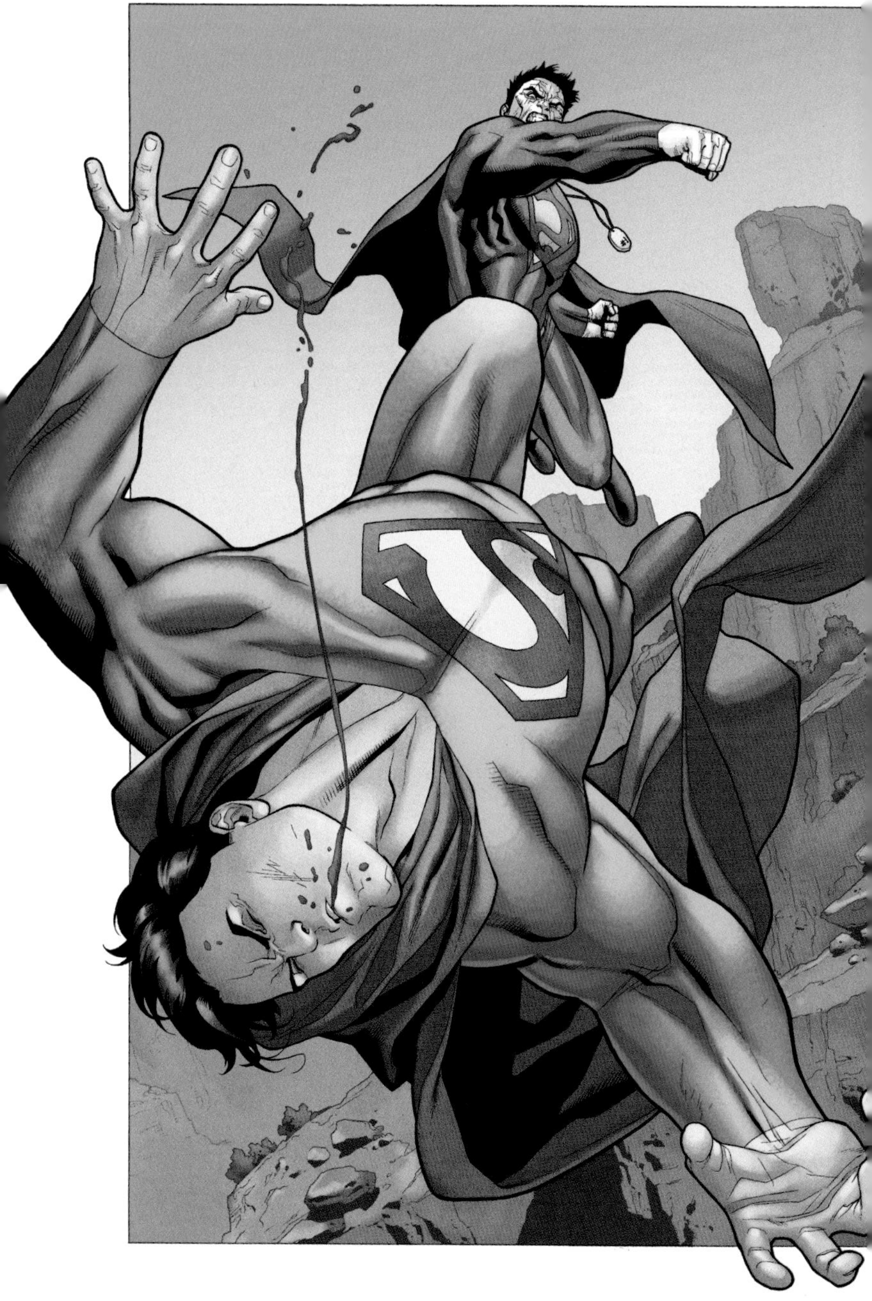

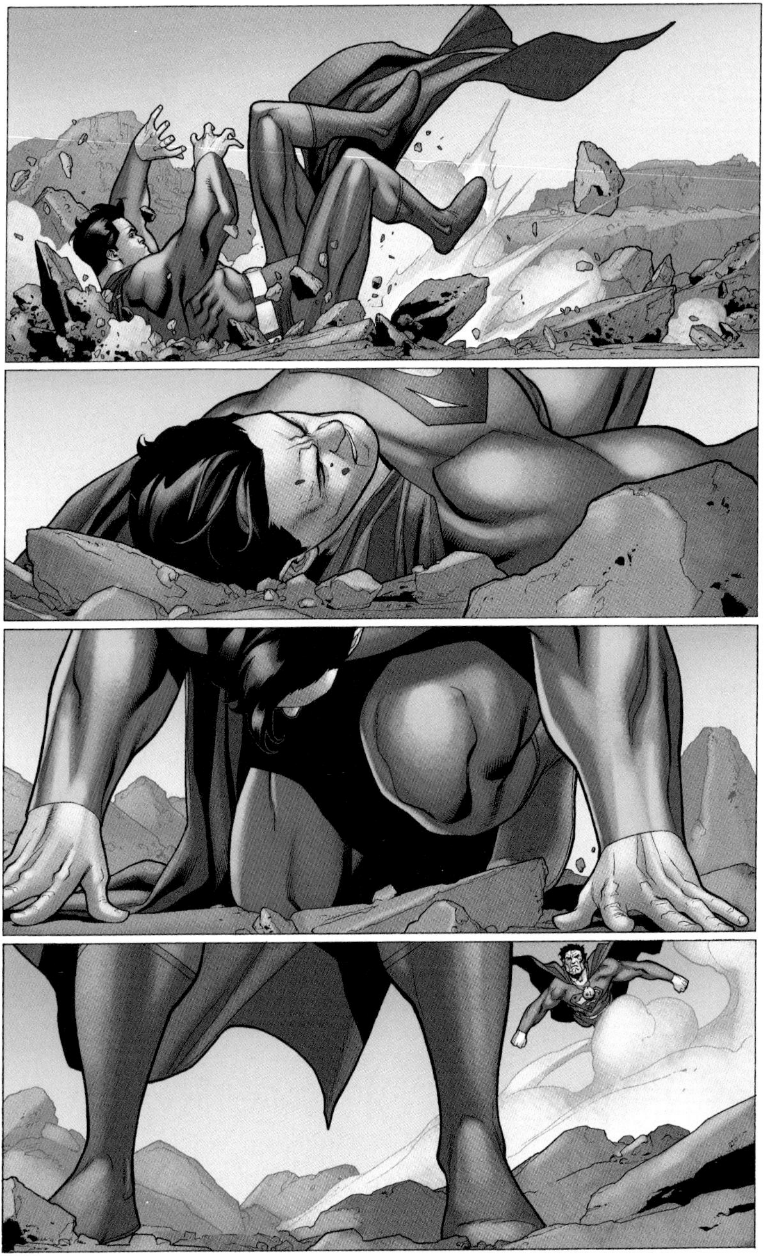

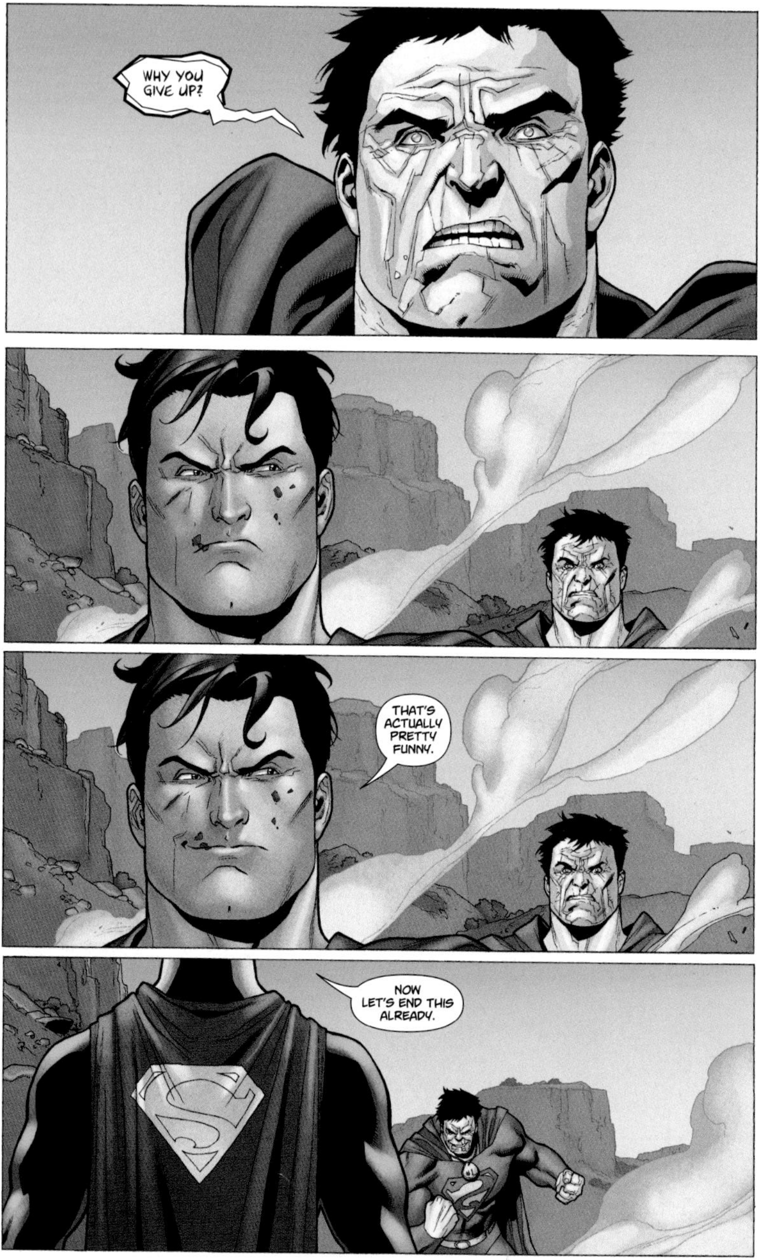
WHY YOU GIVE UP?
THAT'S ACTUALLY PRETTY FUNNY.
NOW LET'S END THIS ALREADY.

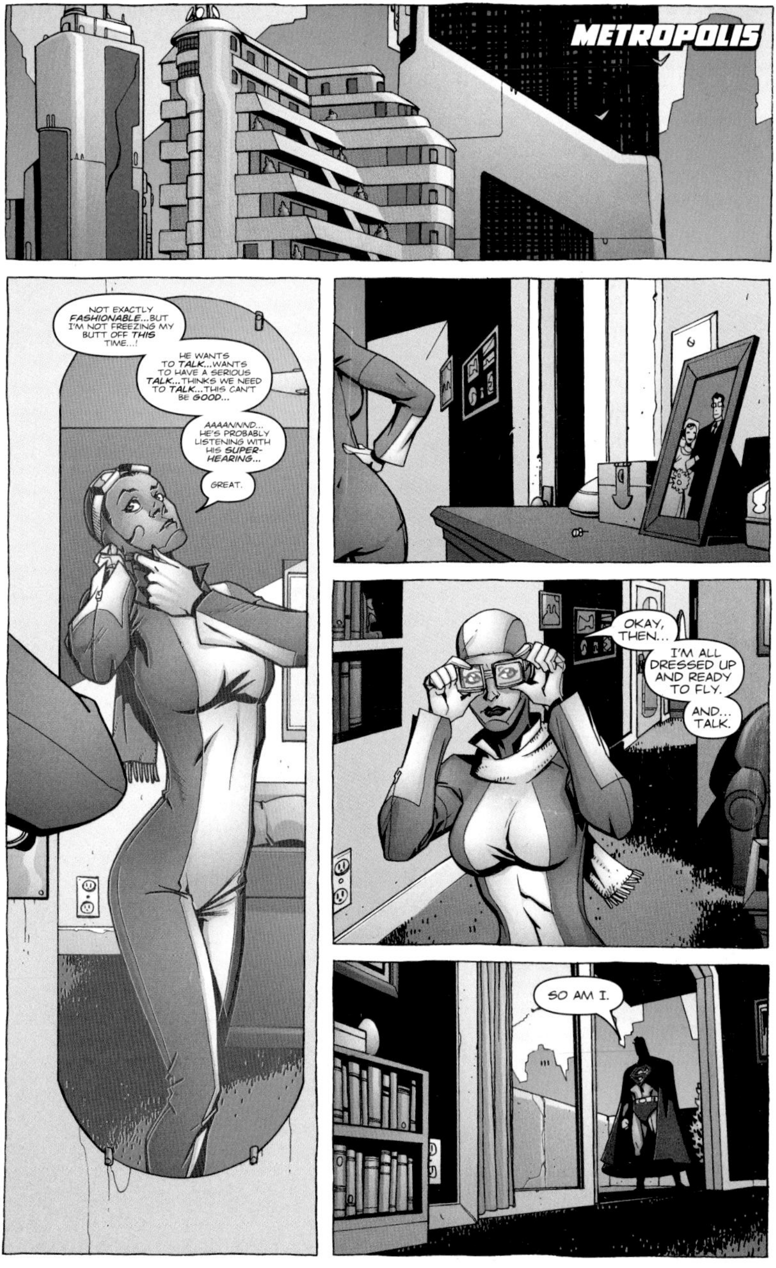
METROPOLIS
NOT EXACTLY FASHIONABLE...BUT I'M NOT FREEZING MY BUTT OFF THIS TIME...!
HE WANTS TO TALK...WANTS TO HAVE A SERIOUS TALK...THINKS WE NEED TO TALK...THIS CAN'T BE GOOD...
AAAANNND... HE'S PROBABLY LISTENING WITH HIS SUPER-HEARING...
GREAT.
OKAY, THEN...
I'M ALL DRESSED UP AND READY TO FLY.
AND... TALK.
SO AM I.

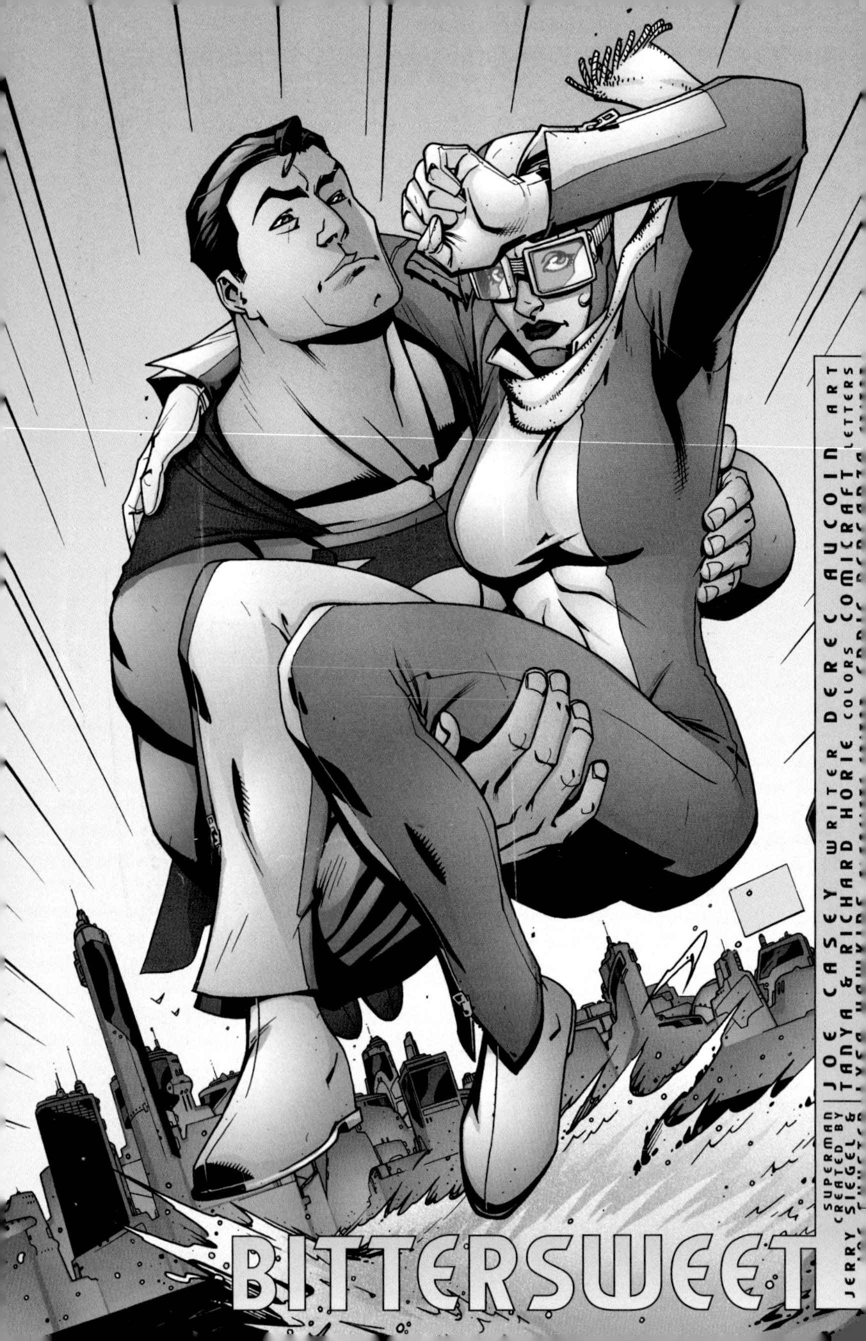
BITTERSWEET
JOE CASEY WRITER DEREC AUCOIN ART
TANYA & RICHARD HORIE COLORS COMICRAFT LETTERS
SUPERMAN CREATED BY JERRY SIEGEL &

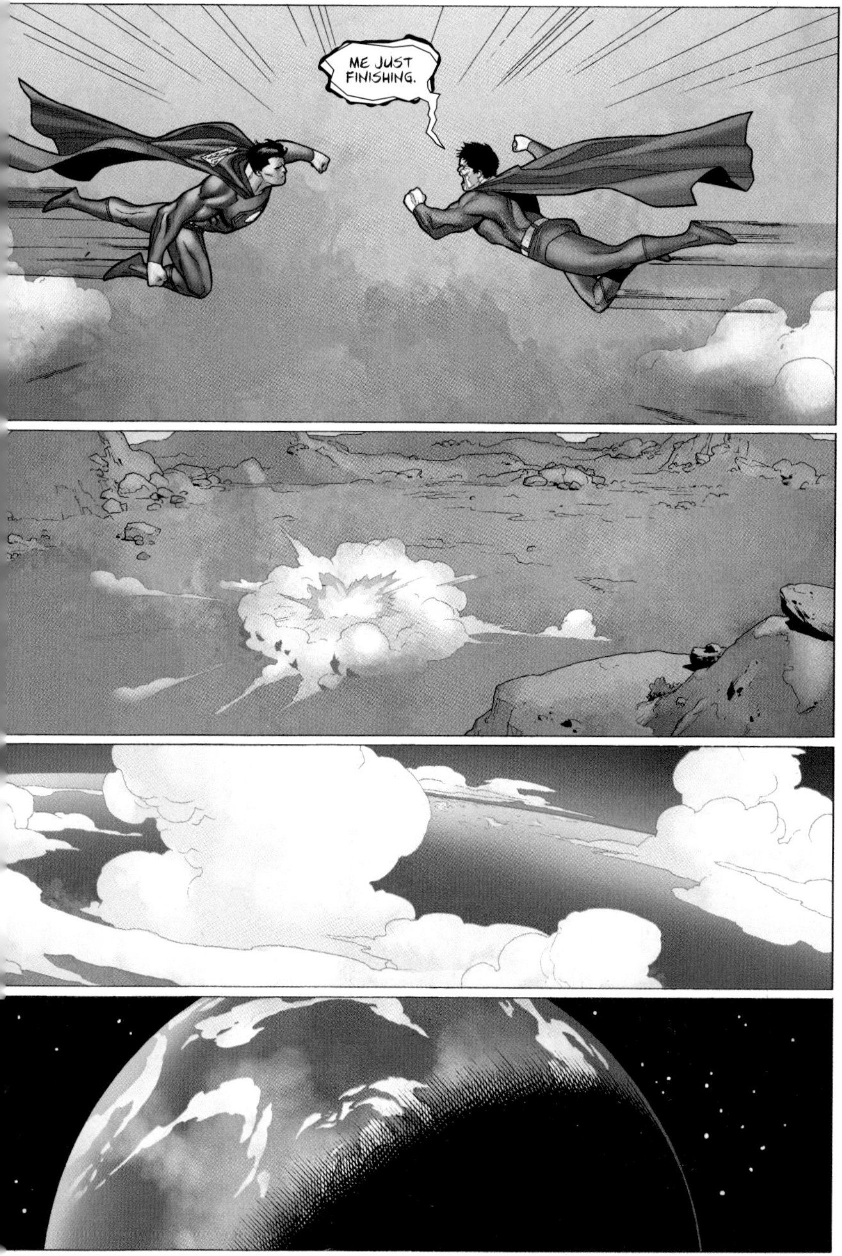
ME JUST FINISHING.

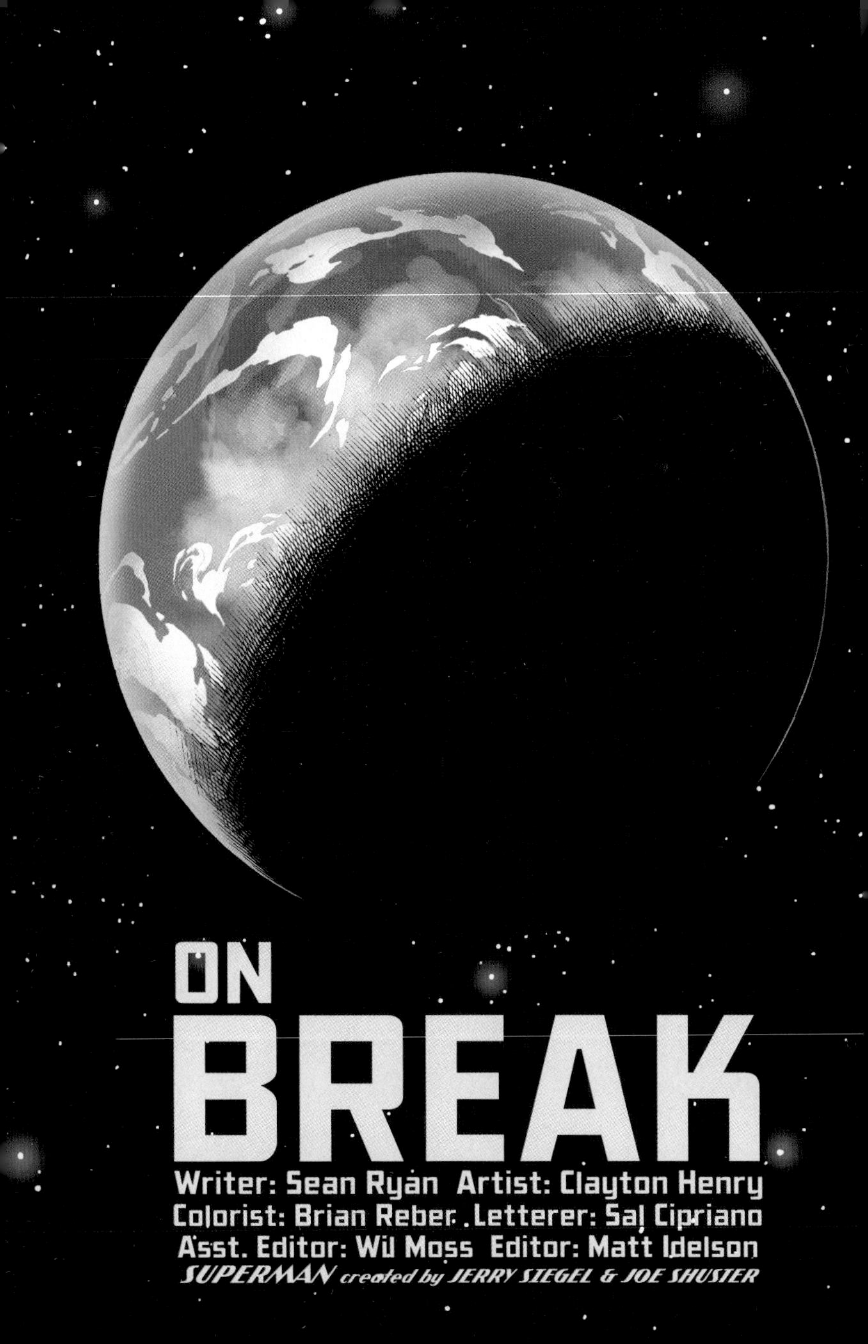

ON BREAK

Writer: Sean Ryan Artist: Clayton Henry
Colorist: Brian Reber Letterer: Sal Cipriano
Asst. Editor: Wil Moss Editor: Matt Idelson
SUPERMAN created by JERRY SIEGEL & JOE SHUSTER

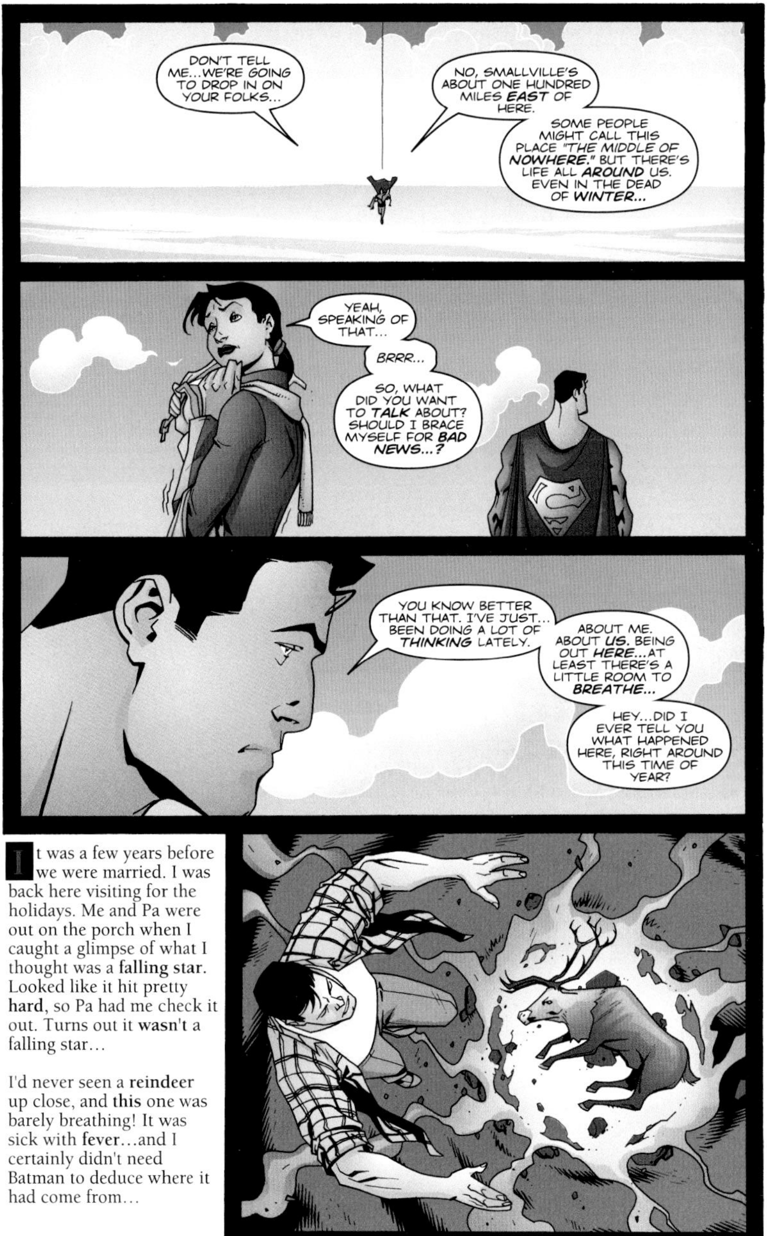
DON'T TELL ME...WE'RE GOING TO DROP IN ON YOUR FOLKS...
NO, SMALLVILLE'S ABOUT ONE HUNDRED MILES EAST OF HERE.
SOME PEOPLE MIGHT CALL THIS PLACE "THE MIDDLE OF NOWHERE." BUT THERE'S LIFE ALL AROUND US. EVEN IN THE DEAD OF WINTER...
YEAH, SPEAKING OF THAT...
BRRR...
SO, WHAT DID YOU WANT TO TALK ABOUT? SHOULD I BRACE MYSELF FOR BAD NEWS...?
YOU KNOW BETTER THAN THAT. I'VE JUST... BEEN DOING A LOT OF THINKING LATELY.
ABOUT ME. ABOUT US. BEING OUT HERE...AT LEAST THERE'S A LITTLE ROOM TO BREATHE...
HEY...DID I EVER TELL YOU WHAT HAPPENED HERE, RIGHT AROUND THIS TIME OF YEAR?
It was a few years before we were married. I was back here visiting for the holidays. Me and Pa were out on the porch when I caught a glimpse of what I thought was a falling star. Looked like it hit pretty hard, so Pa had me check it out. Turns out it wasn't a falling star...
I'd never seen a reindeer up close, and this one was barely breathing! It was sick with fever...and I certainly didn't need Batman to deduce where it had come from...

I followed specific **magnetic waves** that led me to a remote arctic location. I guess I should've known all along where I was headed, but I couldn't help but be **awestruck** once I'd arrived. I could feel the **magic** in the air…

And there he was, practically an amalgamation of all the various **descriptions** he'd been given throughout the ages. I suspect he looks different to **everyone.** To me, he had the warmest **smile** I'd ever seen…

But obviously, this was not the **happiest** of occasions…

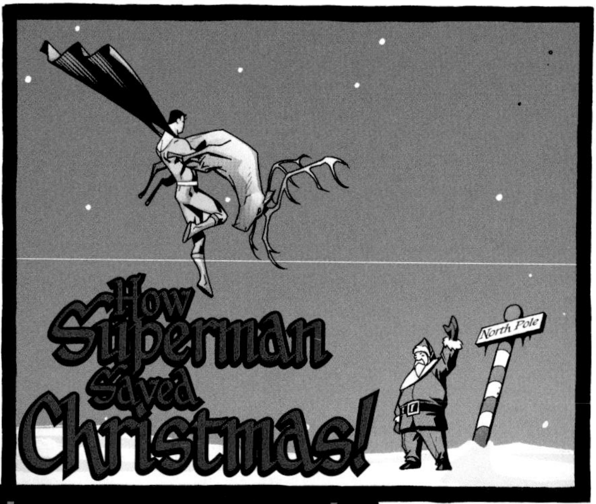
How Superman Saved Christmas!
North Pole

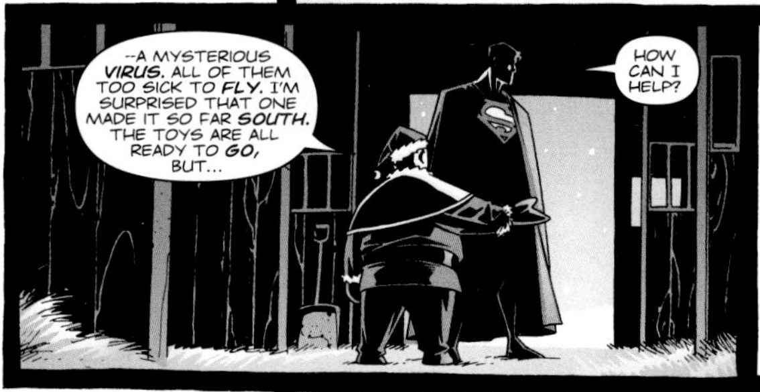
--A MYSTERIOUS *VIRUS.* ALL OF THEM TOO SICK TO *FLY.* I'M SURPRISED THAT ONE MADE IT SO FAR *SOUTH.* THE TOYS ARE ALL READY TO *GO,* BUT...
HOW CAN I HELP?

It was difficult to get past the **sadness** in his voice…

The solution was **obvious**…

I felt like I'd never carried such **precious cargo**. The dreams of so many children all over the world…it all came down to that **one night**.

In that moment, I felt like I was part of something **bigger** than than anything I'd ever experienced. I could **feel** how **special** this was…the sense of **purpose** in what we were doing…

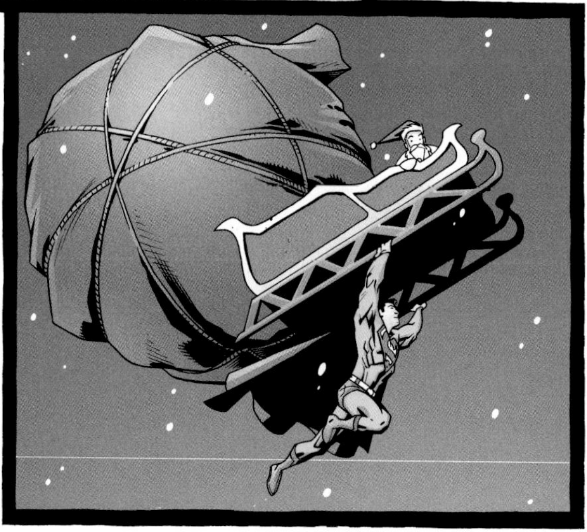

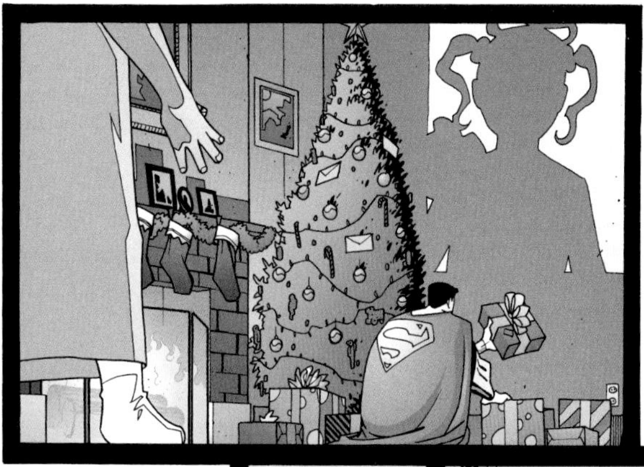

Obviously, time passes much **differently** for him on that night. He's never **rushed.** I had to beg him to let me make a delivery or two…

Of course, he's been doing this a lot longer. I was a rank amateur…

Hopefully, I didn't disappoint anyone…

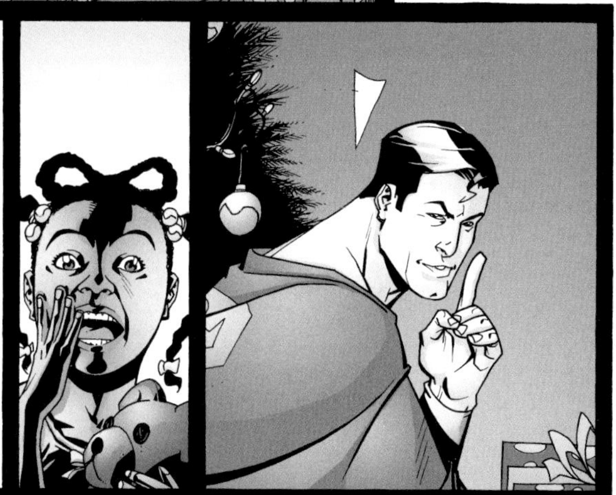

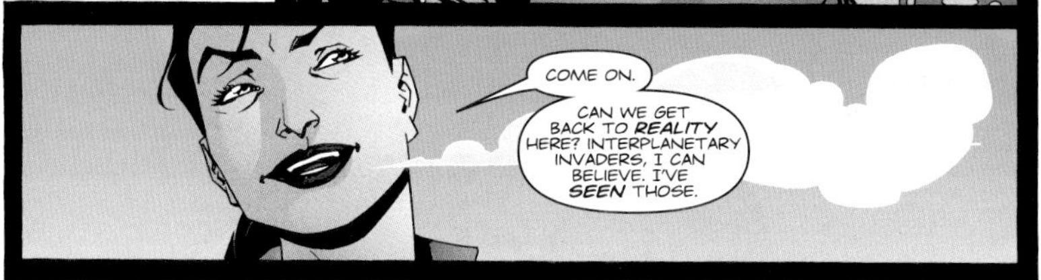
COME ON.
CAN WE GET BACK TO *REALITY* HERE? INTERPLANETARY INVADERS, I CAN BELIEVE. I'VE *SEEN* THOSE.

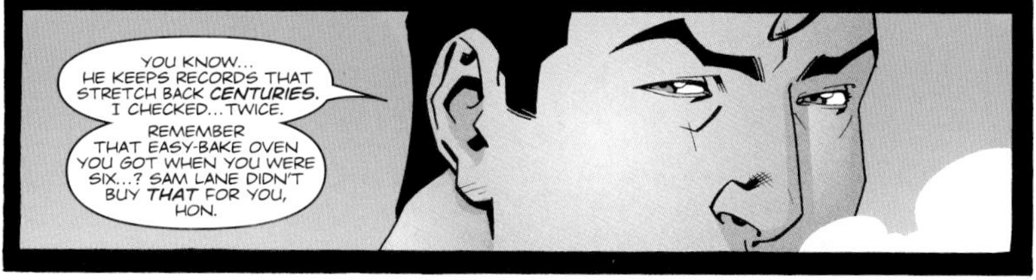
YOU KNOW… HE KEEPS RECORDS THAT STRETCH BACK *CENTURIES.* I CHECKED…TWICE.
REMEMBER THAT EASY-BAKE OVEN YOU GOT WHEN YOU WERE SIX…? SAM LANE DIDN'T BUY *THAT* FOR YOU, HON.

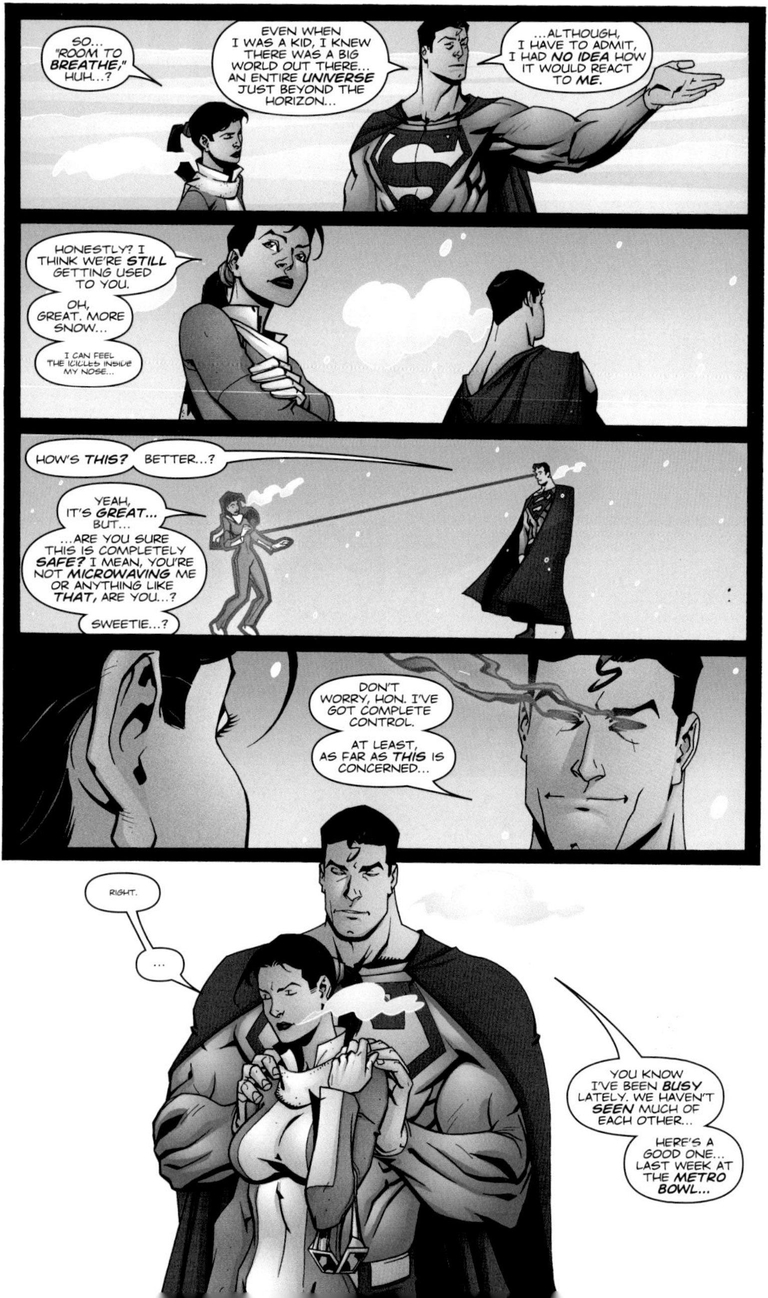
SO... "ROOM TO BREATHE," HUH...?
EVEN WHEN I WAS A KID, I KNEW THERE WAS A BIG WORLD OUT THERE... AN ENTIRE UNIVERSE JUST BEYOND THE HORIZON...
...ALTHOUGH, I HAVE TO ADMIT, I HAD NO IDEA HOW IT WOULD REACT TO ME.
HONESTLY? I THINK WE'RE STILL GETTING USED TO YOU.
OH, GREAT. MORE SNOW...
I CAN FEEL THE ICICLES INSIDE MY NOSE...
HOW'S THIS?
BETTER...?
YEAH, IT'S GREAT... BUT...
...ARE YOU SURE THIS IS COMPLETELY SAFE? I MEAN, YOU'RE NOT MICROWAVING ME OR ANYTHING LIKE THAT, ARE YOU...?
SWEETIE...?
DON'T WORRY, HON. I'VE GOT COMPLETE CONTROL.
AT LEAST, AS FAR AS THIS IS CONCERNED...
RIGHT.
...
YOU KNOW I'VE BEEN BUSY LATELY. WE HAVEN'T SEEN MUCH OF EACH OTHER...
HERE'S A GOOD ONE... LAST WEEK AT THE METRO BOWL...

It was the **Metropolis Meteors** facing down the **Central City Cougars**. The game of the year! If I hadn't had JLA business in Markovia, I would've been right there in the stands. But I'd heard the radio play-by-play over the Atlantic, so I knew instantly when things got **strange** at the forty-yard line…

And when I arrived on the scene, I could hardly believe the spectacle playing itself out on the gridiron…

> EVERYONE STAY CALM! WE'VE GOT SECURITY IN PLACE TO--

> WAIT! LOOK! UP IN THE SKY...!

SECRET OF THE
PHANTOM QUARTERBACK!

> SUPERMAN ATTEMPTS A **TACKLE** AT THE THIRTY-EIGHT YARD LINE--

> HURRGHNN...!

I remembered what Coach Andrews had said back at Smallville High…about an opponent's **center of gravity**. But, **unfortunately**, there was nothing there to take down. Instead, I got a nice jolt of **bio-feedback** that almost caused me to black out. This truly was a phantom creature of some kind. Intangible and indefatigable…

That's when players from **both** teams decided to try and help. Their **hearts** were in the right place. Regardless of the obvious **dangers**… they jumped in just like my old offensive linemen used to. But to **no avail**…

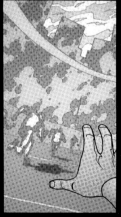

There was no use trying to **outmuscle** this creature. I adjusted my vision to pick up any foreign **energy patterns** that might explain its existence. I found what I was looking for right away…

I could follow that energy pattern straight back to its **source**… which is exactly what I did. In seconds, I was descending toward a quiet neighborhood in **Park Ridge**…

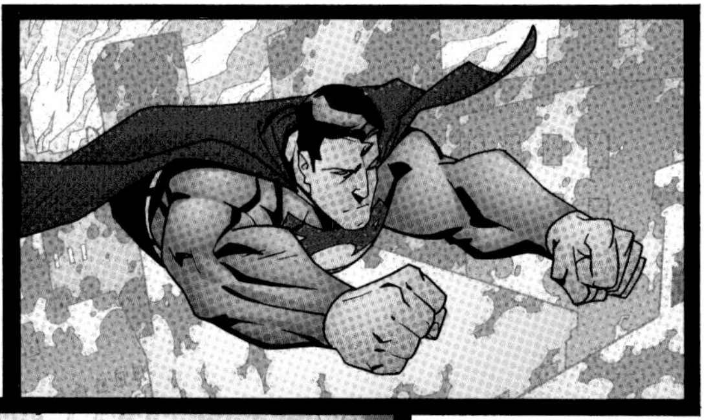

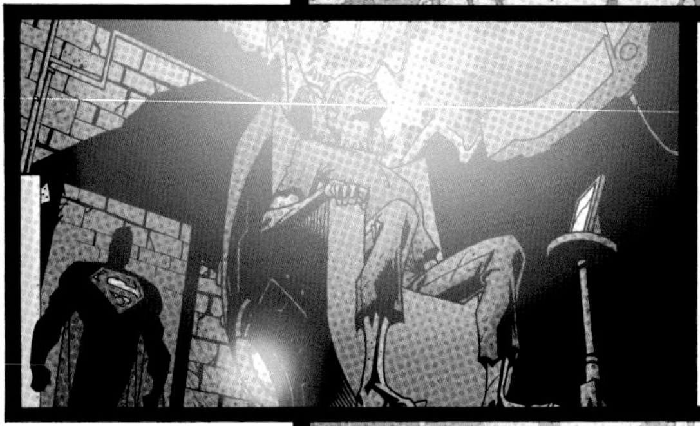

It was just a lonely **basement**…and a normal-looking man hooked up to a very **abnormal**-looking **machine.** He'd been operating the "**Phantom Quarterback**," as though by remote control. At first, I couldn't figure out **why** someone would go to such lengths to cause so much trouble.

But that question was soon **answered** by the photograph I found on the table next to him.

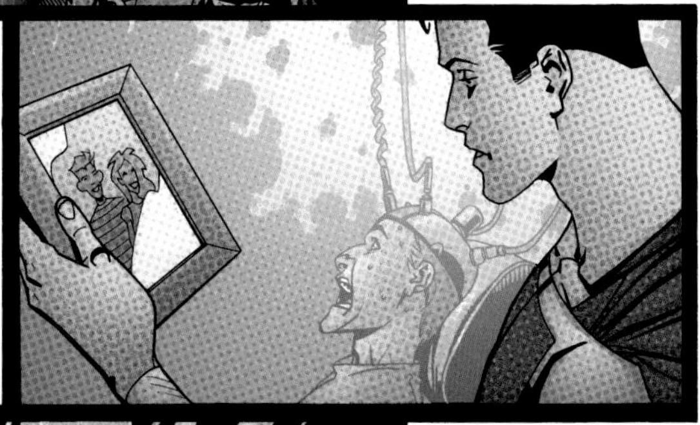

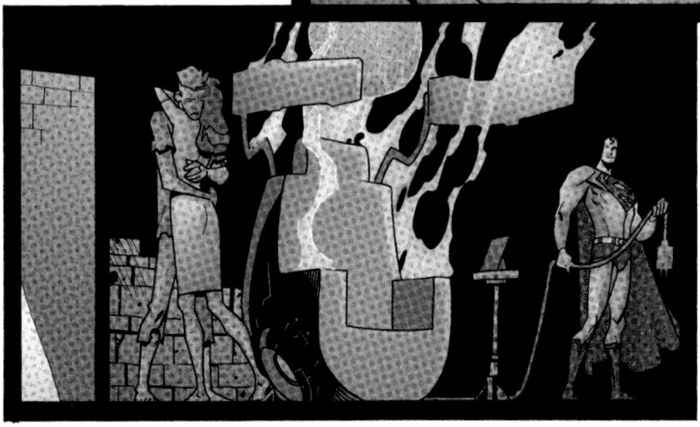

The things we'll do for **love**… the bizarre lengths we'll go to to impress a **woman**…it never ceases to **amaze** me.

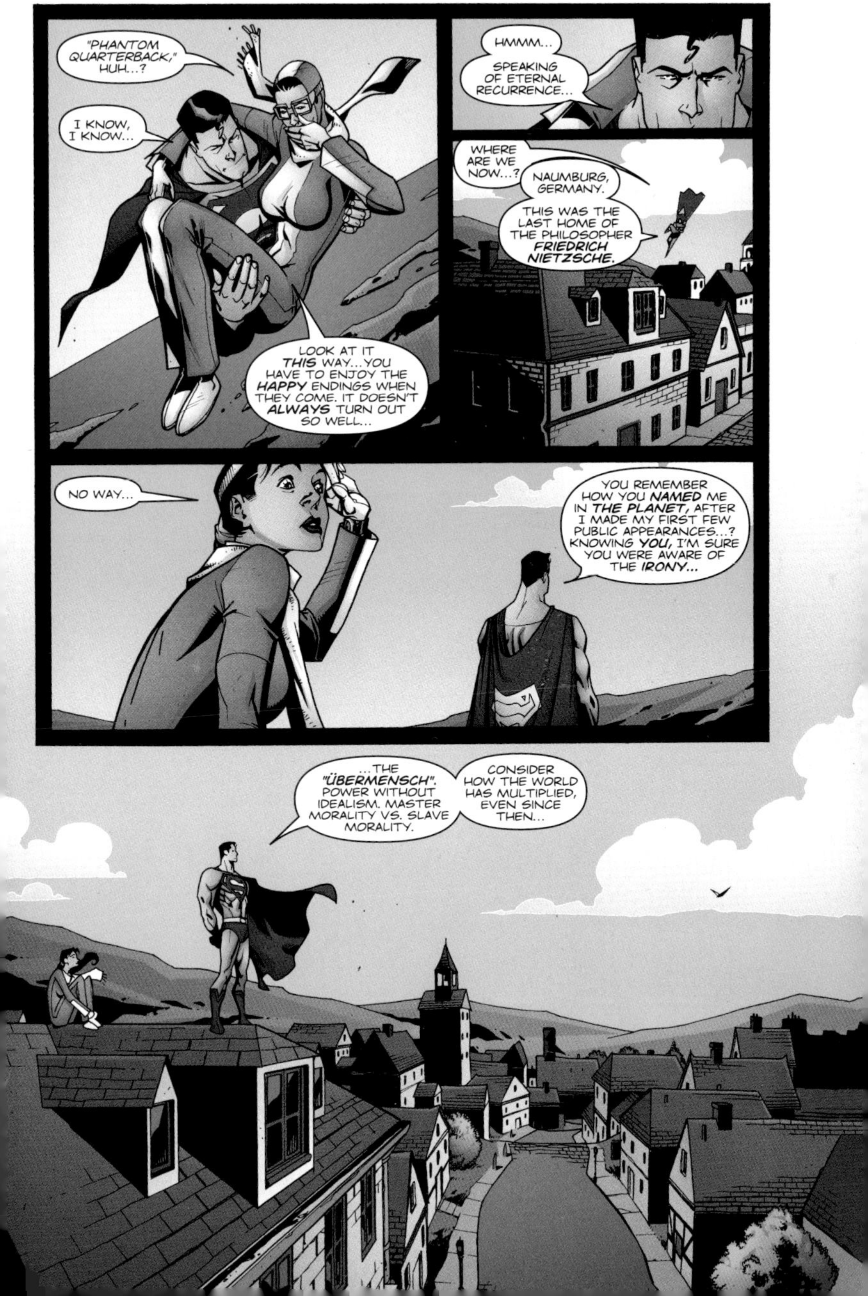
"PHANTOM QUARTERBACK," HUH...?
I KNOW, I KNOW...
LOOK AT IT THIS WAY...YOU HAVE TO ENJOY THE HAPPY ENDINGS WHEN THEY COME. IT DOESN'T ALWAYS TURN OUT SO WELL...
HMMM...
SPEAKING OF ETERNAL RECURRENCE...
WHERE ARE WE NOW...?
NAUMBURG, GERMANY.
THIS WAS THE LAST HOME OF THE PHILOSOPHER FRIEDRICH NIETZSCHE.
NO WAY...
YOU REMEMBER HOW YOU NAMED ME IN THE PLANET, AFTER I MADE MY FIRST FEW PUBLIC APPEARANCES...? KNOWING YOU, I'M SURE YOU WERE AWARE OF THE IRONY...
...THE "ÜBERMENSCH". POWER WITHOUT IDEALISM. MASTER MORALITY VS. SLAVE MORALITY.
CONSIDER HOW THE WORLD HAS MULTIPLIED, EVEN SINCE THEN...

It's a world I've become **identified** with, a perceived overclass of incredible **color** and **imagination.** You know, I've never **asked** to be the one a lot of the others **look** to, for whatever reason. If anything, I try to lead by **example.** It doesn't always work out like that, though…

Case in point…just a few days ago, the entire **superhero community** decided to come looking for me. And it wasn't for **advice.**

It didn't take long to figure out there was some massive **mind control** going on. Even **Batman,** who I'd never seen 'taken over' like that…and he was practically leading the charge. To be perfectly **honest**… I was a little **scared.** These people were my **friends**…and here they were, moving in to **kill** me.

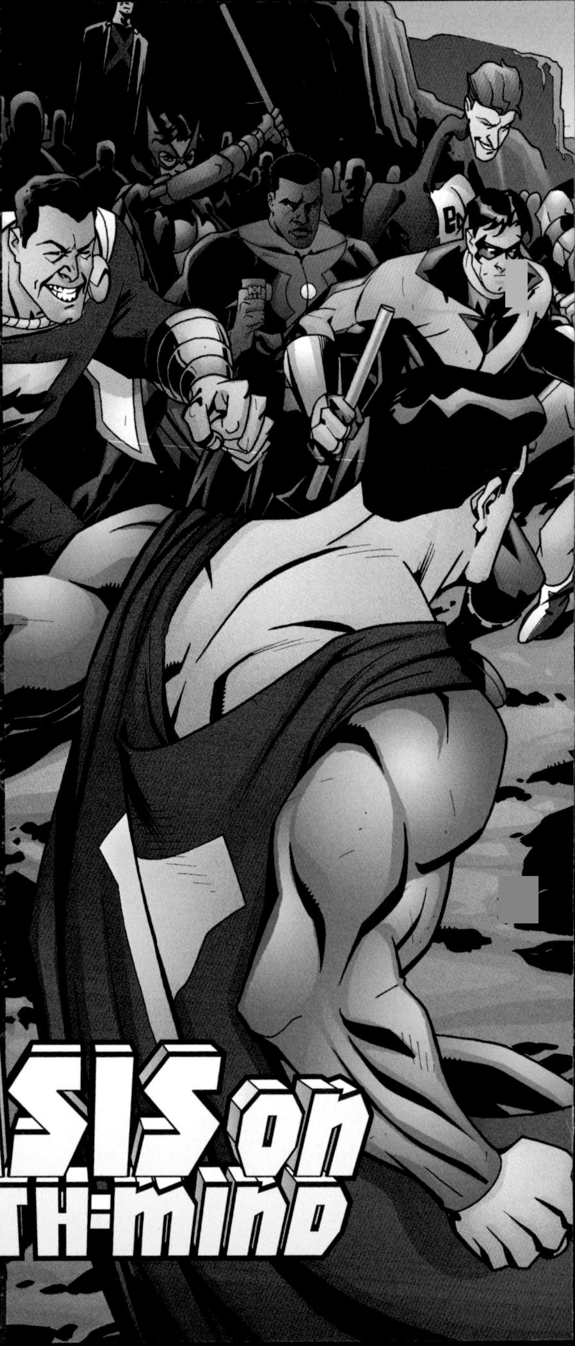

CRISIS ON EARTH-MIND

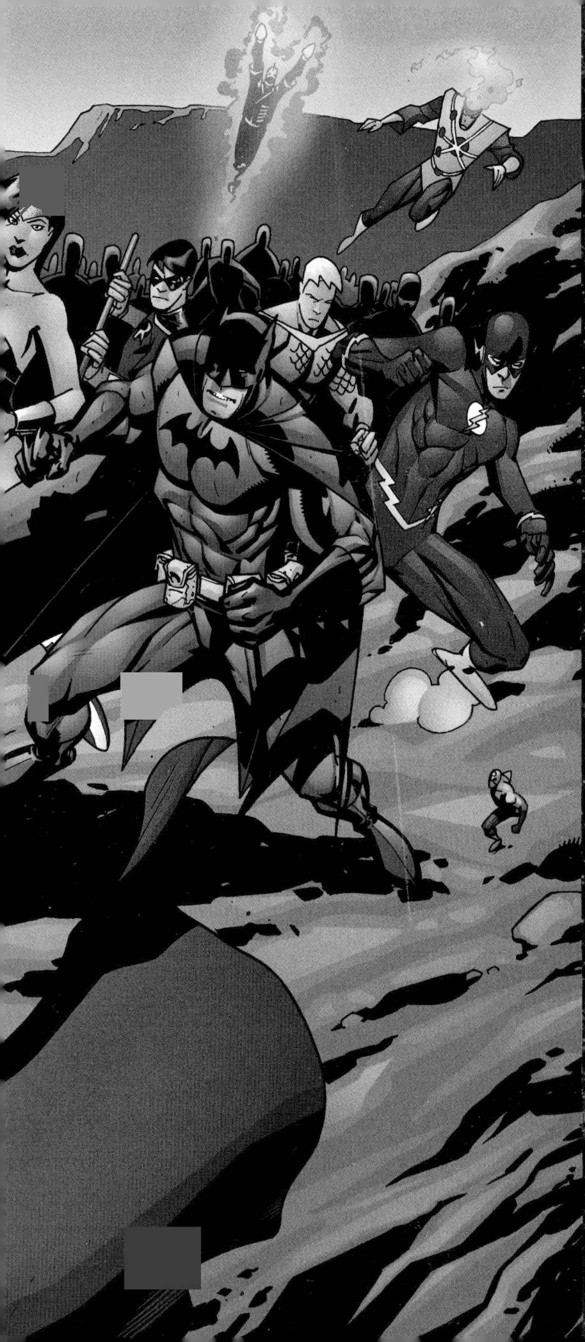

It was certainly a prime opportunity for the kind of "**survival of the fittest**" conflict that a man like Nietzsche would prophesy. A clash of titans that would, in my mind, threaten to **lay waste** everything in its path. These kinds of knock-down, drag-outs tend to result in an inordinate amount of **property damage.** I suppose it goes with the territory…

But I had no intention of **fighting.** There's been too much of that, over the years. too many disagreements leading to **physical** confrontations. Believe me when I tell you…when a **superhero** and **supervillain** engage in open combat, there is no other word to describe it…

…except war.

And, to me, war serves nothing but **itself.** A completely **useless** endeavor…

So, I knew there was a **peaceful** solution to this dilemma. I just had to figure out what it was before my friends could get their hands on me. Luckily, I was feeling the same **psychic tug** that the rest of them had somehow succumbed to. But it was there…I could identify it…and I could **follow** it…

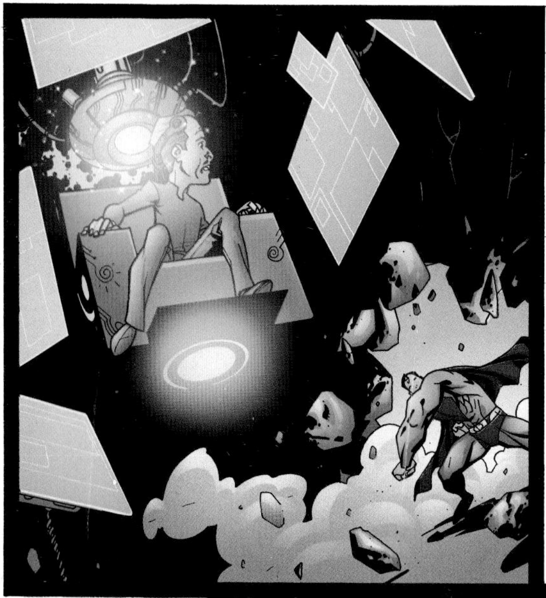

Directly to the secret lab of **Hector Hammond.** An old enemy of **Hal Jordan's**, Hammond was physically inert, but his **mind** had evolved to such a degree that his **telekinesis** was an extremely formidable weapon. **Especially** when it was being augmented by some sort of **mass mind control** device. This one specifically targeted **metahumans** and other heroes of that nature. In fact, the closer I got, the more **powerful** the influence of his machine…

Of course, once I'd **disabled** the machine, all my friends were instantly **freed** of the mind control. Hammond was incarcerated in a specially designed cell that effectively dampened his telekinesis. Believe me, he was safer in **prison**…the look in Batman's eyes once he'd realized what had **happened** to him.

Let's just say, I'd hate to be Hammond if he ever decides to try to **escape.** I'd probably end up saving him from Batman…

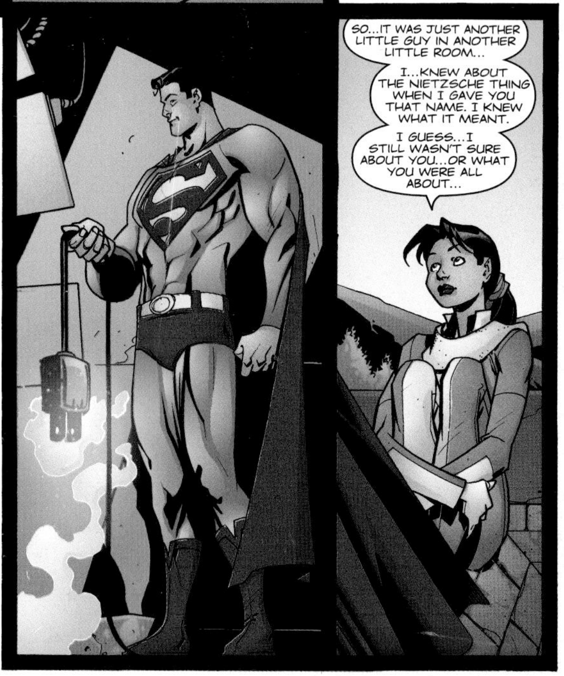
SO...IT WAS JUST ANOTHER LITTLE GUY IN ANOTHER LITTLE ROOM...
I...KNEW ABOUT THE NIETZSCHE THING WHEN I GAVE YOU THAT NAME. I KNEW WHAT IT MEANT.
I GUESS...I STILL WASN'T SURE ABOUT YOU...OR WHAT YOU WERE ALL ABOUT...

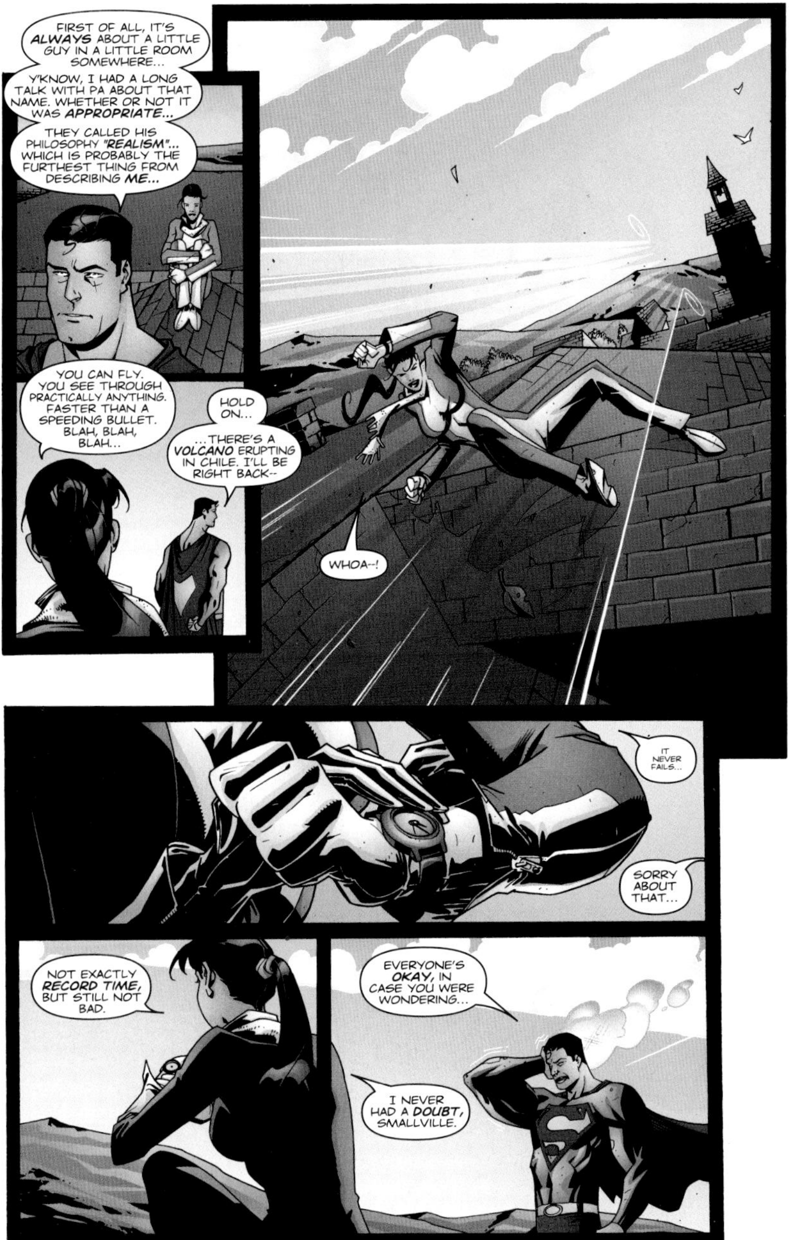
FIRST OF ALL, IT'S ALWAYS ABOUT A LITTLE GUY IN A LITTLE ROOM SOMEWHERE...
Y'KNOW, I HAD A LONG TALK WITH PA ABOUT THAT NAME. WHETHER OR NOT IT WAS APPROPRIATE...
THEY CALLED HIS PHILOSOPHY "REALISM"... WHICH IS PROBABLY THE FURTHEST THING FROM DESCRIBING ME...
YOU CAN FLY. YOU SEE THROUGH PRACTICALLY ANYTHING. FASTER THAN A SPEEDING BULLET. BLAH, BLAH, BLAH...
HOLD ON...
...THERE'S A VOLCANO ERUPTING IN CHILE. I'LL BE RIGHT BACK--
WHOA--!
IT NEVER FAILS...
SORRY ABOUT THAT...
NOT EXACTLY RECORD TIME, BUT STILL NOT BAD.
EVERYONE'S OKAY, IN CASE YOU WERE WONDERING...
I NEVER HAD A DOUBT, SMALLVILLE.

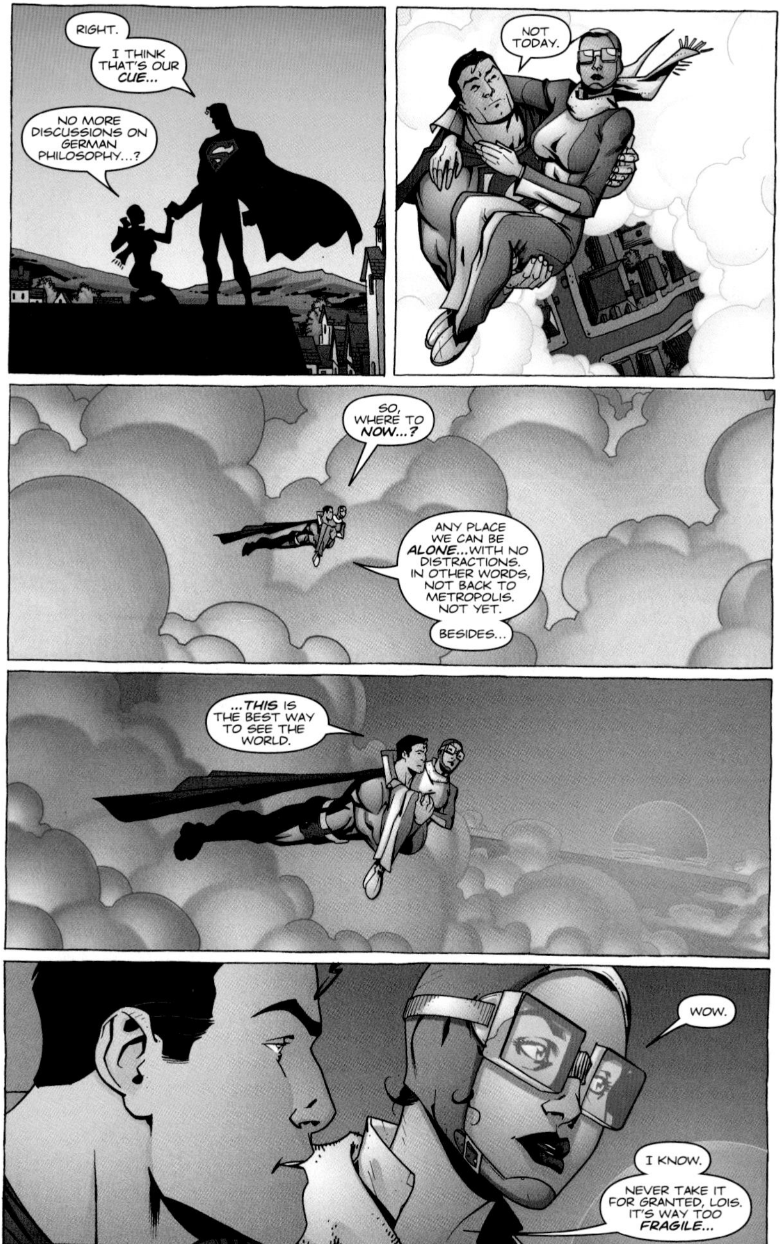
RIGHT.
I THINK THAT'S OUR *CUE...*
NO MORE DISCUSSIONS ON GERMAN PHILOSOPHY...?
NOT TODAY.
SO, WHERE TO *NOW...?*
ANY PLACE WE CAN BE *ALONE...* WITH NO DISTRACTIONS. IN OTHER WORDS, NOT BACK TO METROPOLIS. NOT YET.
BESIDES...
...THIS IS THE BEST WAY TO SEE THE WORLD.
WOW.
I KNOW.
NEVER TAKE IT FOR GRANTED, LOIS. IT'S WAY TOO *FRAGILE...*

Here's a little incident that was never reported: A few weeks ago, the entire **Earth** was at risk when a sudden, inexplicable **phenomenon** occurred. Even in the upper atmosphere, I could feel the **imbalance** of magnetic waves…

Ripples and tremors rising up from the earth's surface.

It was something I'd never felt before--and I've experienced the planet in jeopardy more times than I'd like to count--so when I did a quick check using wide scan **x-ray vision,** I saw a sight that sent **chills** down my spine. The entire elemental makeup of the Earth…**transformed** into some **other** molecular structure. The planet had literally become a **single-celled organism**…and it was beginning to **divide**…!

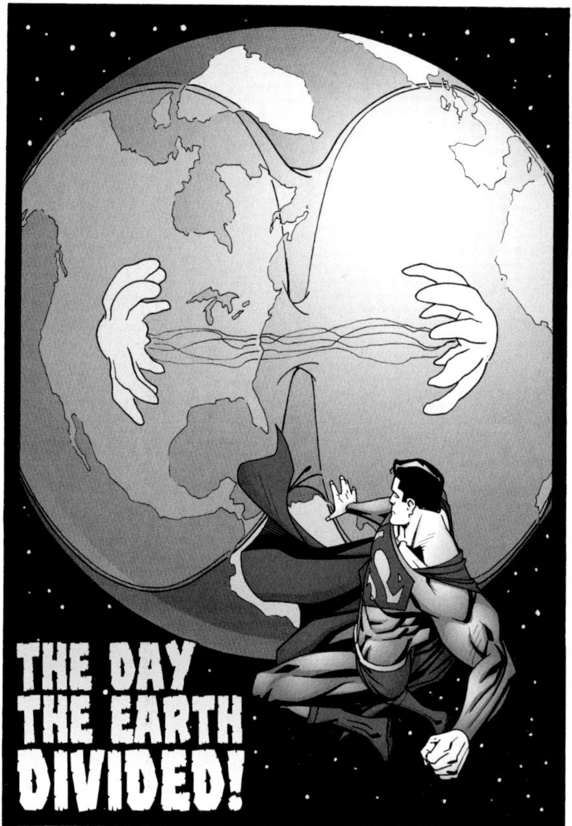
THE DAY
THE EARTH
DIVIDED!

I immediately tried to track the magnetic disturbances to some sort of **origin point.** By the time I'd narrowed it down to the **Amazon Rain Forest**… the entire surface of the Earth was succumbing to the rigors of cellular division on a **planetary** scale…!

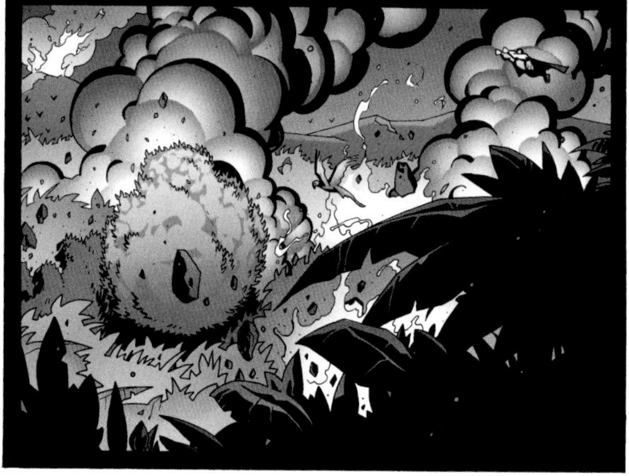

Finally I arrived at what I assumed was my **destination**...an ancient temple dating back several **centuries.** I could see the natives worshipping whatever higher power they believed in. I wondered if this situation was truly **religious** in nature. There was only **one way** to find out...

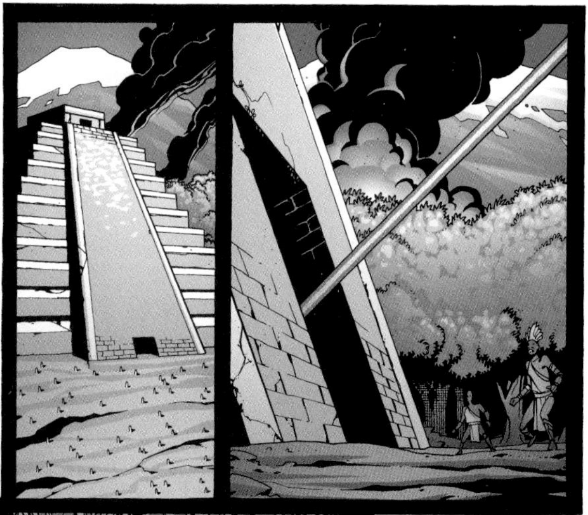

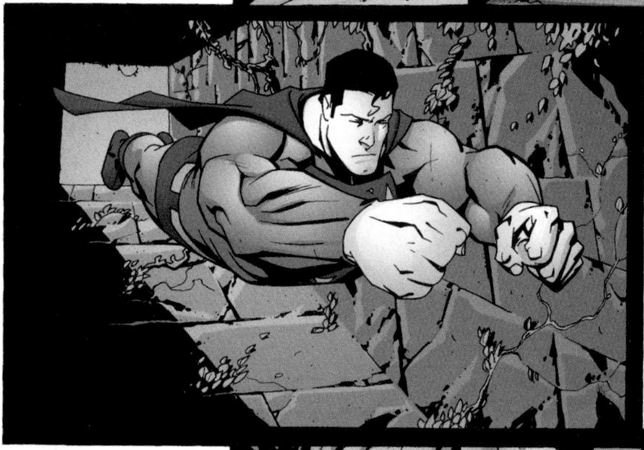

The **pressure** inside the temple was **enormous.** Like being at the center of a **star**... the gravity was literally crushing me...

I found the remains of a giant **starship** that had probably crash-landed here a millennium ago. The temple had been built up around it. Apparently, there was at least one survivor... and this individual was undoubtedly the cause of the planetary crisis...

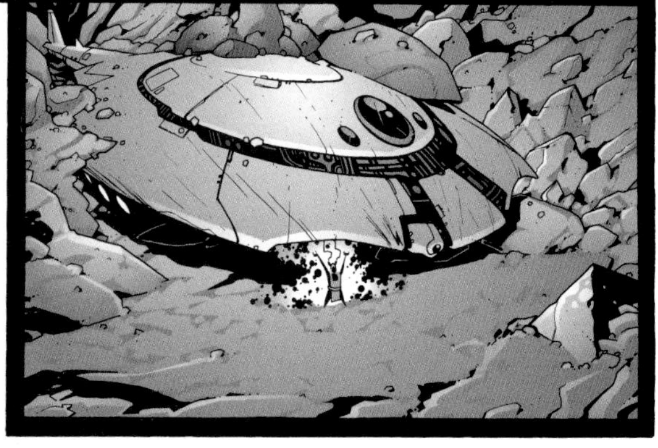

This creature certainly wasn't going to relent without a **fight**. Judging by his wardrobe, this **was** some sort of **religious** ceremony, with the Earth itself offered in sacrifice. I was momentarily **detained** by some sort of psychodramatic c**hess match**…but I was in no mood to play **games**…

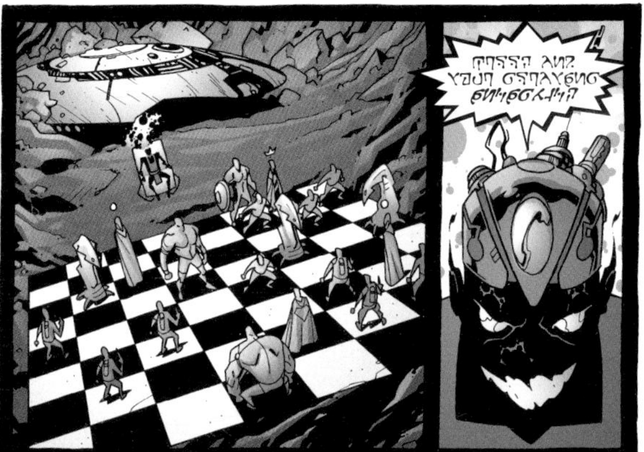

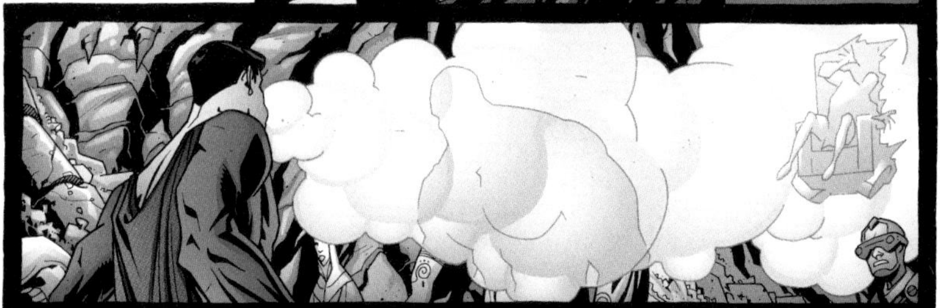

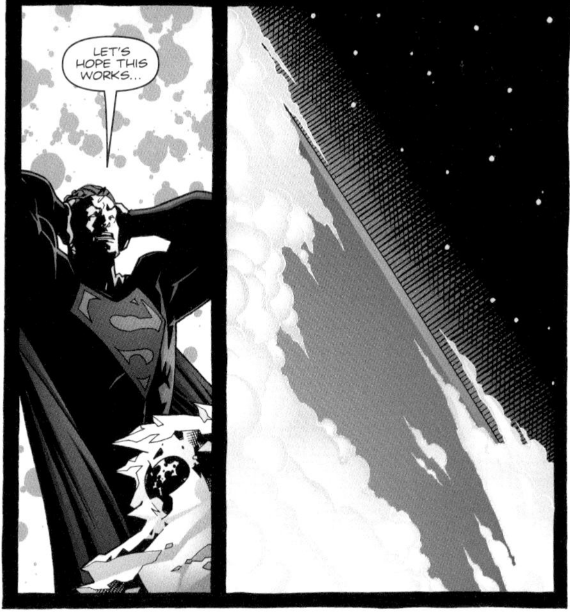
LET'S HOPE THIS WORKS...

Needless to say, a little **brainpower** can go a long way. I used the creature's alien technology to **reverse** the cellular division and **restore** the earth to its natural elemental state. All I had to do was **imagine** it…and soon it became **reality**…

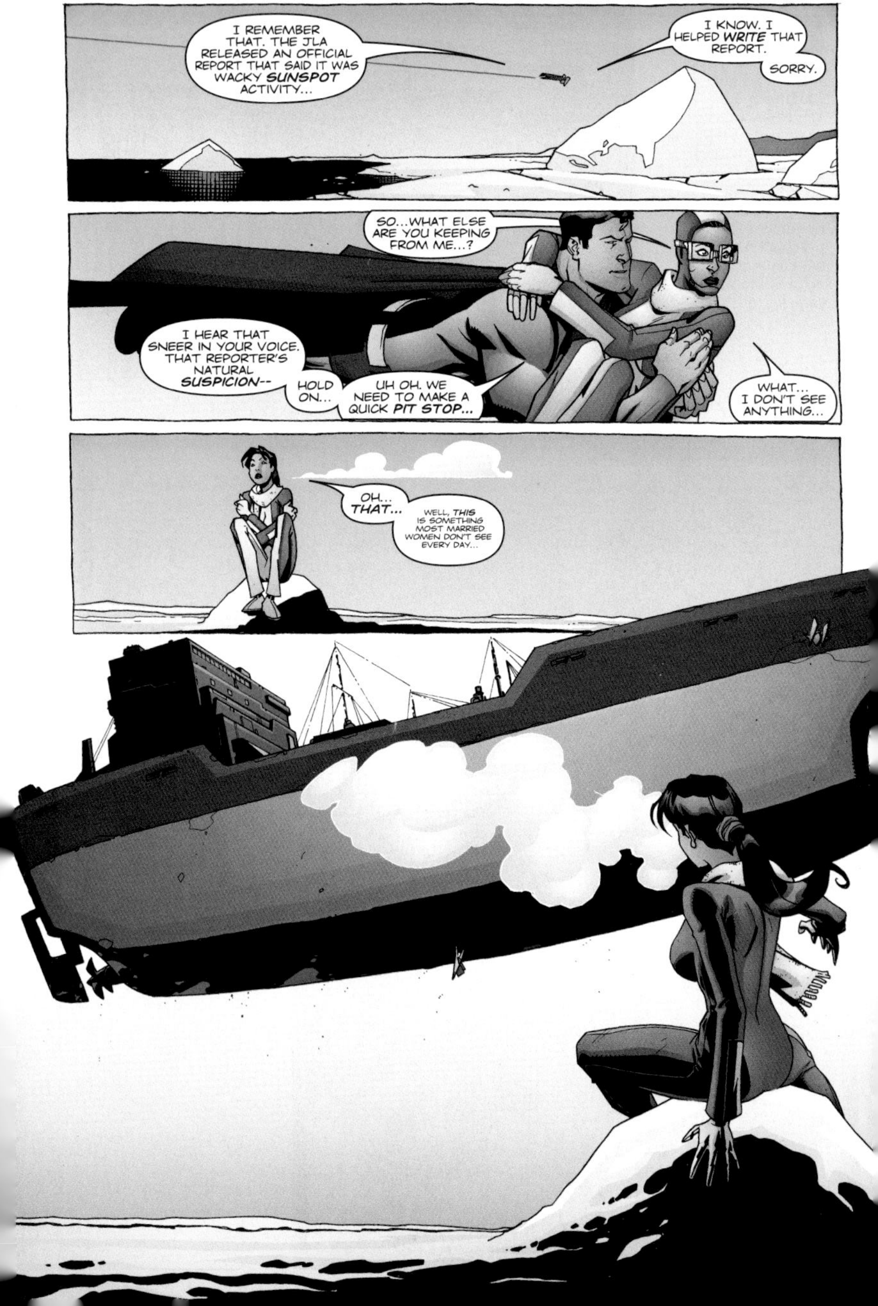
I REMEMBER THAT. THE JLA RELEASED AN OFFICIAL REPORT THAT SAID IT WAS WACKY SUNSPOT ACTIVITY...
I KNOW. I HELPED WRITE THAT REPORT.
SORRY.
SO...WHAT ELSE ARE YOU KEEPING FROM ME...?
I HEAR THAT SNEER IN YOUR VOICE. THAT REPORTER'S NATURAL SUSPICION--
HOLD ON...
UH OH. WE NEED TO MAKE A QUICK PIT STOP...
WHAT... I DON'T SEE ANYTHING...
OH... THAT...
WELL, THIS IS SOMETHING MOST MARRIED WOMEN DON'T SEE EVERY DAY...

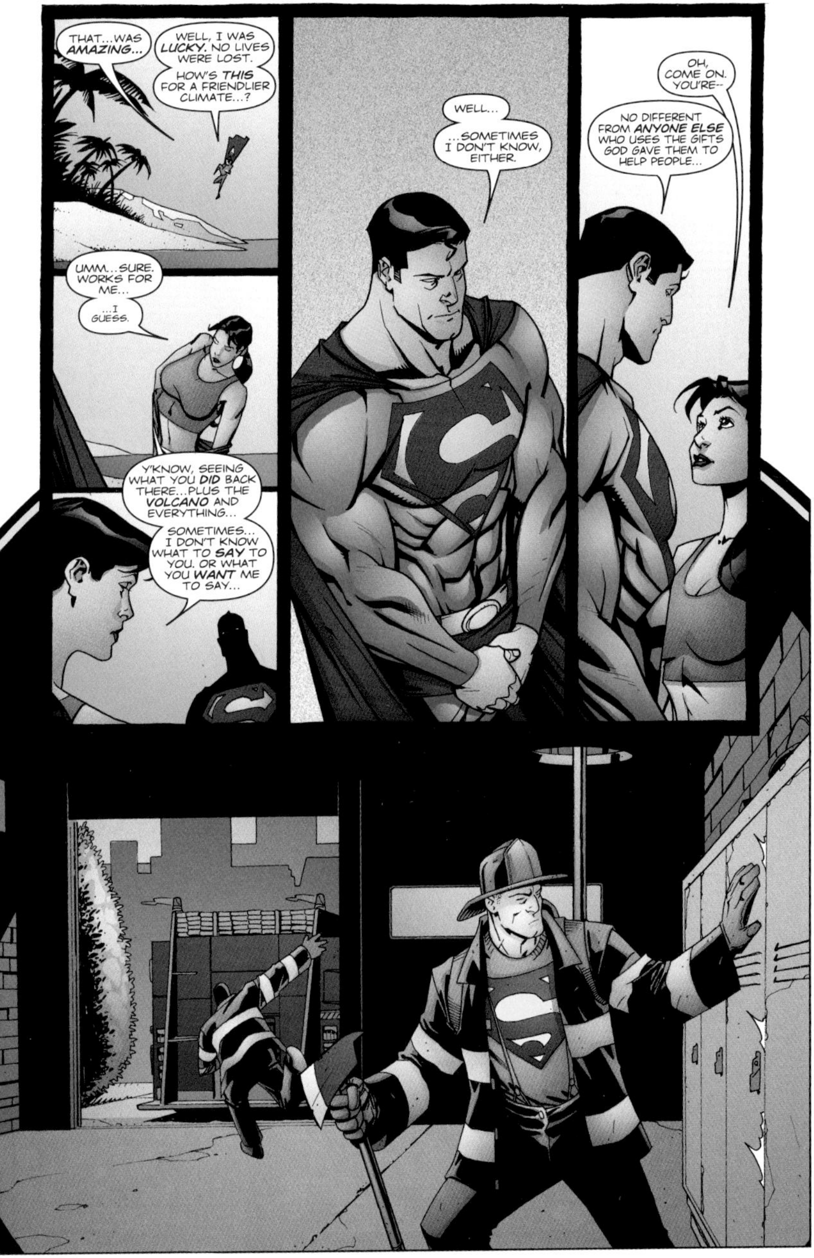
THAT...WAS AMAZING...
WELL, I WAS LUCKY. NO LIVES WERE LOST.
HOW'S THIS FOR A FRIENDLIER CLIMATE...?
UMM...SURE. WORKS FOR ME...
...I GUESS.
Y'KNOW, SEEING WHAT YOU DID BACK THERE...PLUS THE VOLCANO AND EVERYTHING...
SOMETIMES... I DON'T KNOW WHAT TO SAY TO YOU. OR WHAT YOU WANT ME TO SAY...
WELL...
...SOMETIMES I DON'T KNOW, EITHER.
OH, COME ON. YOU'RE--
NO DIFFERENT FROM ANYONE ELSE WHO USES THE GIFTS GOD GAVE THEM TO HELP PEOPLE...

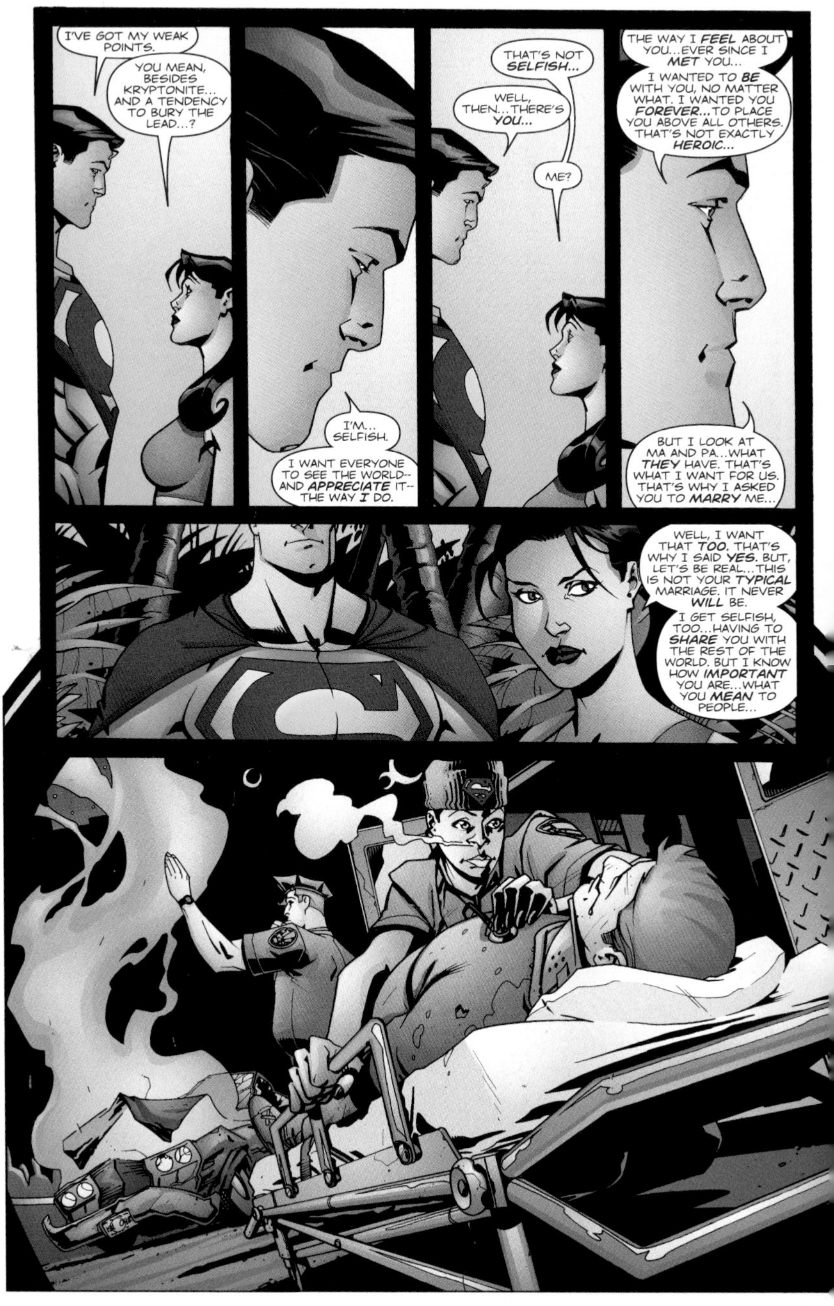
I'VE GOT MY WEAK POINTS.
YOU MEAN, BESIDES KRYPTONITE... AND A TENDENCY TO BURY THE LEAD...?
I'M... SELFISH.
I WANT EVERYONE TO SEE THE WORLD-- AND APPRECIATE IT-- THE WAY I DO.
THAT'S NOT SELFISH...
WELL, THEN...THERE'S YOU...
ME?
THE WAY I FEEL ABOUT YOU...EVER SINCE I MET YOU...
I WANTED TO BE WITH YOU, NO MATTER WHAT. I WANTED YOU FOREVER...TO PLACE YOU ABOVE ALL OTHERS. THAT'S NOT EXACTLY HEROIC...
BUT I LOOK AT MA AND PA...WHAT THEY HAVE. THAT'S WHAT I WANT FOR US. THAT'S WHY I ASKED YOU TO MARRY ME...
WELL, I WANT THAT TOO. THAT'S WHY I SAID YES. BUT, LET'S BE REAL...THIS IS NOT YOUR TYPICAL MARRIAGE. IT NEVER WILL BE.
I GET SELFISH, TOO...HAVING TO SHARE YOU WITH THE REST OF THE WORLD. BUT I KNOW HOW IMPORTANT YOU ARE...WHAT YOU MEAN TO PEOPLE...

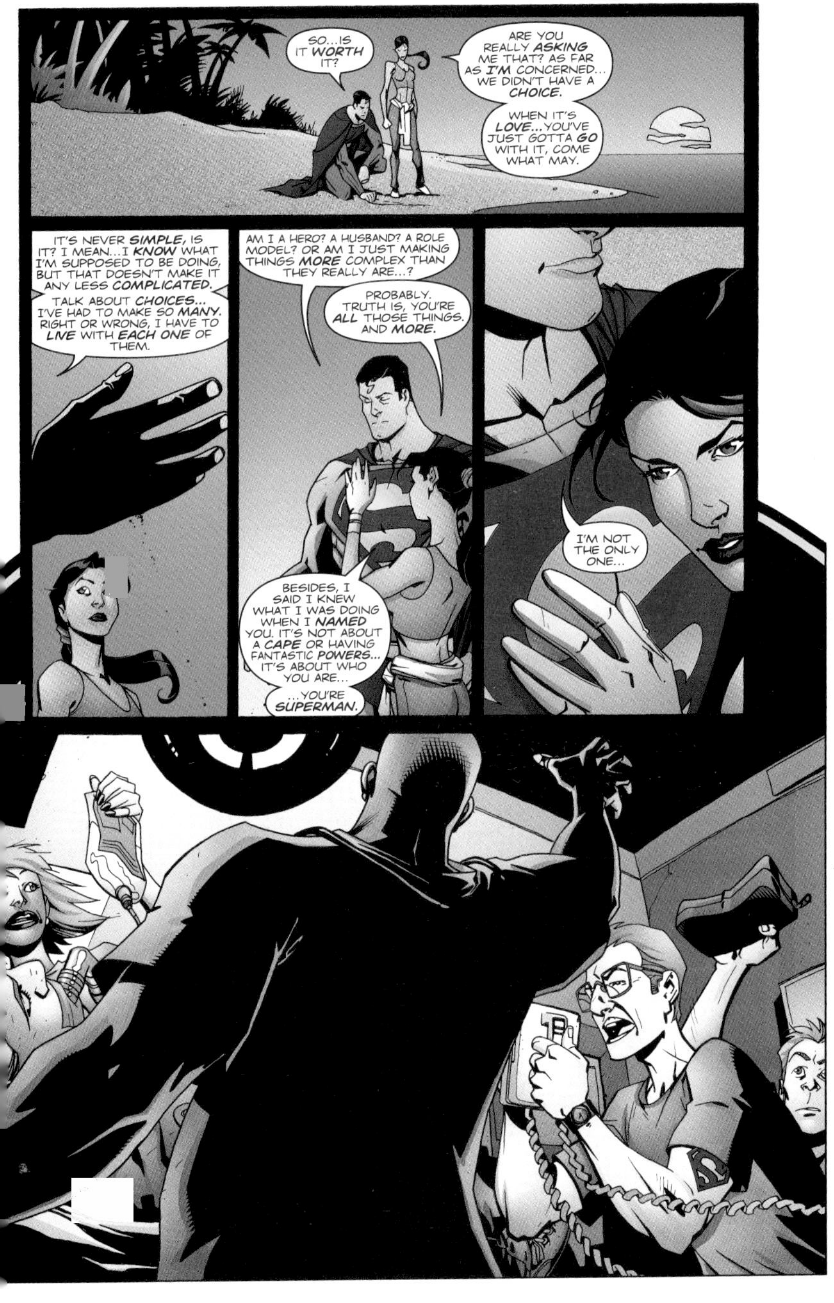

SO...IS IT WORTH IT?
ARE YOU REALLY ASKING ME THAT? AS FAR AS I'M CONCERNED... WE DIDN'T HAVE A CHOICE.
WHEN IT'S LOVE...YOU'VE JUST GOTTA GO WITH IT, COME WHAT MAY.
IT'S NEVER SIMPLE, IS IT? I MEAN...I KNOW WHAT I'M SUPPOSED TO BE DOING, BUT THAT DOESN'T MAKE IT ANY LESS COMPLICATED.
TALK ABOUT CHOICES... I'VE HAD TO MAKE SO MANY. RIGHT OR WRONG, I HAVE TO LIVE WITH EACH ONE OF THEM.
AM I A HERO? A HUSBAND? A ROLE MODEL? OR AM I JUST MAKING THINGS MORE COMPLEX THAN THEY REALLY ARE...?
PROBABLY. TRUTH IS, YOU'RE ALL THOSE THINGS. AND MORE.
BESIDES, I SAID I KNEW WHAT I WAS DOING WHEN I NAMED YOU. IT'S NOT ABOUT A CAPE OR HAVING FANTASTIC POWERS... IT'S ABOUT WHO YOU ARE...
...YOU'RE SUPERMAN.
I'M NOT THE ONLY ONE...

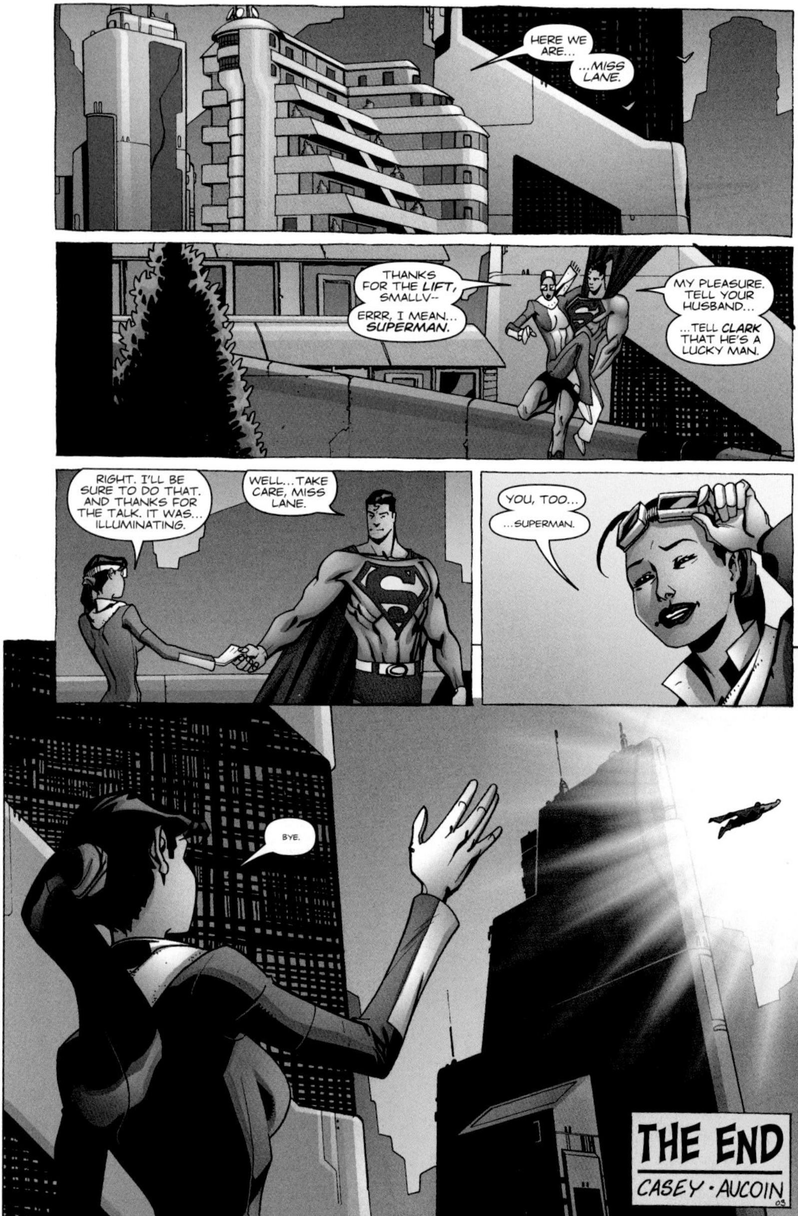
HERE WE ARE...
...MISS LANE.
THANKS FOR THE LIFT, SMALLV--
ERRR, I MEAN... SUPERMAN.
MY PLEASURE. TELL YOUR HUSBAND...
...TELL CLARK THAT HE'S A LUCKY MAN.
RIGHT. I'LL BE SURE TO DO THAT. AND THANKS FOR THE TALK. IT WAS... ILLUMINATING.
WELL...TAKE CARE, MISS LANE.
YOU, TOO...
...SUPERMAN.
BYE.
THE END
CASEY • AUCOIN
03

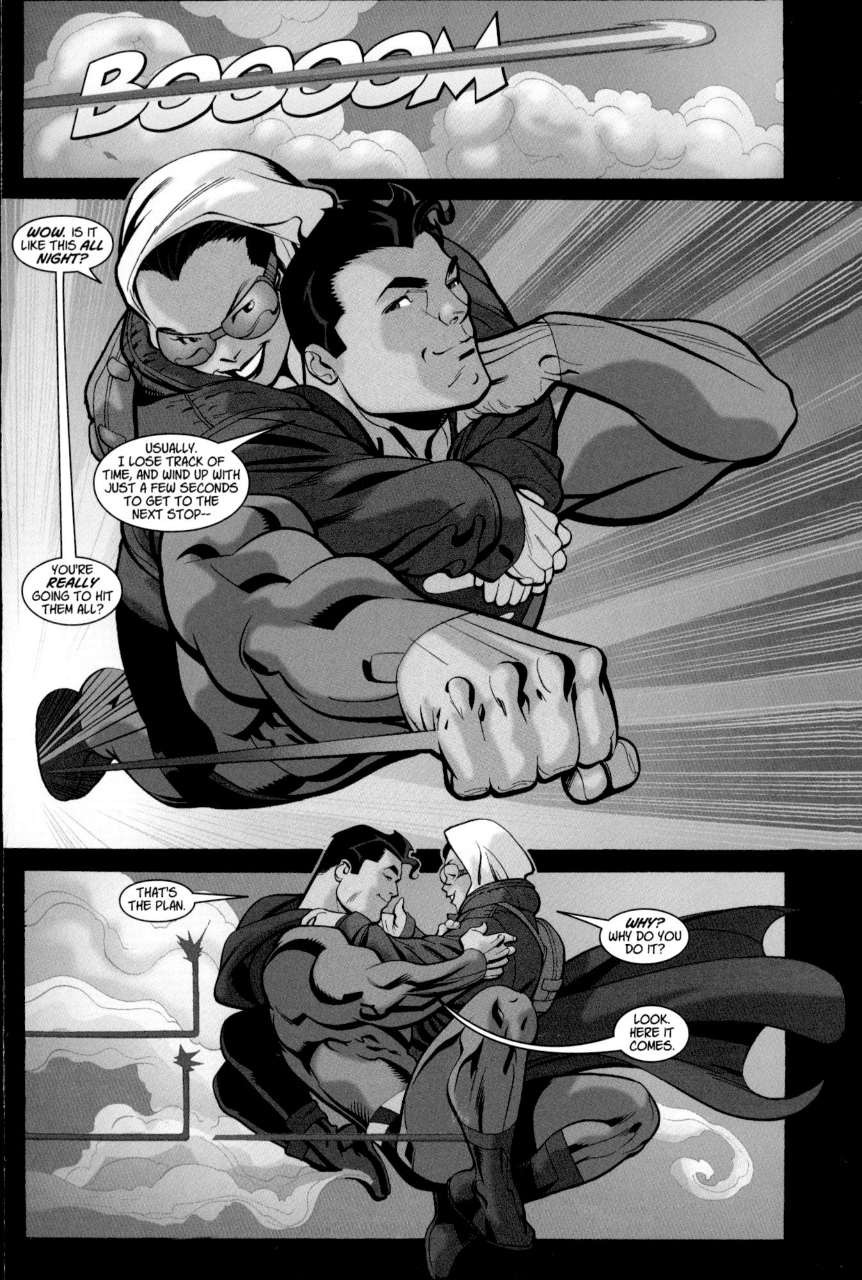
BOOOOOM
WOW. IS IT LIKE THIS ALL NIGHT?
USUALLY. I LOSE TRACK OF TIME, AND WIND UP WITH JUST A FEW SECONDS TO GET TO THE NEXT STOP--
YOU'RE REALLY GOING TO HIT THEM ALL?
THAT'S THE PLAN.
WHY? WHY DO YOU DO IT?
LOOK. HERE IT COMES.

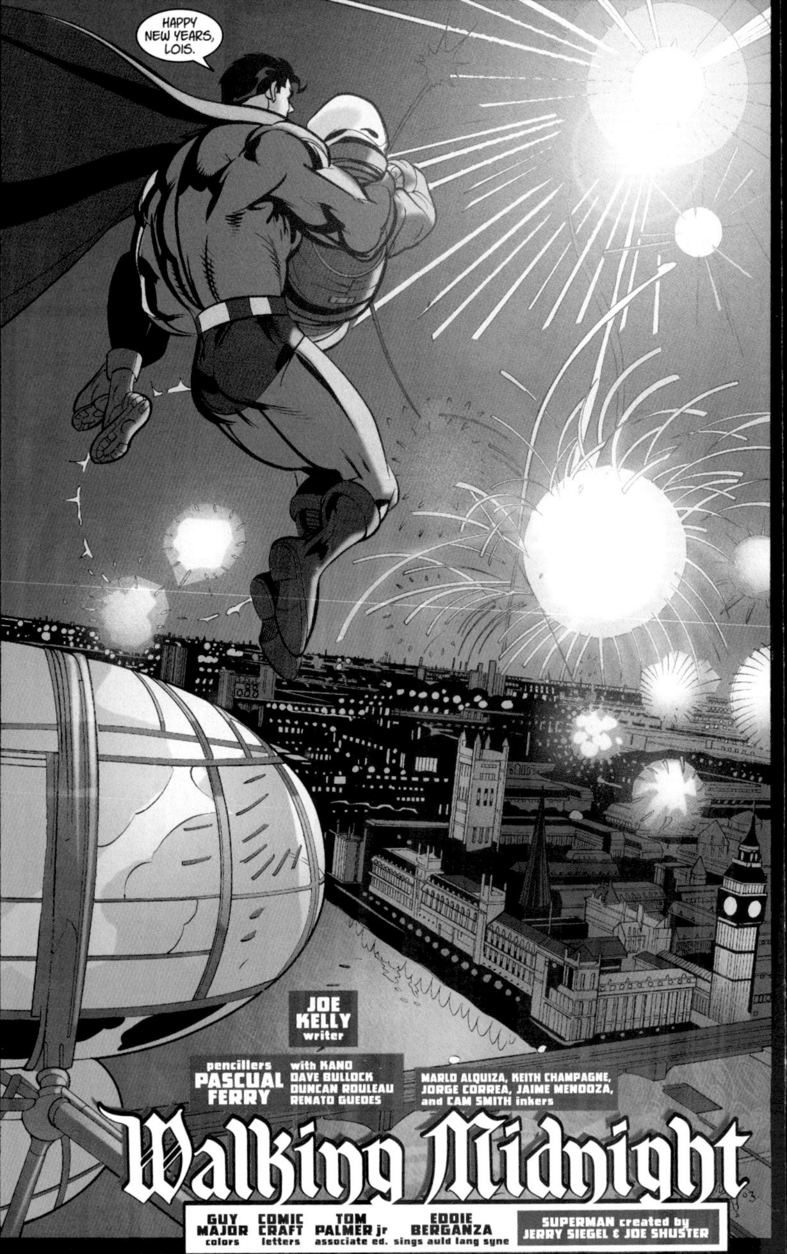
HAPPY NEW YEARS, LOIS.
JOE KELLY writer
pencillers PASCUAL FERRY with KANO DAVE BULLOCK DUNCAN ROULEAU RENATO GUEDES
MARLO ALQUIZA, KEITH CHAMPAGNE, JORGE CORREA, JAIME MENDOZA, and CAM SMITH inkers
Walking Midnight
GUY MAJOR colors
COMIC CRAFT letters
TOM PALMER jr associate ed.
EDDIE BERGANZA sings auld lang syne
SUPERMAN created by JERRY SIEGEL & JOE SHUSTER

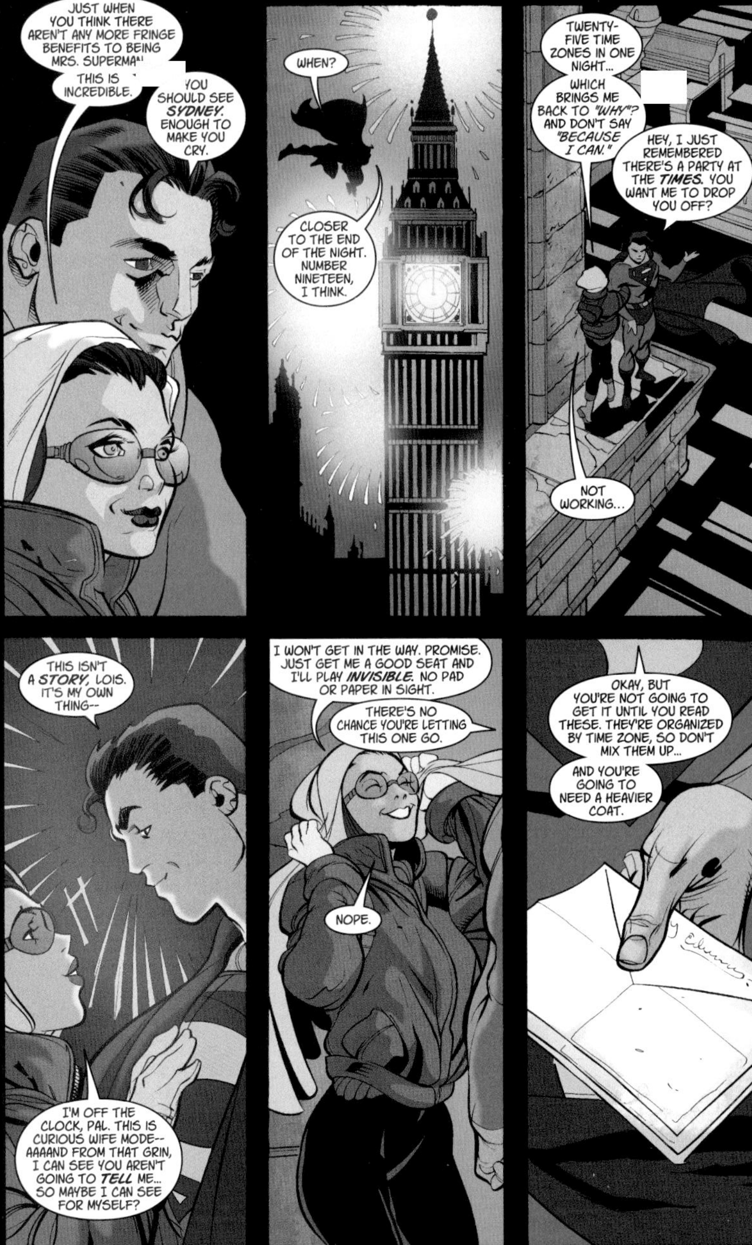
JUST WHEN YOU THINK THERE AREN'T ANY MORE FRINGE BENEFITS TO BEING MRS. SUPERMA
THIS IS INCREDIBLE.
YOU SHOULD SEE SYDNEY. ENOUGH TO MAKE YOU CRY.
WHEN?
CLOSER TO THE END OF THE NIGHT. NUMBER NINETEEN, I THINK.
TWENTY-FIVE TIME ZONES IN ONE NIGHT...
WHICH BRINGS ME BACK TO "WHY"? AND DON'T SAY "BECAUSE I CAN."
HEY, I JUST REMEMBERED THERE'S A PARTY AT THE TIMES. YOU WANT ME TO DROP YOU OFF?
NOT WORKING...
THIS ISN'T A STORY, LOIS. IT'S MY OWN THING--
I'M OFF THE CLOCK, PAL. THIS IS CURIOUS WIFE MODE-- AAAAND FROM THAT GRIN, I CAN SEE YOU AREN'T GOING TO TELL ME... SO MAYBE I CAN SEE FOR MYSELF?
I WON'T GET IN THE WAY. PROMISE. JUST GET ME A GOOD SEAT AND I'LL PLAY INVISIBLE. NO PAD OR PAPER IN SIGHT.
THERE'S NO CHANCE YOU'RE LETTING THIS ONE GO.
NOPE.
OKAY, BUT YOU'RE NOT GOING TO GET IT UNTIL YOU READ THESE. THEY'RE ORGANIZED BY TIME ZONE, SO DON'T MIX THEM UP...
AND YOU'RE GOING TO NEED A HEAVIER COAT.

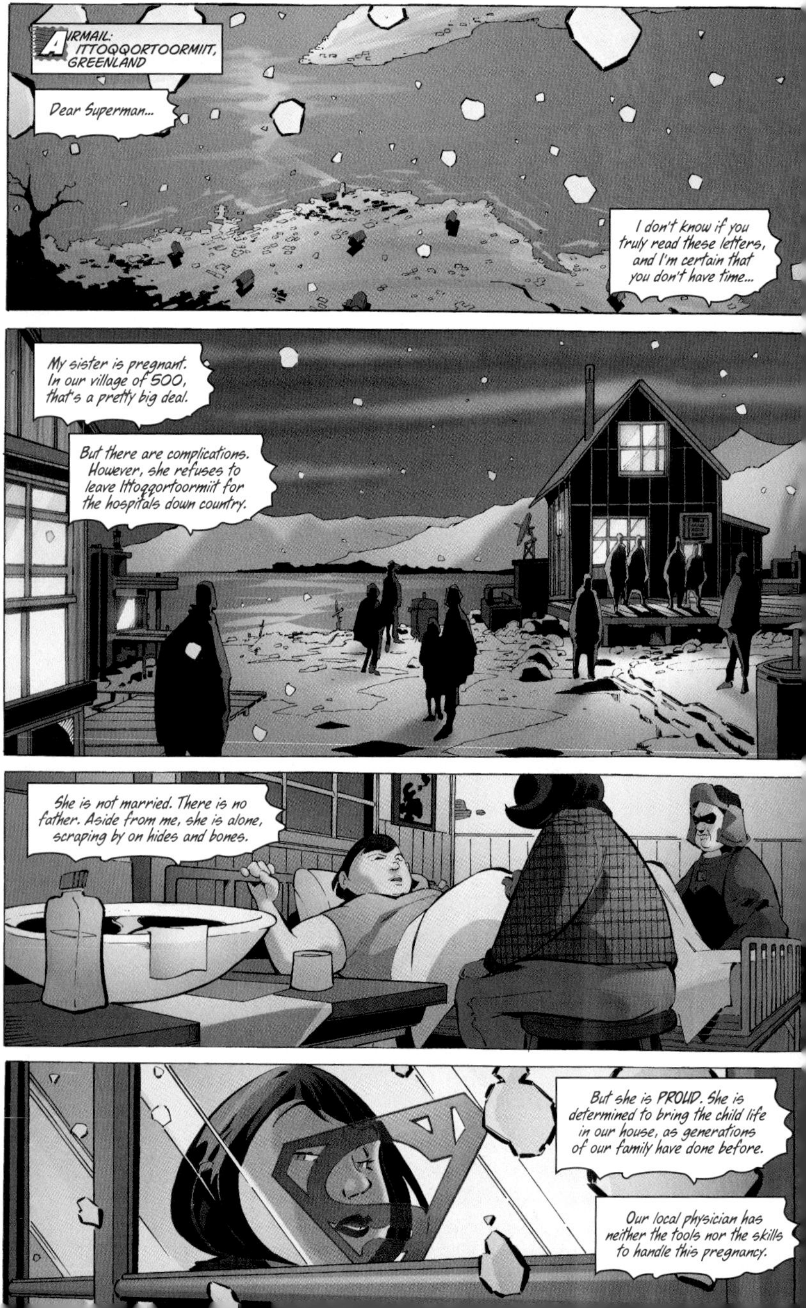
AIRMAIL: ITTOQQORTOORMIIT, GREENLAND
Dear Superman...
I don't know if you truly read these letters, and I'm certain that you don't have time...
My sister is pregnant. In our village of 500, that's a pretty big deal.
But there are complications. However, she refuses to leave Ittoqqortoormiit for the hospitals down country.
She is not married. There is no father. Aside from me, she is alone, scraping by on hides and bones.
But she is PROUD. She is determined to bring the child life in our house, as generations of our family have done before.
Our local physician has neither the tools nor the skills to handle this pregnancy.

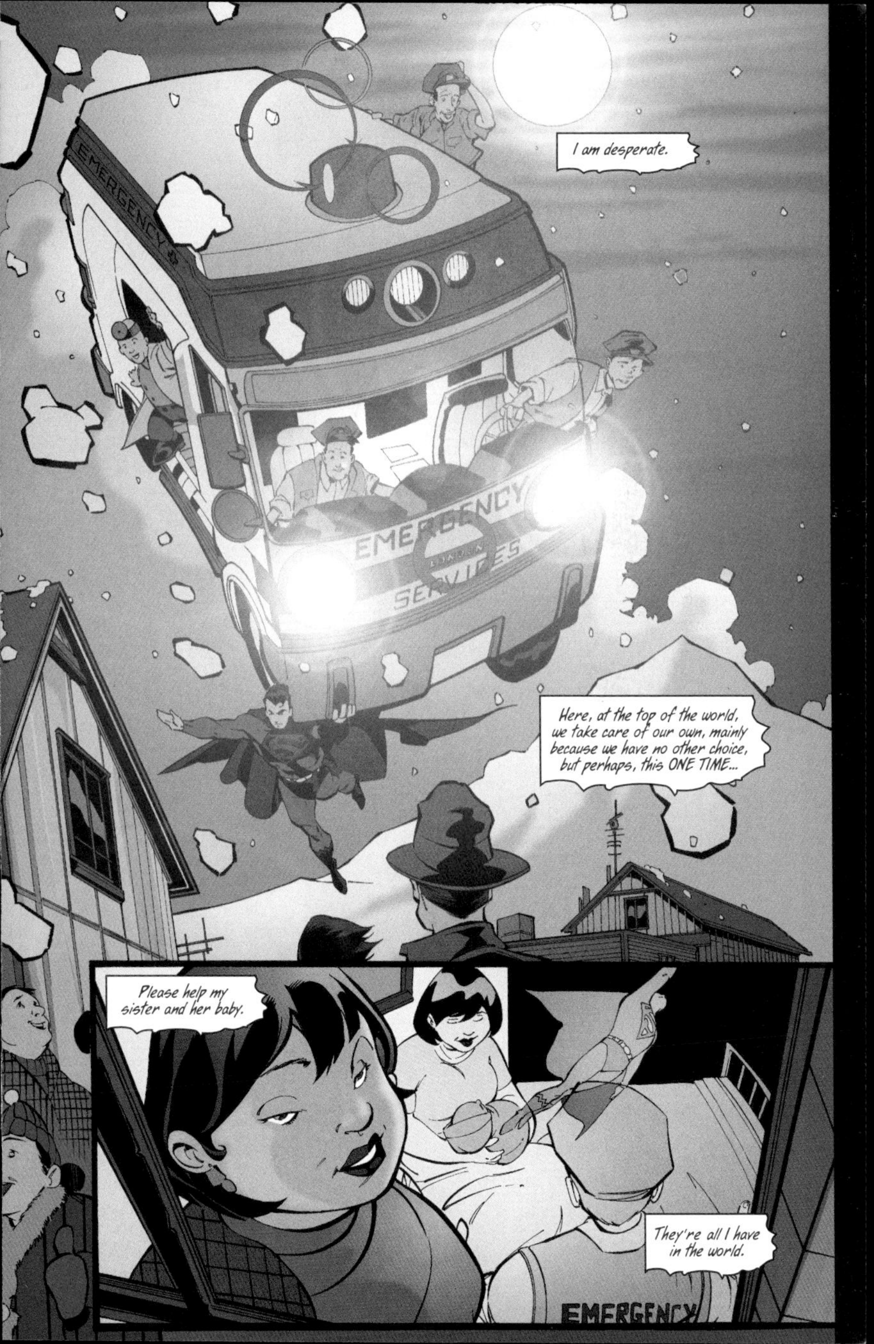
I am desperate.
EMERGENCY
EMERGENCY
EMERGENCY
SERVICES
Here, at the top of the world, we take care of our own, mainly because we have no other choice, but perhaps, this ONE TIME...
Please help my sister and her baby.
They're all I have in the world.
EMERGENCY

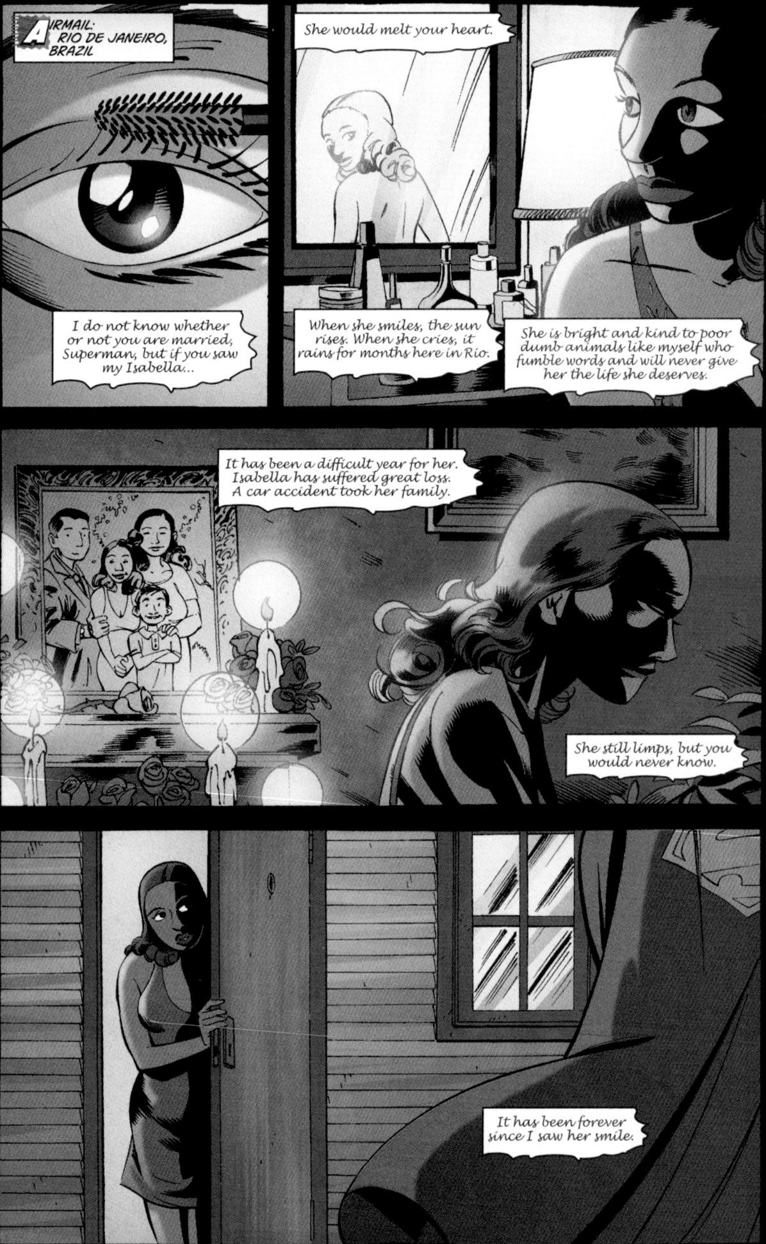
AIRMAIL: RIO DE JANEIRO, BRAZIL
I do not know whether or not you are married, Superman, but if you saw my Isabella...
She would melt your heart.
When she smiles, the sun rises. When she cries, it rains for months here in Rio.
She is bright and kind to poor dumb animals like myself who fumble words and will never give her the life she deserves.
It has been a difficult year for her. Isabella has suffered great loss. A car accident took her family.
She still limps, but you would never know.
It has been forever since I saw her smile.

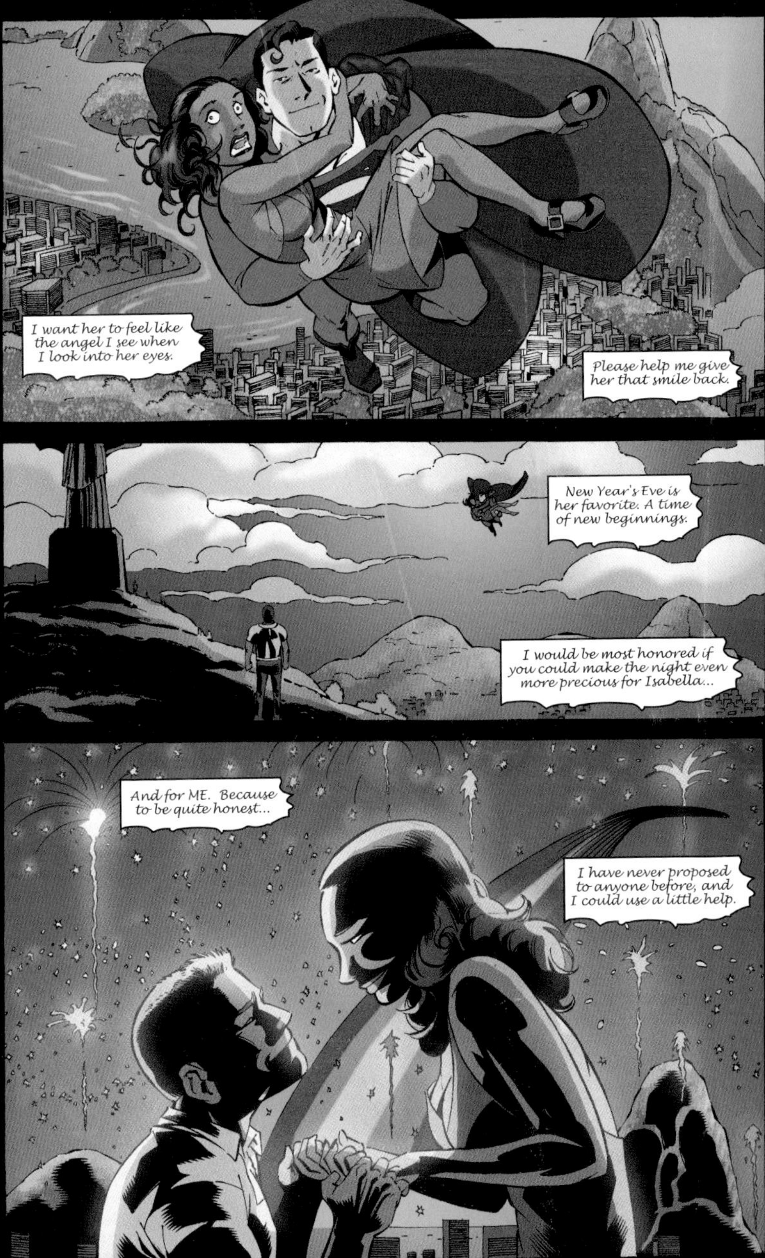
I want her to feel like the angel I see when I look into her eyes.
Please help me give her that smile back.
New Year's Eve is her favorite. A time of new beginnings.
I would be most honored if you could make the night even more precious for Isabella...
And for ME. Because to be quite honest...
I have never proposed to anyone before, and I could use a little help.

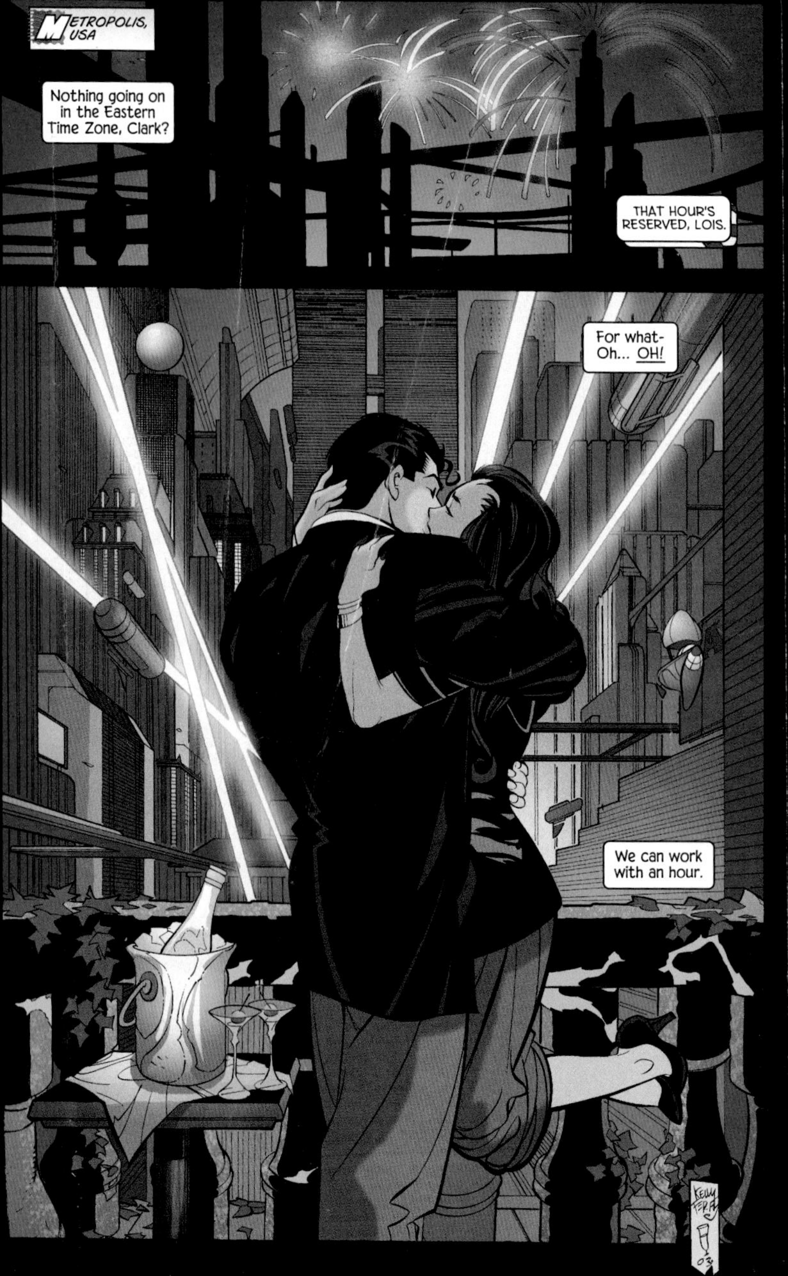

METROPOLIS, USA
Nothing going on in the Eastern Time Zone, Clark?
THAT HOUR'S RESERVED, LOIS.
For what- Oh... OH!
We can work with an hour.

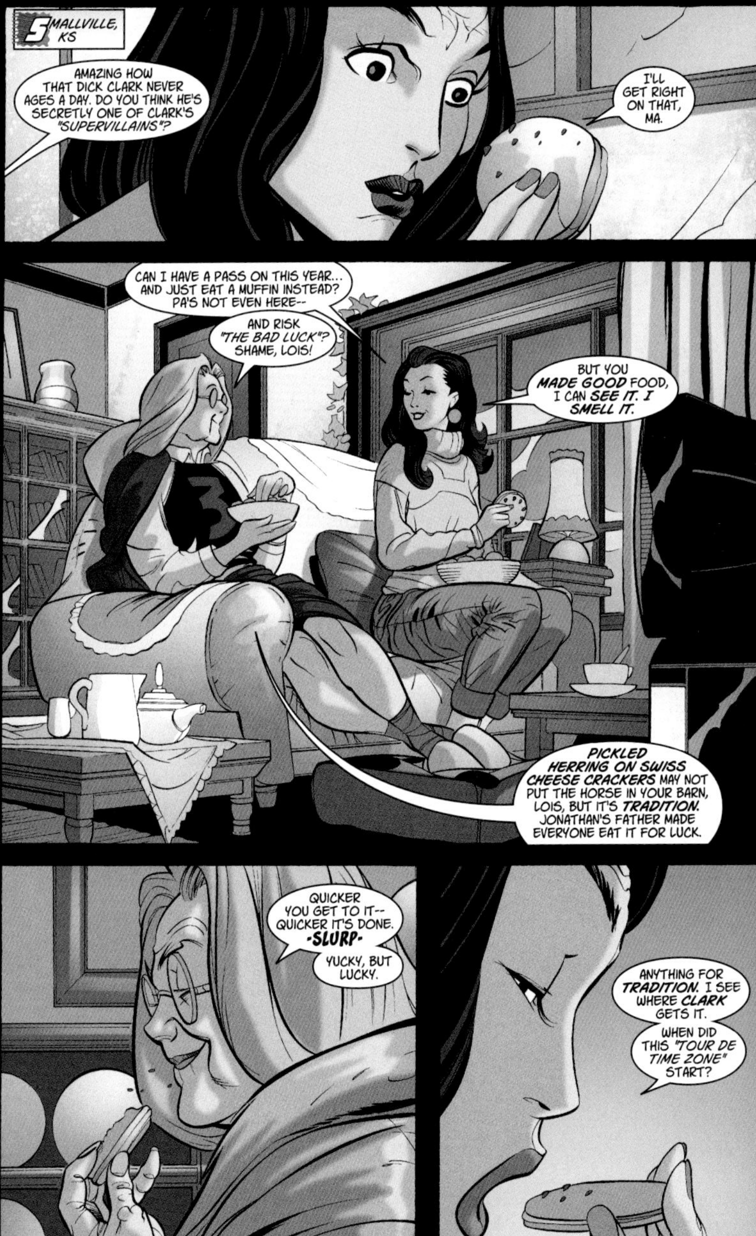
SMALLVILLE, KS
AMAZING HOW THAT DICK CLARK NEVER AGES A DAY. DO YOU THINK HE'S SECRETLY ONE OF CLARK'S "SUPERVILLAINS"?
I'LL GET RIGHT ON THAT, MA.
CAN I HAVE A PASS ON THIS YEAR... AND JUST EAT A MUFFIN INSTEAD? PA'S NOT EVEN HERE--
AND RISK "THE BAD LUCK"? SHAME, LOIS!
BUT YOU MADE GOOD FOOD, I CAN SEE IT. I SMELL IT.
PICKLED HERRING ON SWISS CHEESE CRACKERS MAY NOT PUT THE HORSE IN YOUR BARN, LOIS, BUT IT'S TRADITION. JONATHAN'S FATHER MADE EVERYONE EAT IT FOR LUCK.
QUICKER YOU GET TO IT-- QUICKER IT'S DONE.
-SLURP-
YUCKY, BUT LUCKY.
ANYTHING FOR TRADITION. I SEE WHERE CLARK GETS IT.
WHEN DID THIS "TOUR DE TIME ZONE" START?

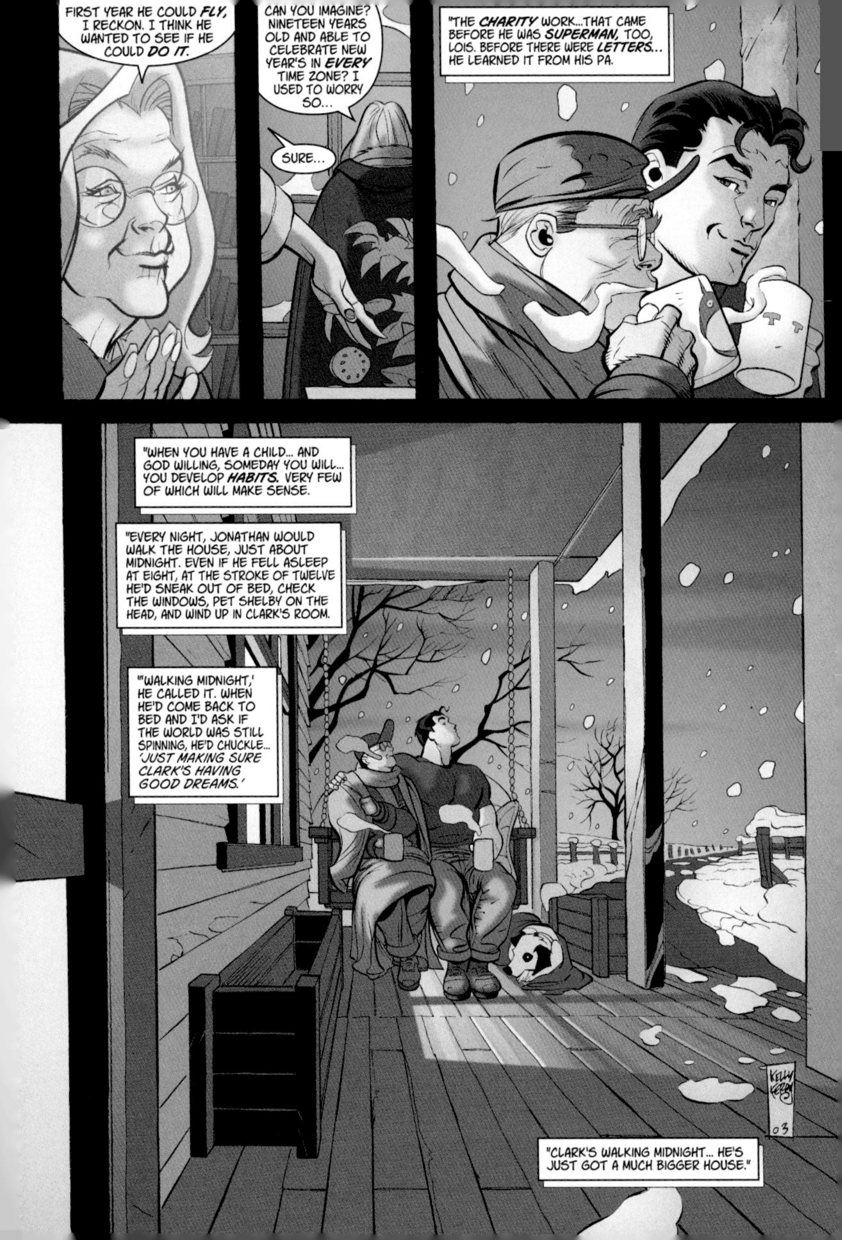
FIRST YEAR HE COULD FLY, I RECKON. I THINK HE WANTED TO SEE IF HE COULD DO IT.
CAN YOU IMAGINE? NINETEEN YEARS OLD AND ABLE TO CELEBRATE NEW YEAR'S IN EVERY TIME ZONE? I USED TO WORRY SO...
SURE...
"THE CHARITY WORK...THAT CAME BEFORE HE WAS SUPERMAN, TOO, LOIS. BEFORE THERE WERE LETTERS... HE LEARNED IT FROM HIS PA.
"WHEN YOU HAVE A CHILD... AND GOD WILLING, SOMEDAY YOU WILL... YOU DEVELOP HABITS. VERY FEW OF WHICH WILL MAKE SENSE.
"EVERY NIGHT, JONATHAN WOULD WALK THE HOUSE, JUST ABOUT MIDNIGHT. EVEN IF HE FELL ASLEEP AT EIGHT, AT THE STROKE OF TWELVE HE'D SNEAK OUT OF BED, CHECK THE WINDOWS, PET SHELBY ON THE HEAD, AND WIND UP IN CLARK'S ROOM.
"'WALKING MIDNIGHT,' HE CALLED IT. WHEN HE'D COME BACK TO BED AND I'D ASK IF THE WORLD WAS STILL SPINNING, HE'D CHUCKLE... 'JUST MAKING SURE CLARK'S HAVING GOOD DREAMS.'
KELLY KERSCHL 03
"CLARK'S WALKING MIDNIGHT... HE'S JUST GOT A MUCH BIGGER HOUSE."

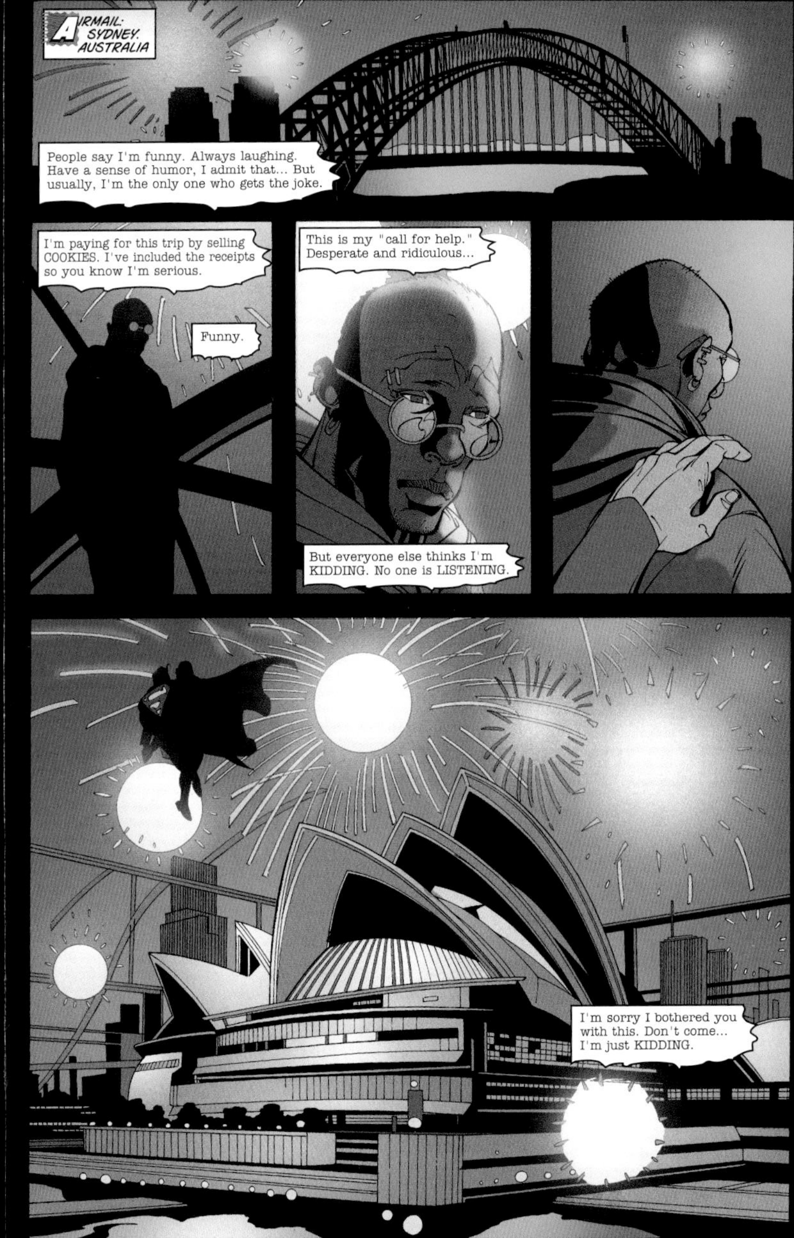
AIRMAIL: SYDNEY. AUSTRALIA
People say I'm funny. Always laughing. Have a sense of humor, I admit that... But usually, I'm the only one who gets the joke.
I'm paying for this trip by selling COOKIES. I've included the receipts so you know I'm serious.
Funny.
This is my "call for help." Desperate and ridiculous...
But everyone else thinks I'm KIDDING. No one is LISTENING.
I'm sorry I bothered you with this. Don't come... I'm just KIDDING.

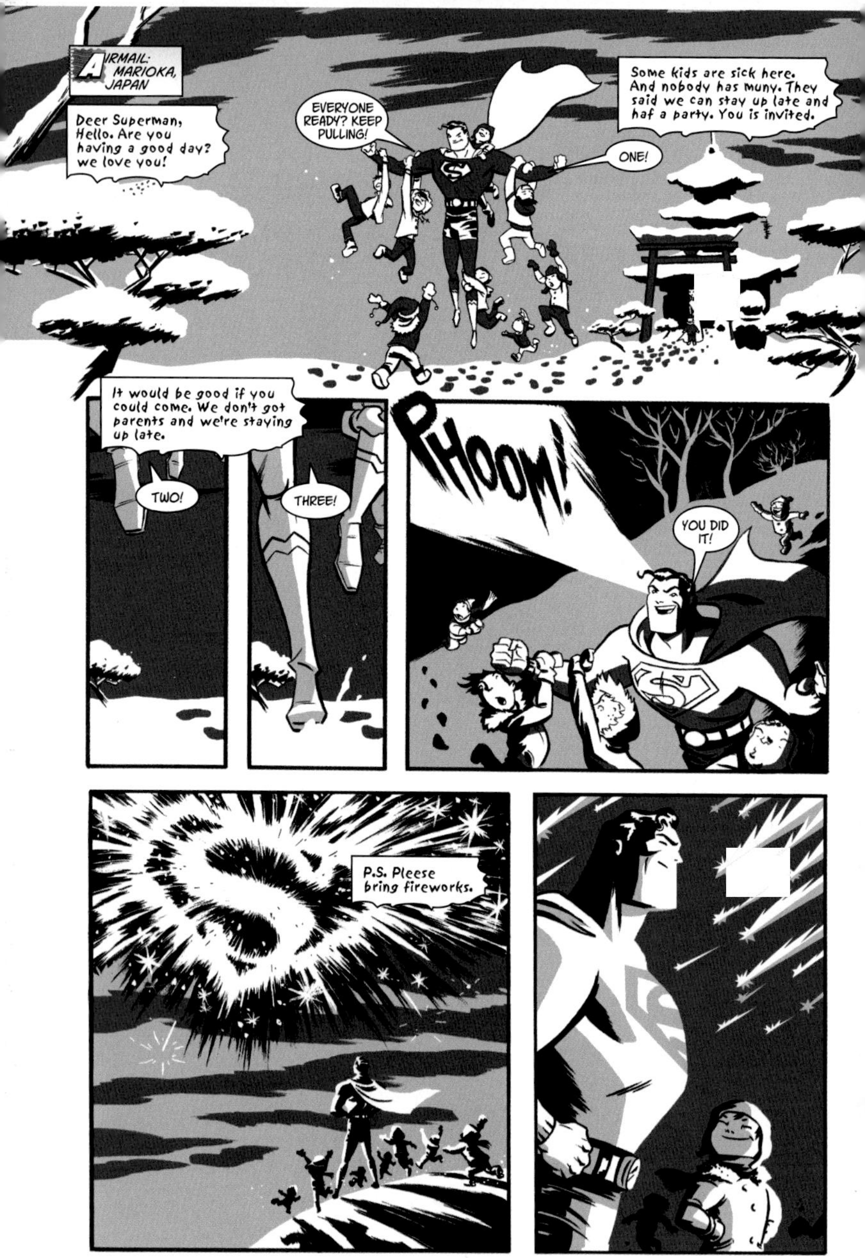
AIRMAIL: MARIOKA, JAPAN
Deer Superman, Hello. Are you having a good day? we love you!
EVERYONE READY? KEEP PULLING!
Some kids are sick here. And nobody has muny. They said we can stay up late and haf a party. You is invited.
ONE!
It would be good if you could come. We don't got parents and we're staying up late.
TWO!
THREE!
PHOOM!
YOU DID IT!
P.S. Pleese bring fireworks.

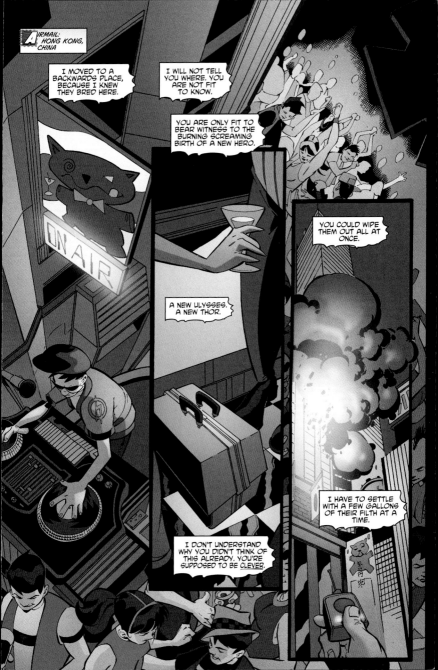

AIRMAIL: HONG KONG, CHINA

I MOVED TO A BACKWARDS PLACE, BECAUSE I KNEW THEY BRED HERE.

I WILL NOT TELL YOU WHERE. YOU ARE NOT FIT TO KNOW.

YOU ARE ONLY FIT TO BEAR WITNESS TO THE BURNING SCREAMING BIRTH OF A NEW HERO.

YOU COULD WIPE THEM OUT ALL AT ONCE.

A NEW ULYSSES. A NEW THOR.

I HAVE TO SETTLE WITH A FEW GALLONS OF THEIR FILTH AT A TIME.

I DON'T UNDERSTAND WHY YOU DIDN'T THINK OF THIS ALREADY. YOU'RE SUPPOSED TO BE CLEVER.

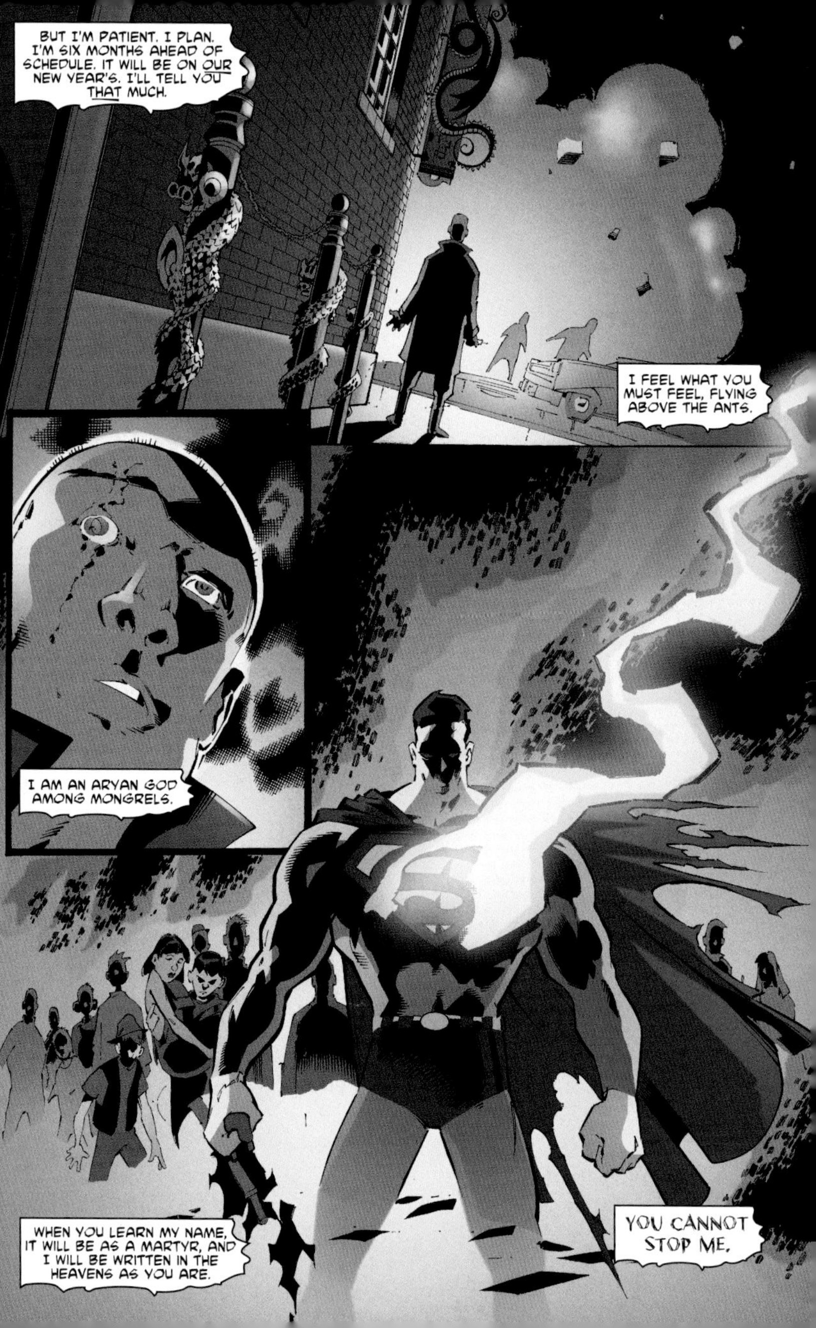
BUT I'M PATIENT. I PLAN. I'M SIX MONTHS AHEAD OF SCHEDULE. IT WILL BE ON OUR NEW YEAR'S. I'LL TELL YOU THAT MUCH.
I FEEL WHAT YOU MUST FEEL, FLYING ABOVE THE ANTS.
I AM AN ARYAN GOD AMONG MONGRELS.
WHEN YOU LEARN MY NAME, IT WILL BE AS A MARTYR, AND I WILL BE WRITTEN IN THE HEAVENS AS YOU ARE.
YOU CANNOT STOP ME.

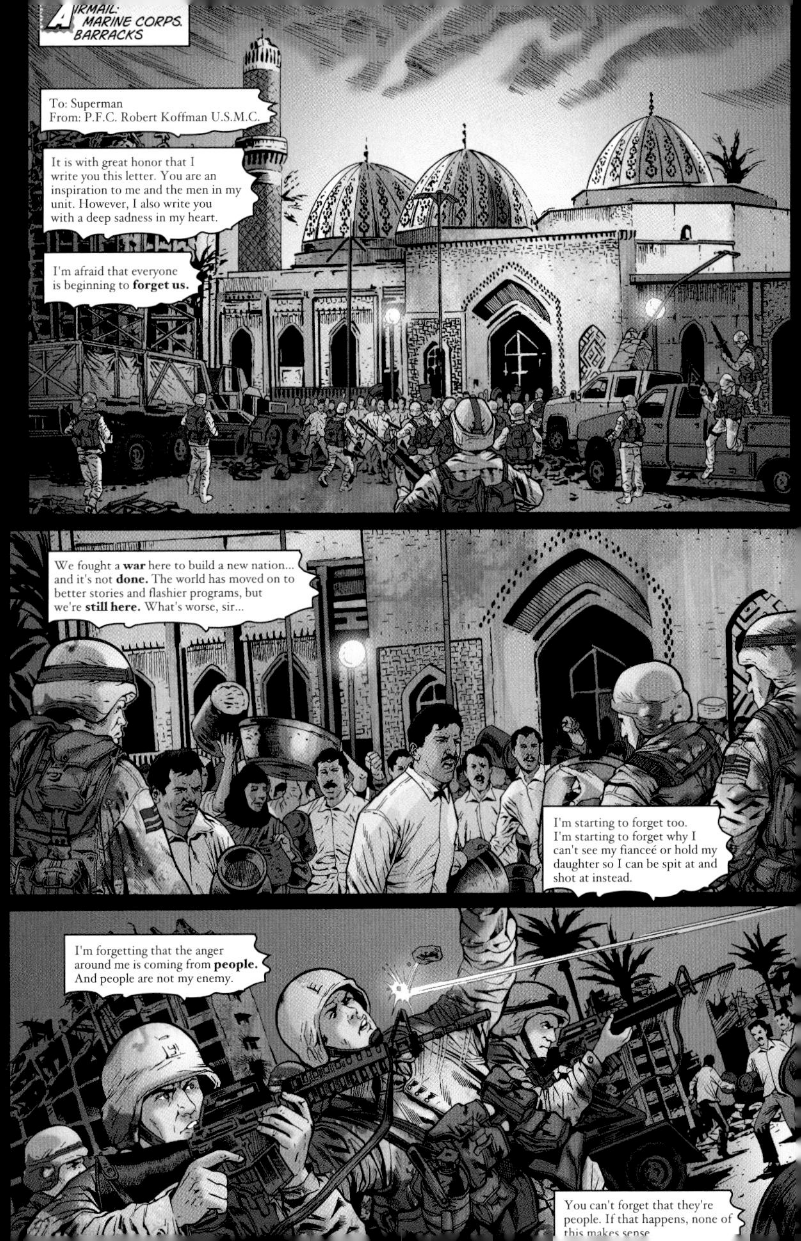
AIRMAIL: MARINE CORPS. BARRACKS
To: Superman
From: P.F.C. Robert Koffman U.S.M.C.
It is with great honor that I write you this letter. You are an inspiration to me and the men in my unit. However, I also write you with a deep sadness in my heart.
I'm afraid that everyone is beginning to **forget us.**
We fought a **war** here to build a new nation... and it's not **done.** The world has moved on to better stories and flashier programs, but we're **still here.** What's worse, sir...
I'm starting to forget too. I'm starting to forget why I can't see my fianceé or hold my daughter so I can be spit at and shot at instead.
I'm forgetting that the anger around me is coming from **people.** And people are not my enemy.
You can't forget that they're people. If that happens, none of this makes sense.

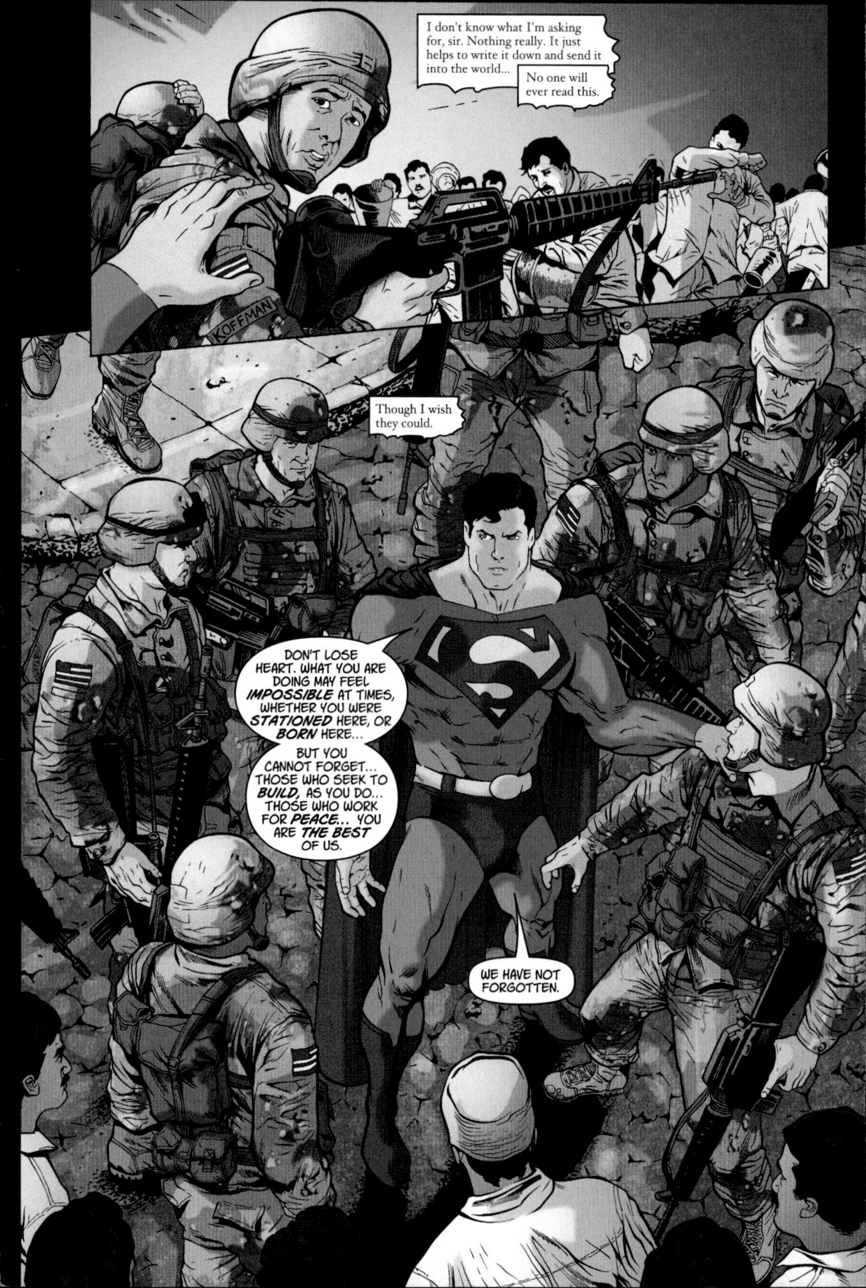

I don't know what I'm asking for, sir. Nothing really. It just helps to write it down and send it into the world...
No one will ever read this.
KOFFMAN
Though I wish they could.
DON'T LOSE HEART. WHAT YOU ARE DOING MAY FEEL IMPOSSIBLE AT TIMES, WHETHER YOU WERE STATIONED HERE, OR BORN HERE...
BUT YOU CANNOT FORGET... THOSE WHO SEEK TO BUILD, AS YOU DO... THOSE WHO WORK FOR PEACE... YOU ARE THE BEST OF US.
WE HAVE NOT FORGOTTEN.

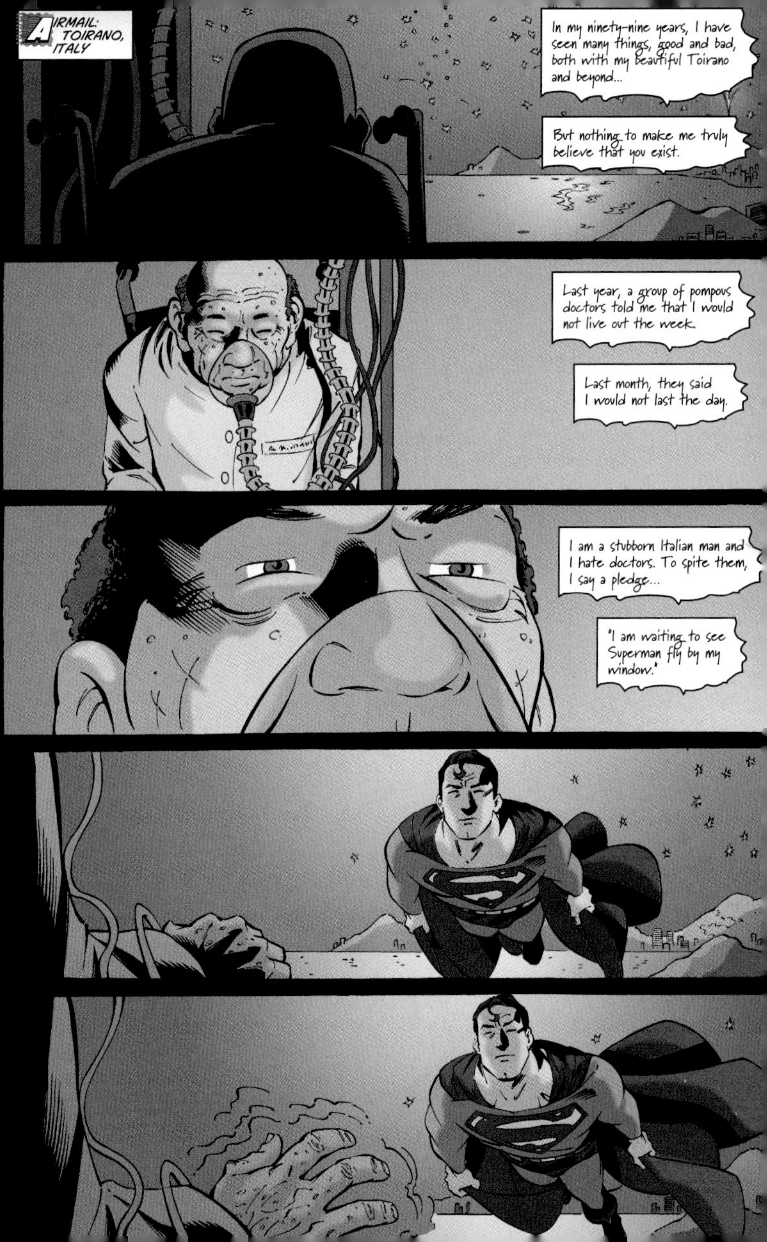
AIRMAIL: TOIRANO, ITALY
In my ninety-nine years, I have seen many things, good and bad, both with my beautiful Toirano and beyond...
But nothing to make me truly believe that you exist.
Last year, a group of pompous doctors told me that I would not live out the week.
Last month, they said I would not last the day.
I am a stubborn Italian man and I hate doctors. To spite them, I say a pledge...
"I am waiting to see Superman fly by my window."

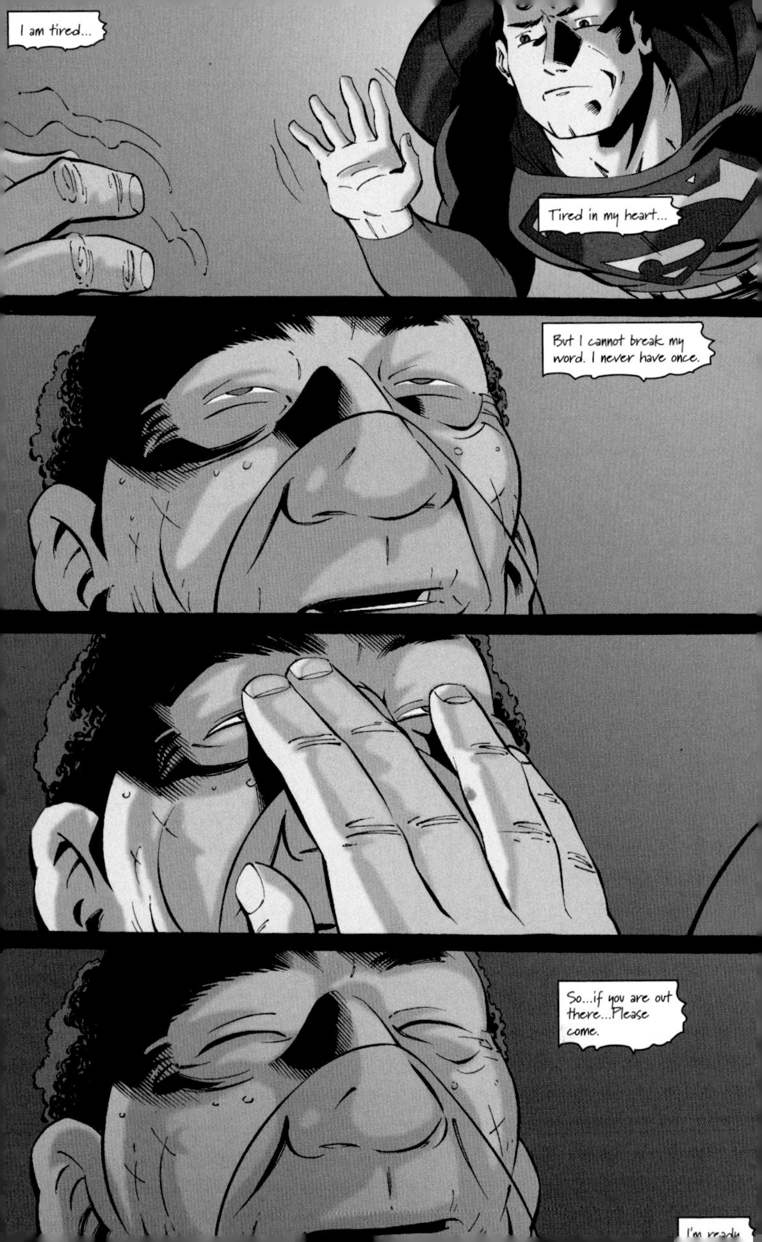

I am tired...
Tired in my heart...
But I cannot break my word. I never have once.
So...if you are out there...Please come.
I'm ready

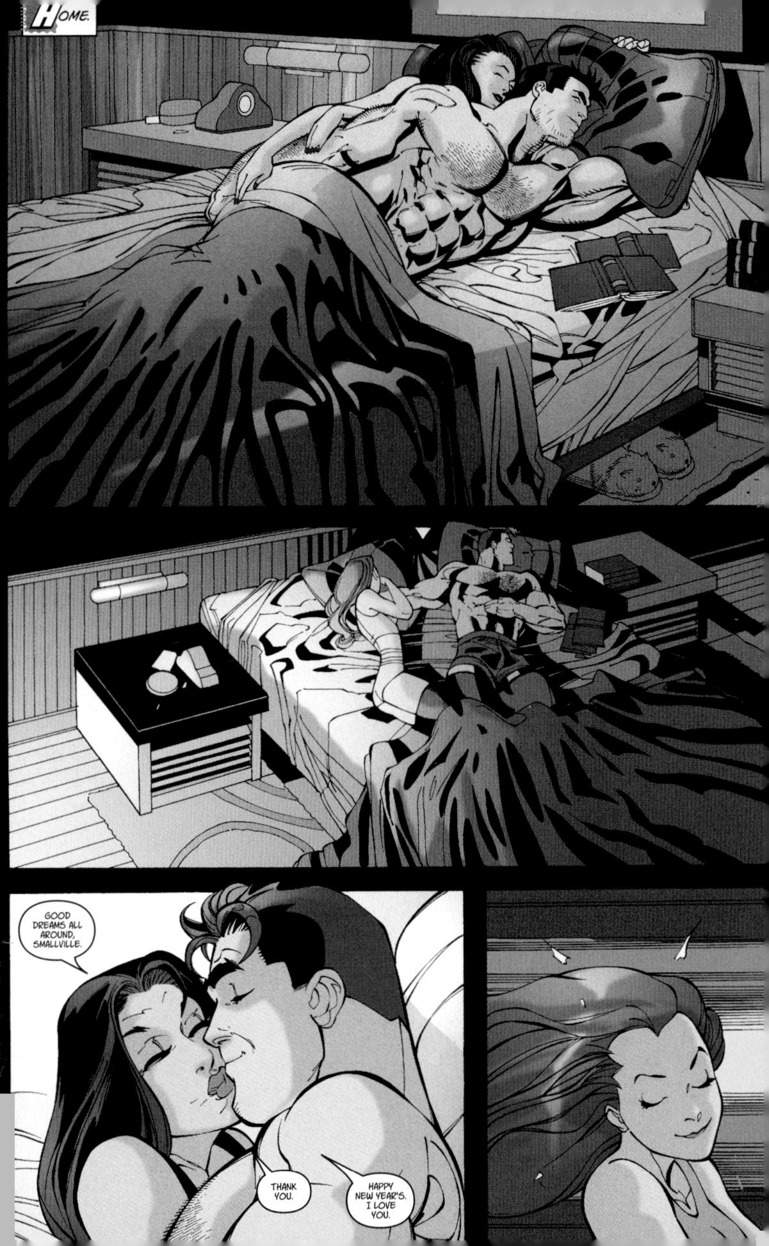
HOME.
GOOD DREAMS ALL AROUND, SMALLVILLE.
THANK YOU.
HAPPY NEW YEAR'S. I LOVE YOU.

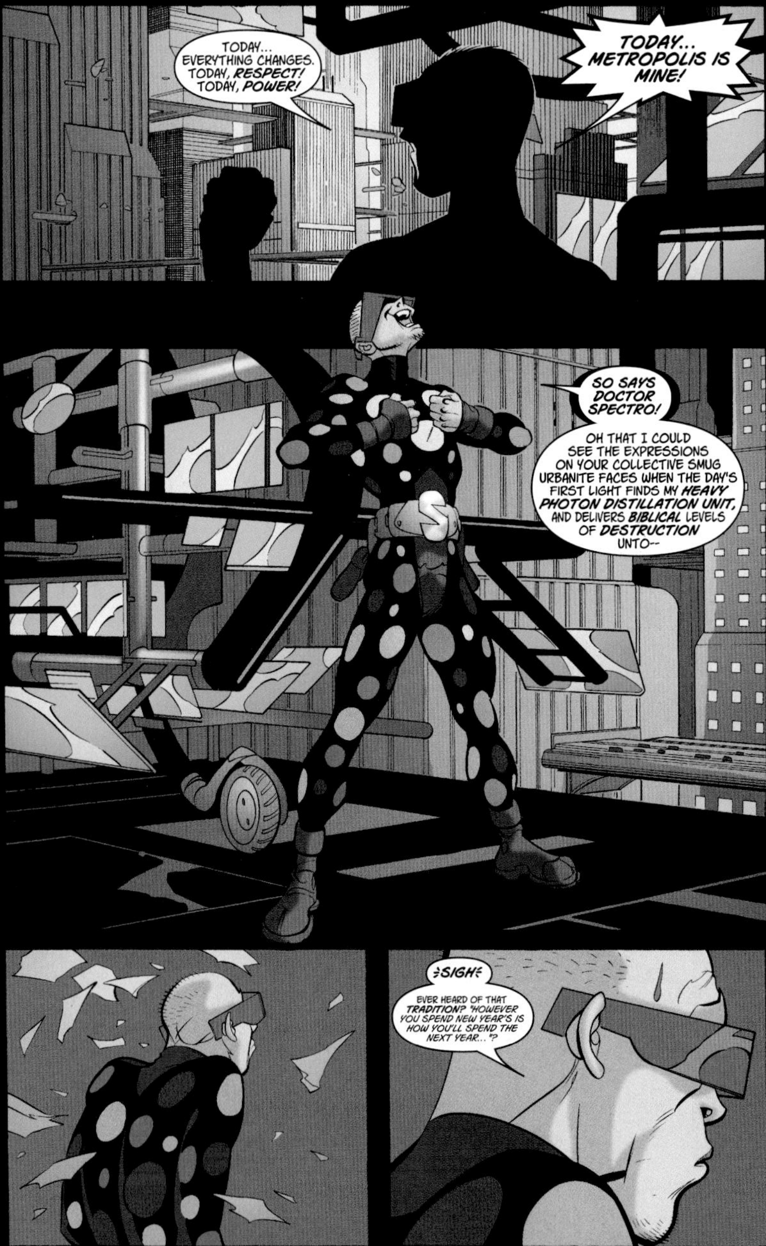
TODAY... EVERYTHING CHANGES. TODAY, RESPECT! TODAY, POWER!
TODAY... METROPOLIS IS MINE!
SO SAYS DOCTOR SPECTRO!
OH THAT I COULD SEE THE EXPRESSIONS ON YOUR COLLECTIVE SMUG URBANITE FACES WHEN THE DAY'S FIRST LIGHT FINDS MY HEAVY PHOTON DISTILLATION UNIT, AND DELIVERS BIBLICAL LEVELS OF DESTRUCTION UNTO--
SIGH
EVER HEARD OF THAT TRADITION? "HOWEVER YOU SPEND NEW YEAR'S IS HOW YOU'LL SPEND THE NEXT YEAR..."?

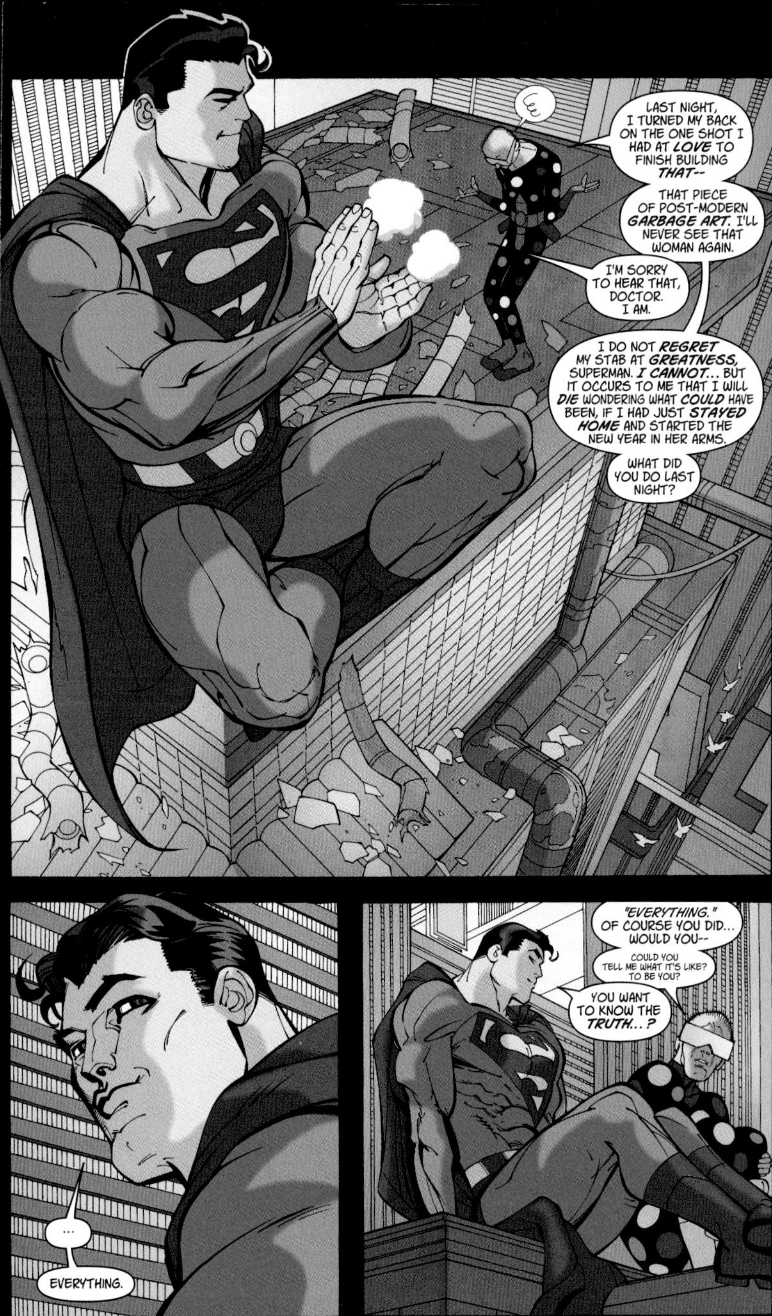

LAST NIGHT, I TURNED MY BACK ON THE ONE SHOT I HAD AT LOVE TO FINISH BUILDING THAT--
THAT PIECE OF POST-MODERN GARBAGE ART. I'LL NEVER SEE THAT WOMAN AGAIN.
I'M SORRY TO HEAR THAT, DOCTOR. I AM.
I DO NOT REGRET MY STAB AT GREATNESS, SUPERMAN. I CANNOT... BUT IT OCCURS TO ME THAT I WILL DIE WONDERING WHAT COULD HAVE BEEN, IF I HAD JUST STAYED HOME AND STARTED THE NEW YEAR IN HER ARMS.
WHAT DID YOU DO LAST NIGHT?
...
EVERYTHING.
"EVERYTHING." OF COURSE YOU DID... WOULD YOU--
COULD YOU TELL ME WHAT IT'S LIKE? TO BE YOU?
YOU WANT TO KNOW THE TRUTH...?

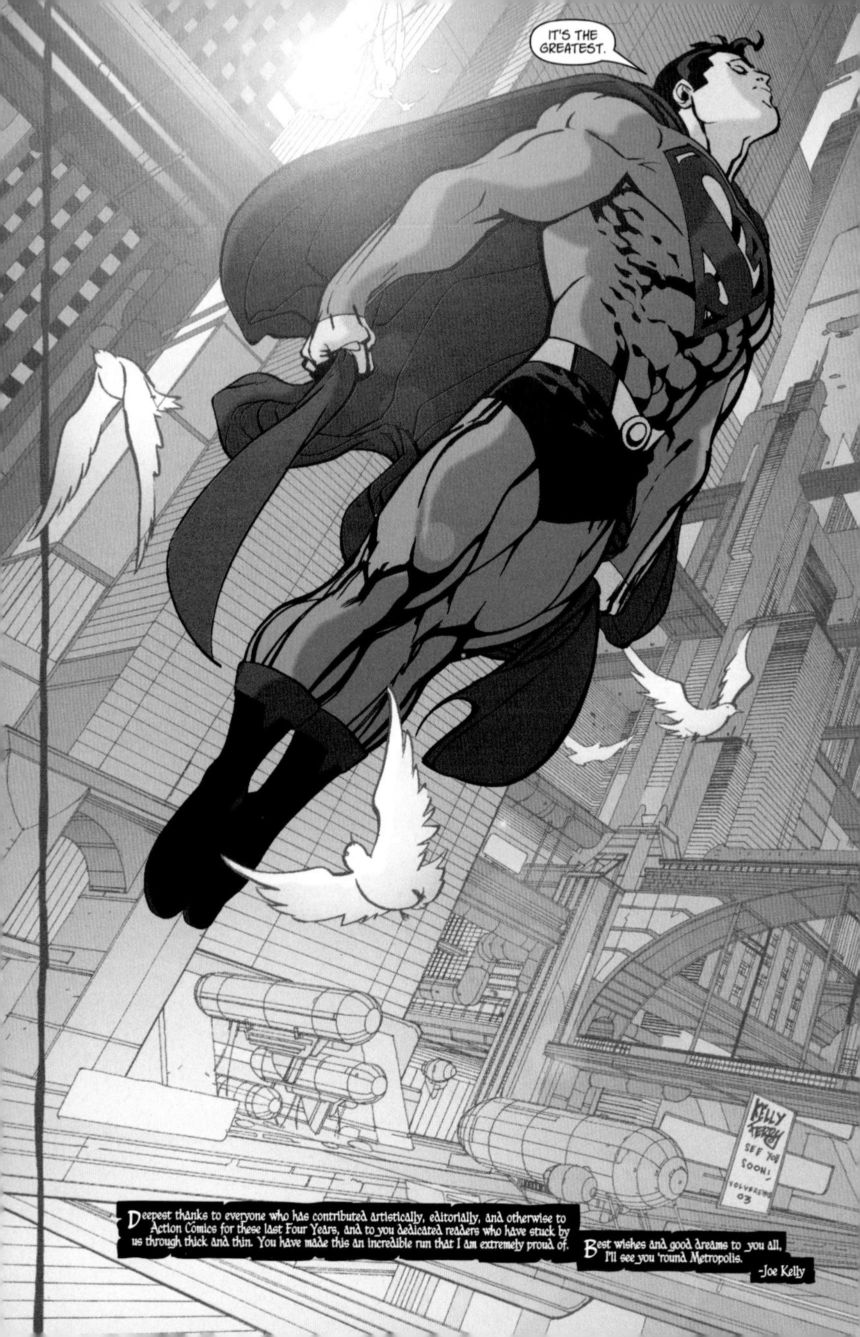
IT'S THE GREATEST.
KELLY
SEE YOU SOON!
Deepest thanks to everyone who has contributed artistically, editorially, and otherwise to Action Comics for these last Four Years, and to you dedicated readers who have stuck by us through thick and thin. You have made this an incredible run that I am extremely proud of.
Best wishes and good dreams to you all, I'll see you 'round Metropolis.
-Joe Kelly

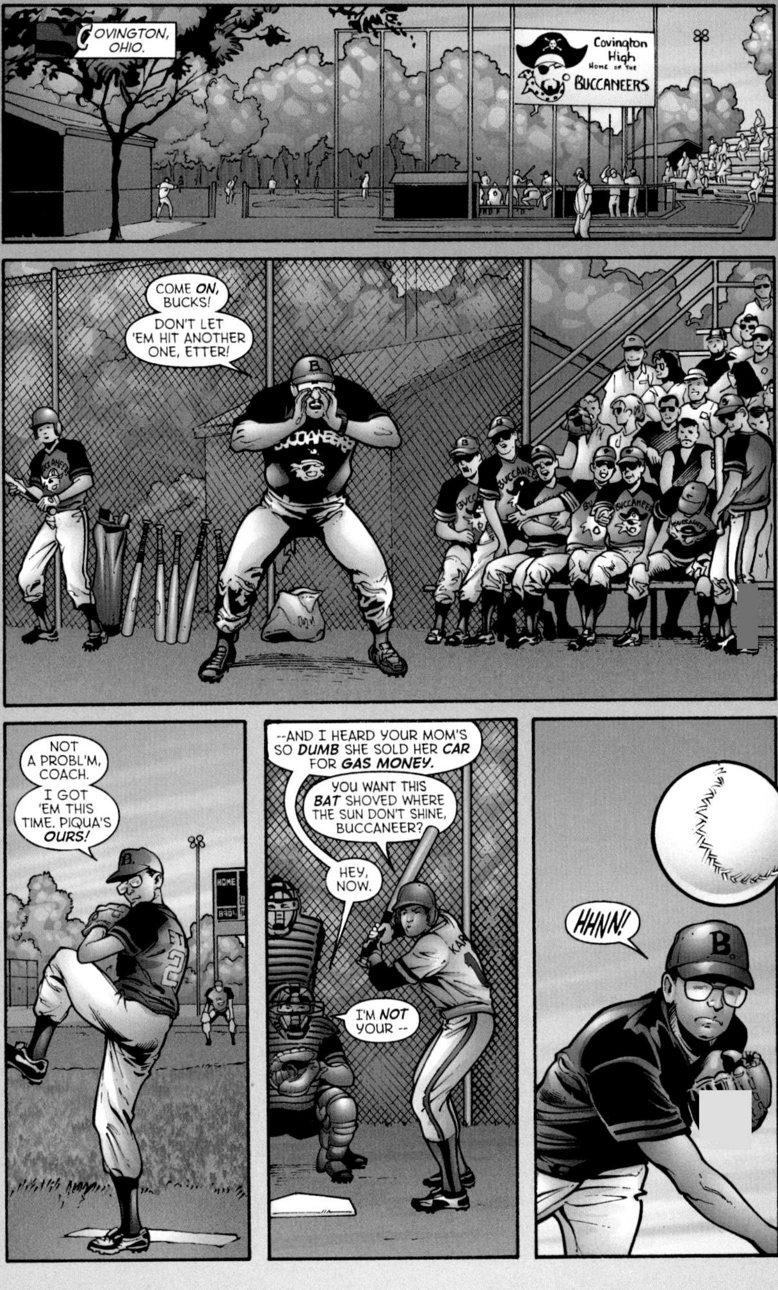
COVINGTON, OHIO.
Covington High HOME OF THE BUCCANEERS
COME ON, BUCKS!
DON'T LET 'EM HIT ANOTHER ONE, ETTER!
NOT A PROBL'M, COACH.
I GOT 'EM THIS TIME. PIQUA'S OURS!
--AND I HEARD YOUR MOM'S SO DUMB SHE SOLD HER CAR FOR GAS MONEY.
YOU WANT THIS BAT SHOVED WHERE THE SUN DON'T SHINE, BUCCANEER?
HEY, NOW.
I'M NOT YOUR --
HHNN!

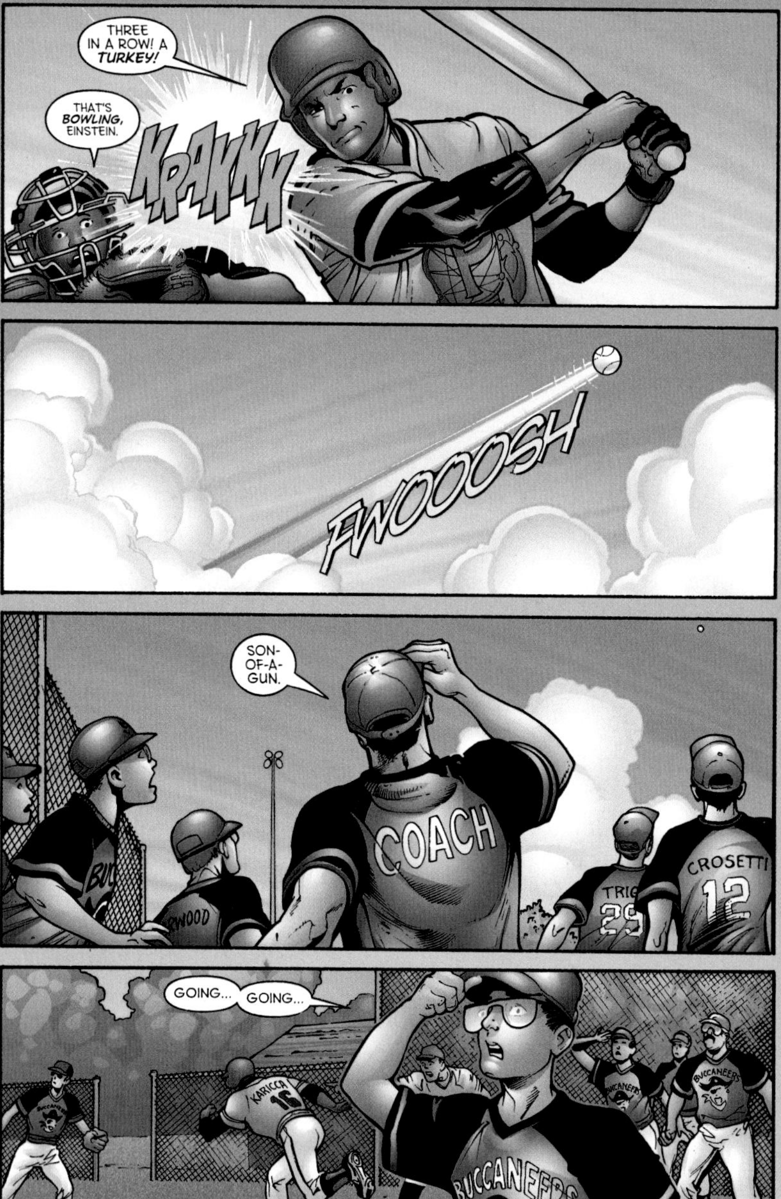

THREE IN A ROW! A *TURKEY!*
THAT'S *BOWLING,* EINSTEIN.
KRAKKKK
FWOOOSH
SON-OF-A-GUN.
COACH
TRIG 29
CROSETTI 12
GOING...
GOING...
KARICCA 16
BUCCANEERS

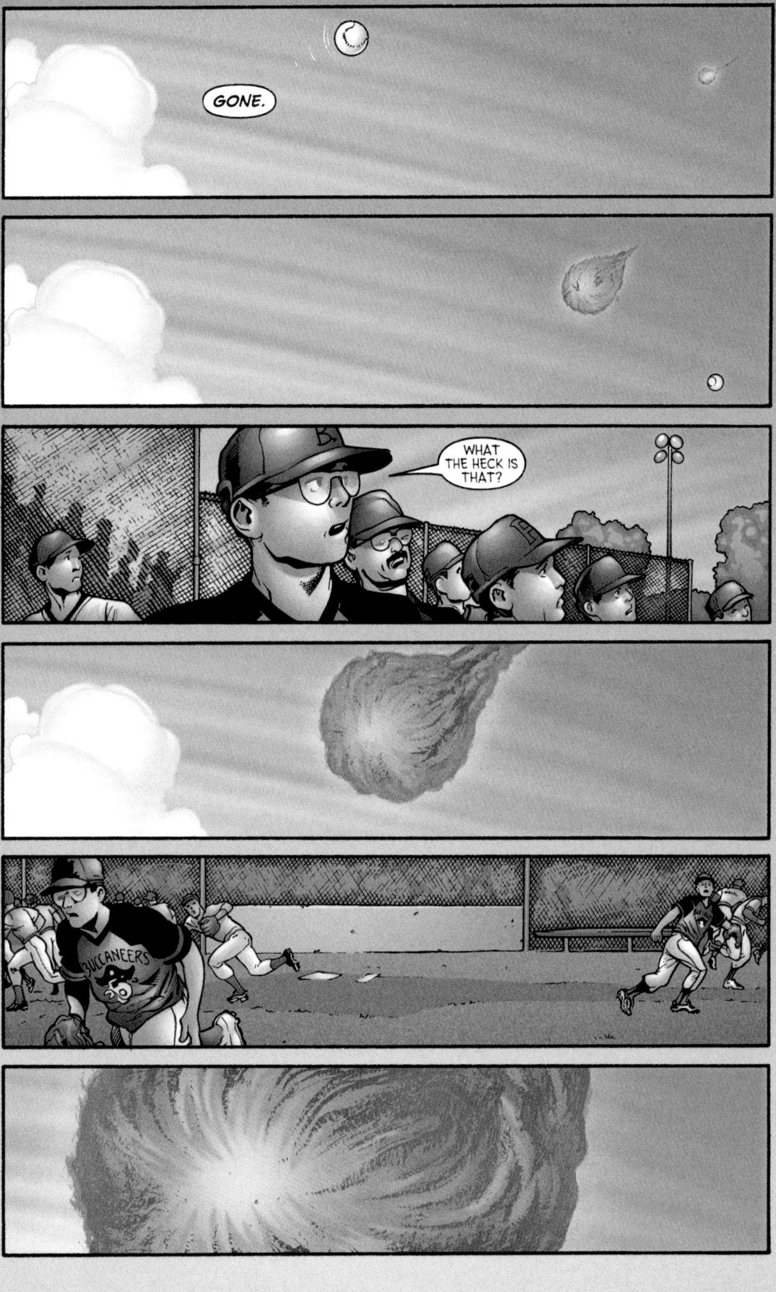
GONE.
WHAT THE HECK IS THAT?
BUCCANEERS

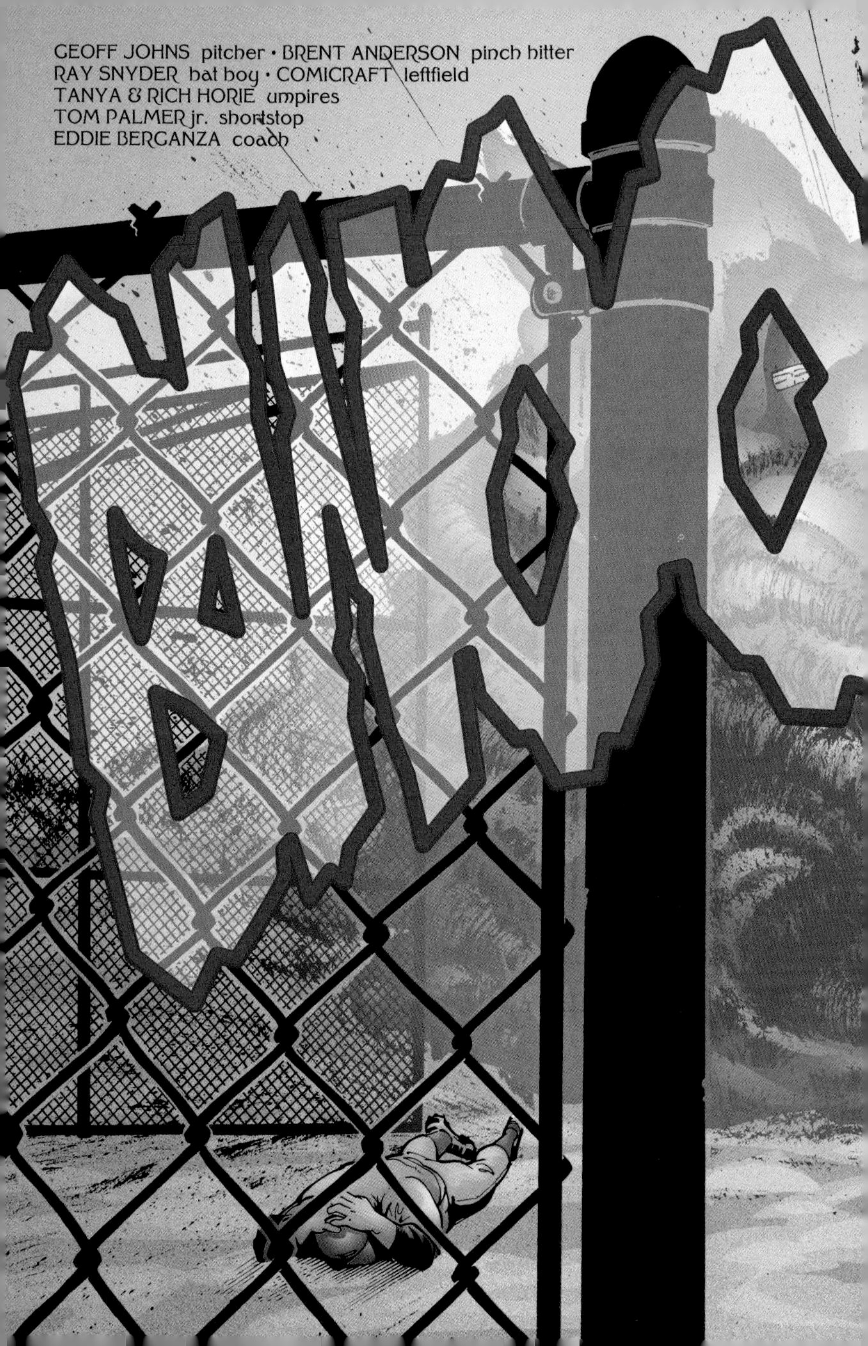
GEOFF JOHNS pitcher • BRENT ANDERSON pinch hitter
RAY SNYDER bat boy • COMICRAFT leftfield
TANYA & RICH HORIE umpires
TOM PALMER jr. shortstop
EDDIE BERGANZA coach

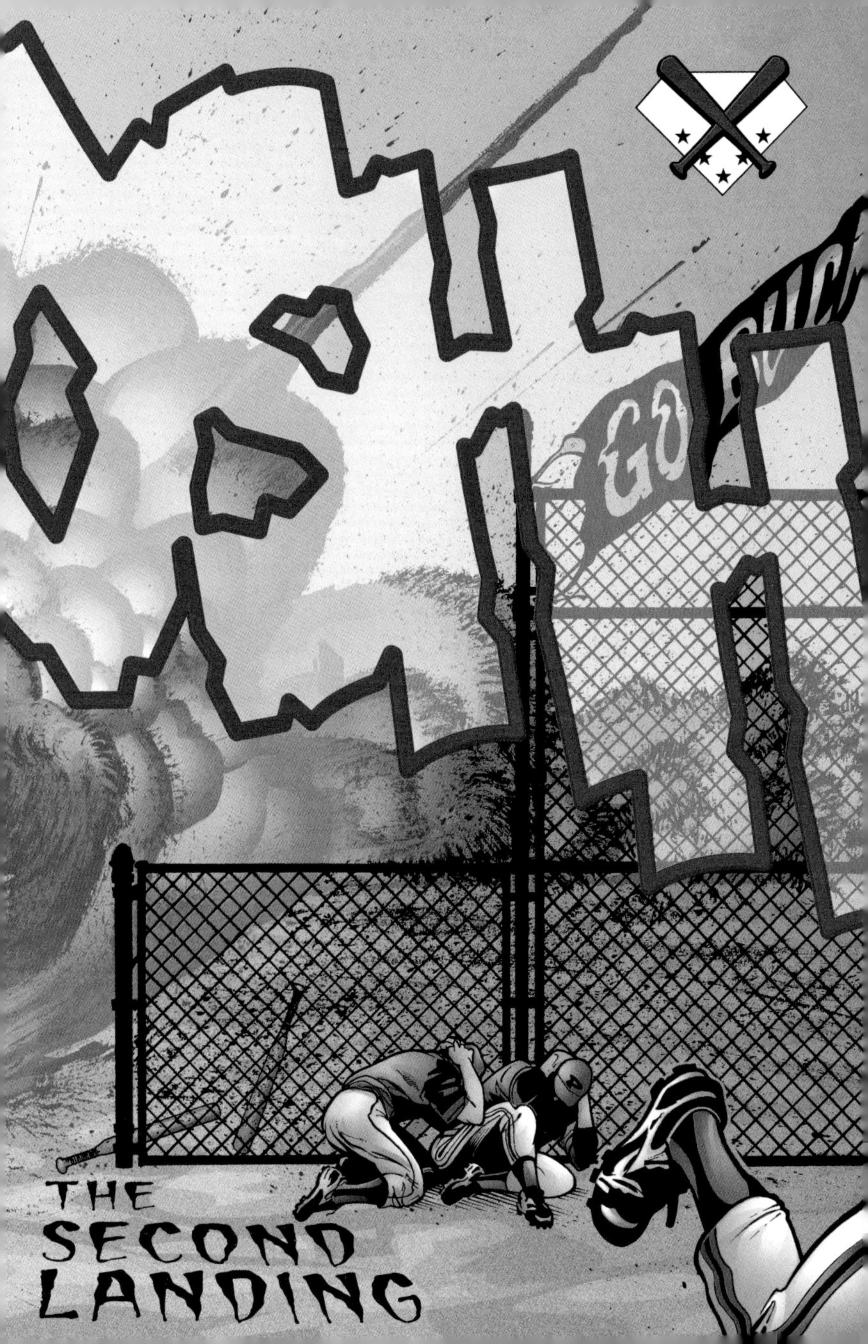
GO
THE SECOND LANDING

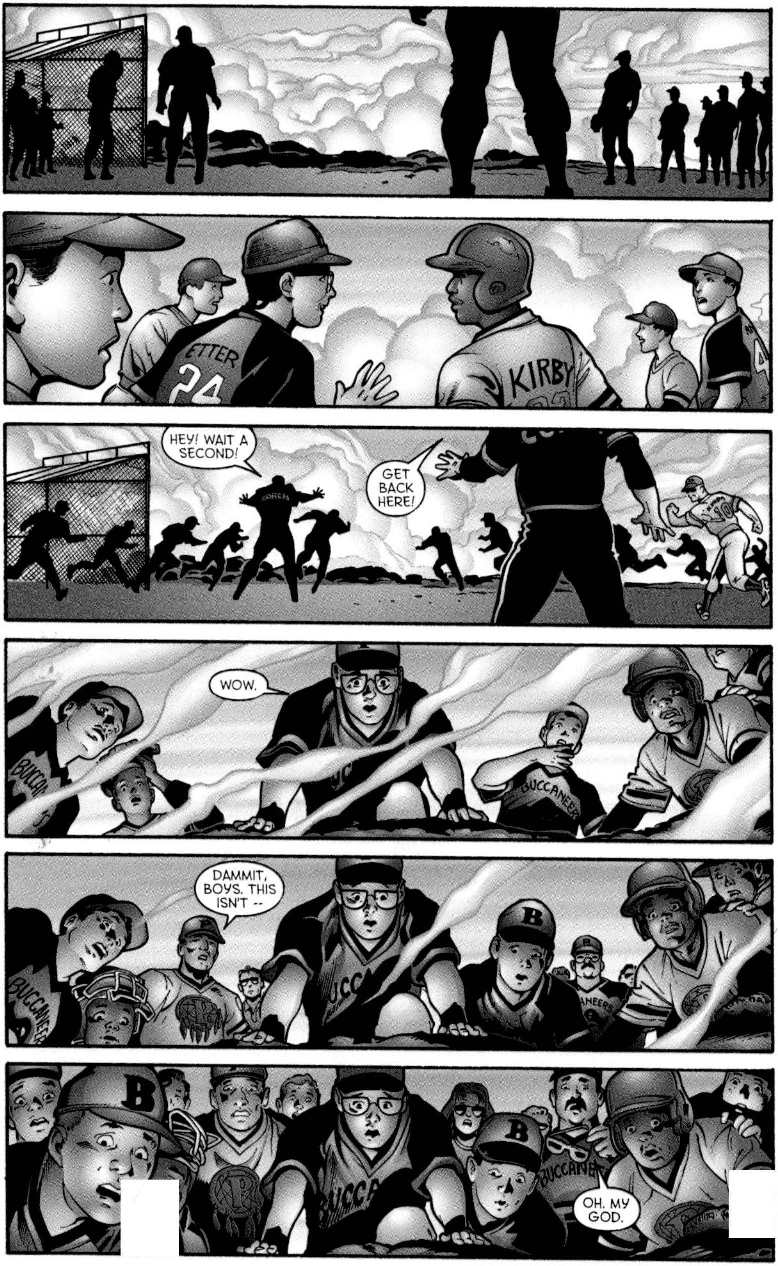
HEY! WAIT A SECOND!
GET BACK HERE!
WOW.
DAMMIT, BOYS. THIS ISN'T --
OH. MY GOD.

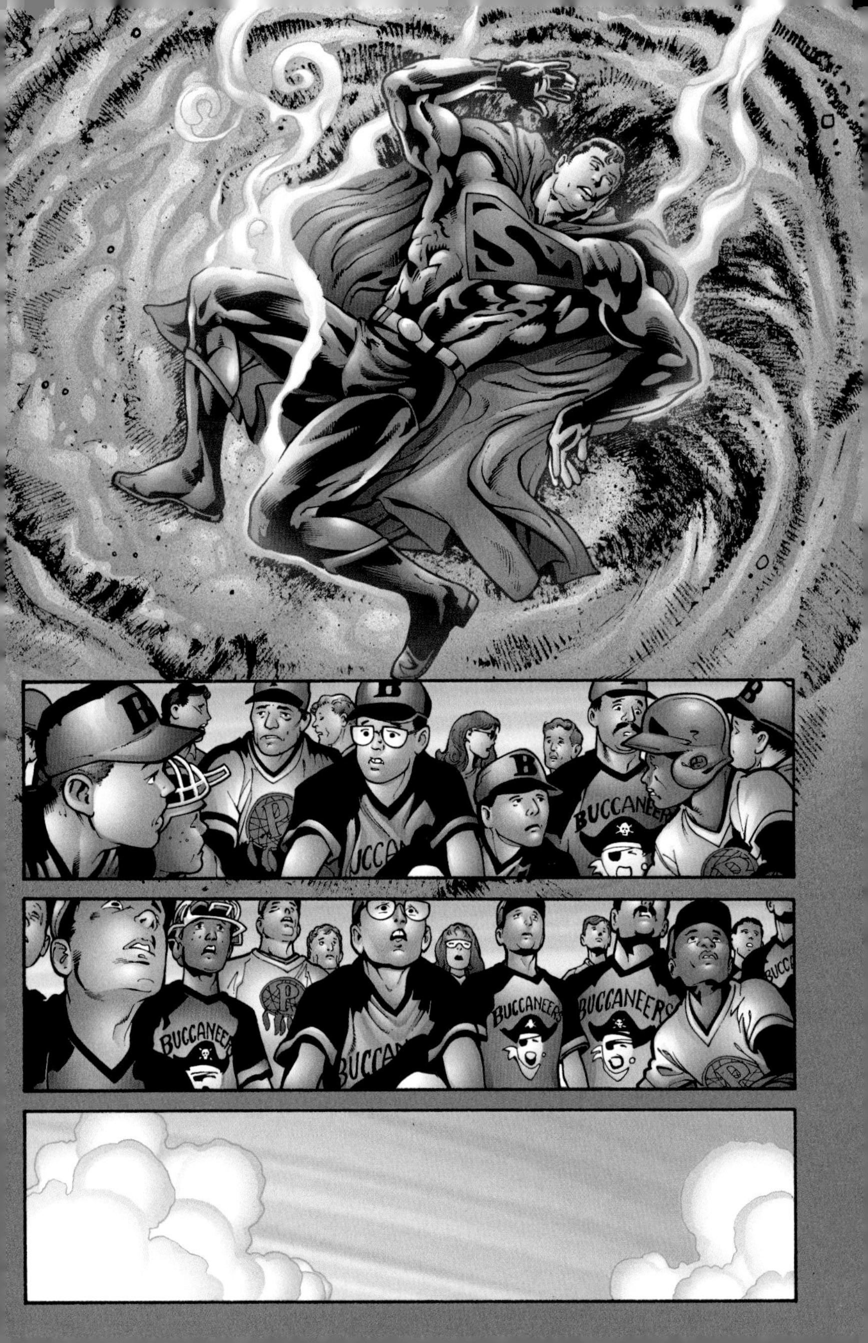
BUCCANEERS
BUCCANEERS
BUCCANEERS
BUCCANEERS

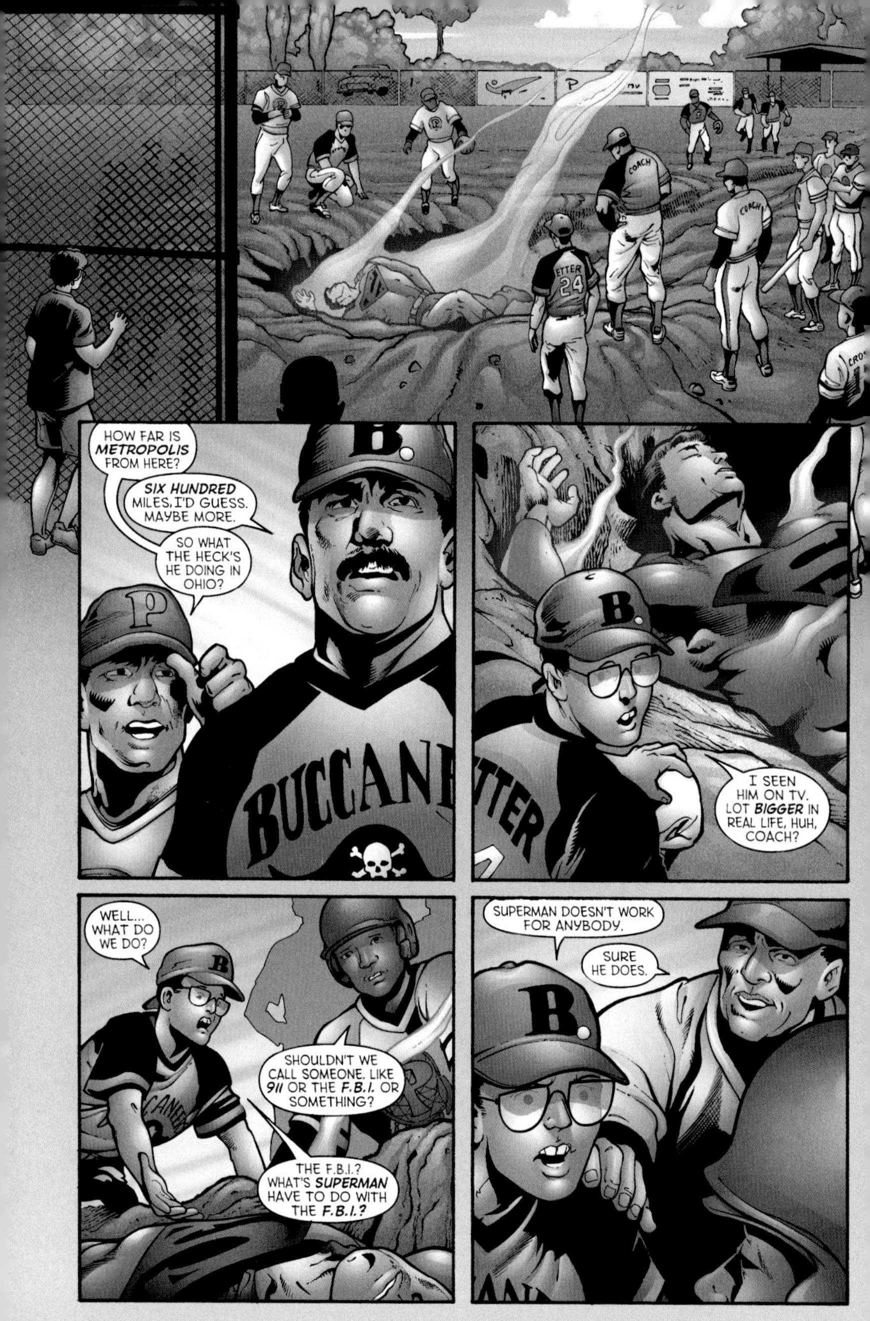
HOW FAR IS METROPOLIS FROM HERE?
SIX HUNDRED MILES, I'D GUESS. MAYBE MORE.
SO WHAT THE HECK'S HE DOING IN OHIO?
I SEEN HIM ON TV. LOT BIGGER IN REAL LIFE, HUH, COACH?
WELL... WHAT DO WE DO?
SHOULDN'T WE CALL SOMEONE. LIKE 911 OR THE F.B.I. OR SOMETHING?
THE F.B.I.? WHAT'S SUPERMAN HAVE TO DO WITH THE F.B.I.?
SUPERMAN DOESN'T WORK FOR ANYBODY.
SURE HE DOES.

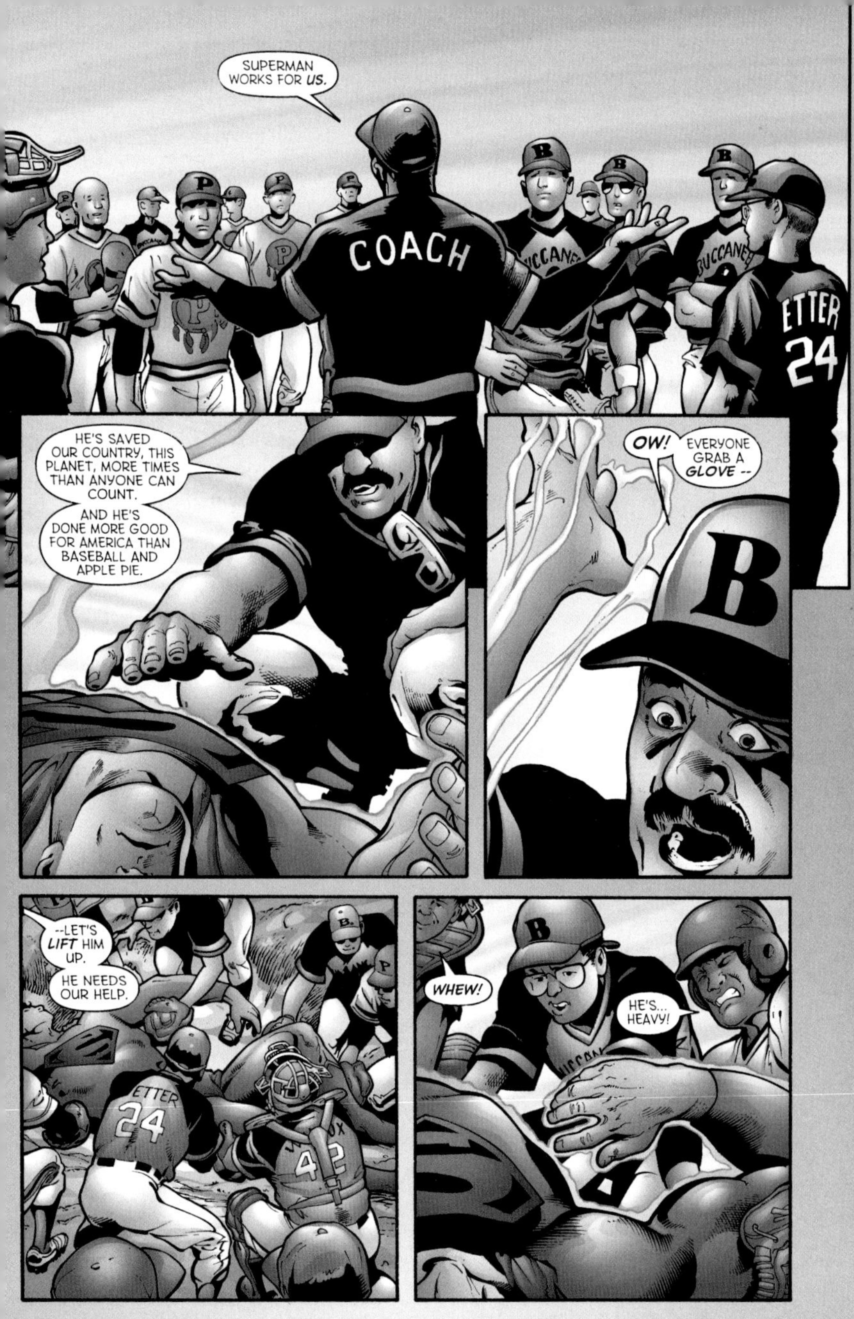
SUPERMAN WORKS FOR US.
COACH
ETTER 24
HE'S SAVED OUR COUNTRY, THIS PLANET, MORE TIMES THAN ANYONE CAN COUNT.
AND HE'S DONE MORE GOOD FOR AMERICA THAN BASEBALL AND APPLE PIE.
OW!
EVERYONE GRAB A GLOVE --
--LET'S LIFT HIM UP.
HE NEEDS OUR HELP.
ETTER 24
WHEW!
HE'S... HEAVY!

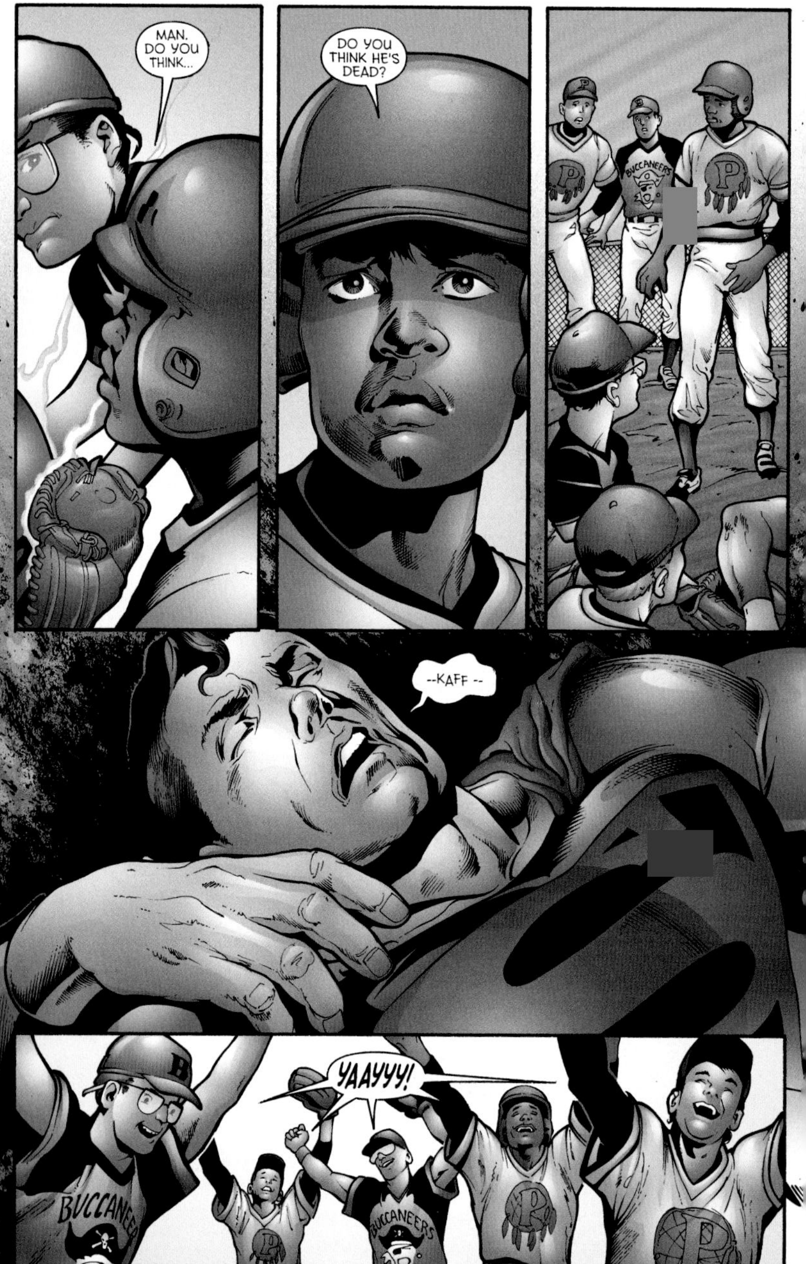
MAN. DO YOU THINK...
DO YOU THINK HE'S DEAD?
--KAFF --
YAAYYY!

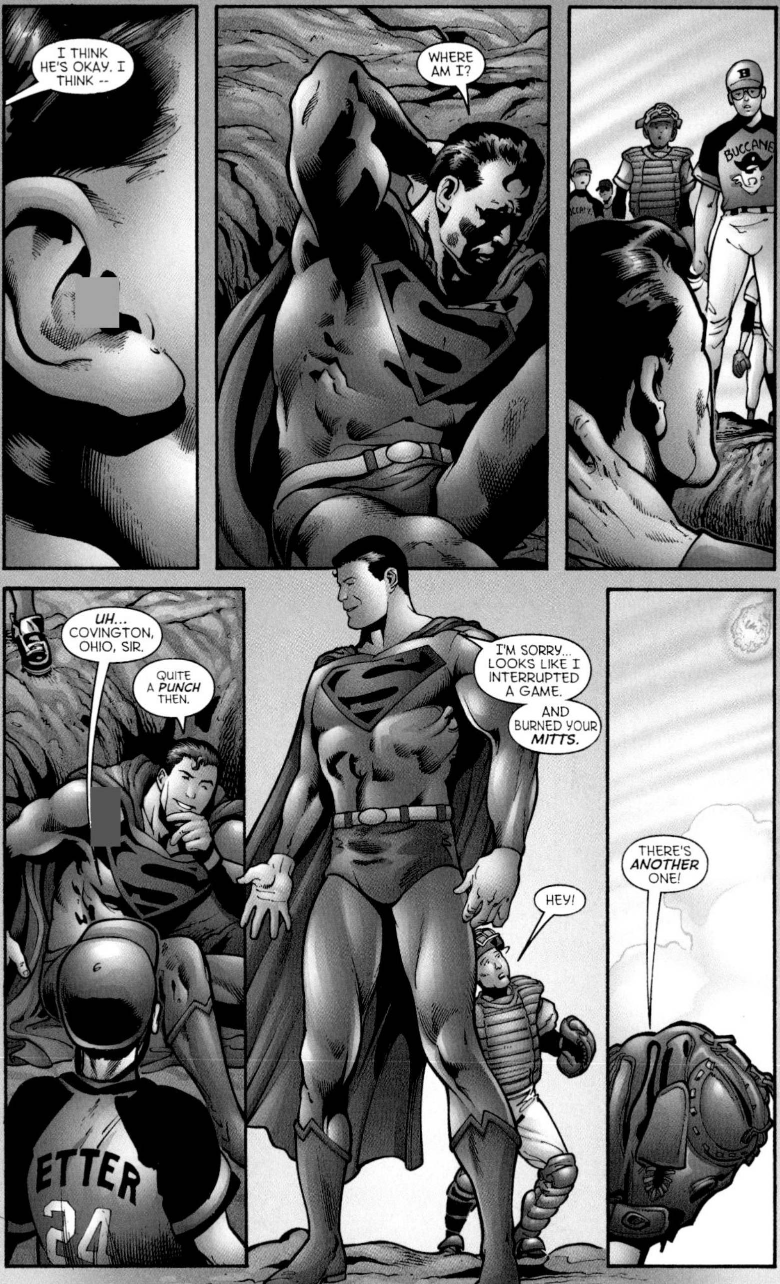
I THINK HE'S OKAY. I THINK --
WHERE AM I?
UH... COVINGTON, OHIO, SIR.
QUITE A *PUNCH* THEN.
I'M SORRY... LOOKS LIKE I INTERRUPTED A GAME.
AND BURNED YOUR ***MITTS.***
HEY!
THERE'S ***ANOTHER*** ONE!

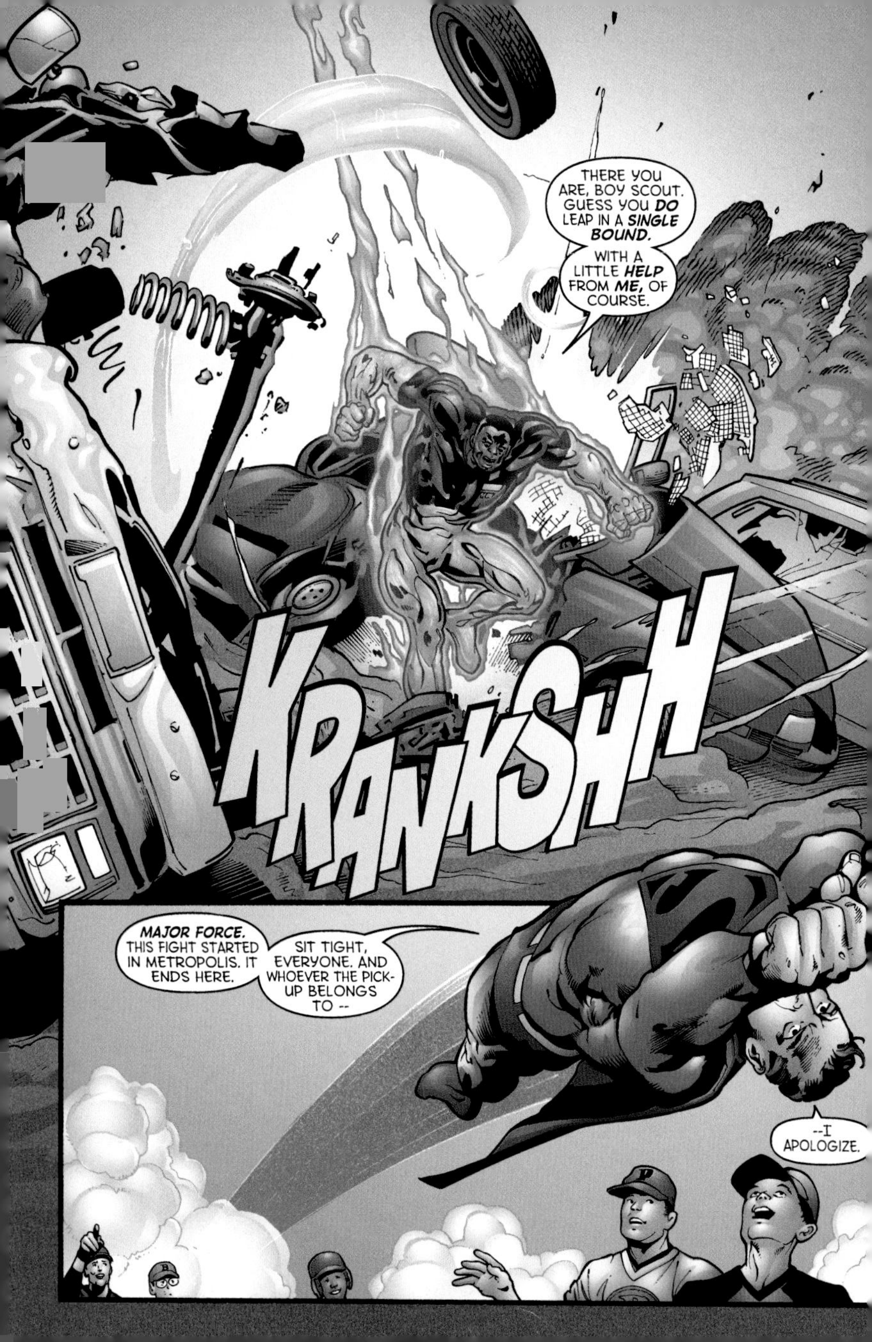
THERE YOU ARE, BOY SCOUT. GUESS YOU DO LEAP IN A SINGLE BOUND.
WITH A LITTLE HELP FROM ME, OF COURSE.
KRANKSHH
MAJOR FORCE. THIS FIGHT STARTED IN METROPOLIS. IT ENDS HERE.
SIT TIGHT, EVERYONE. AND WHOEVER THE PICK-UP BELONGS TO --
--I APOLOGIZE.

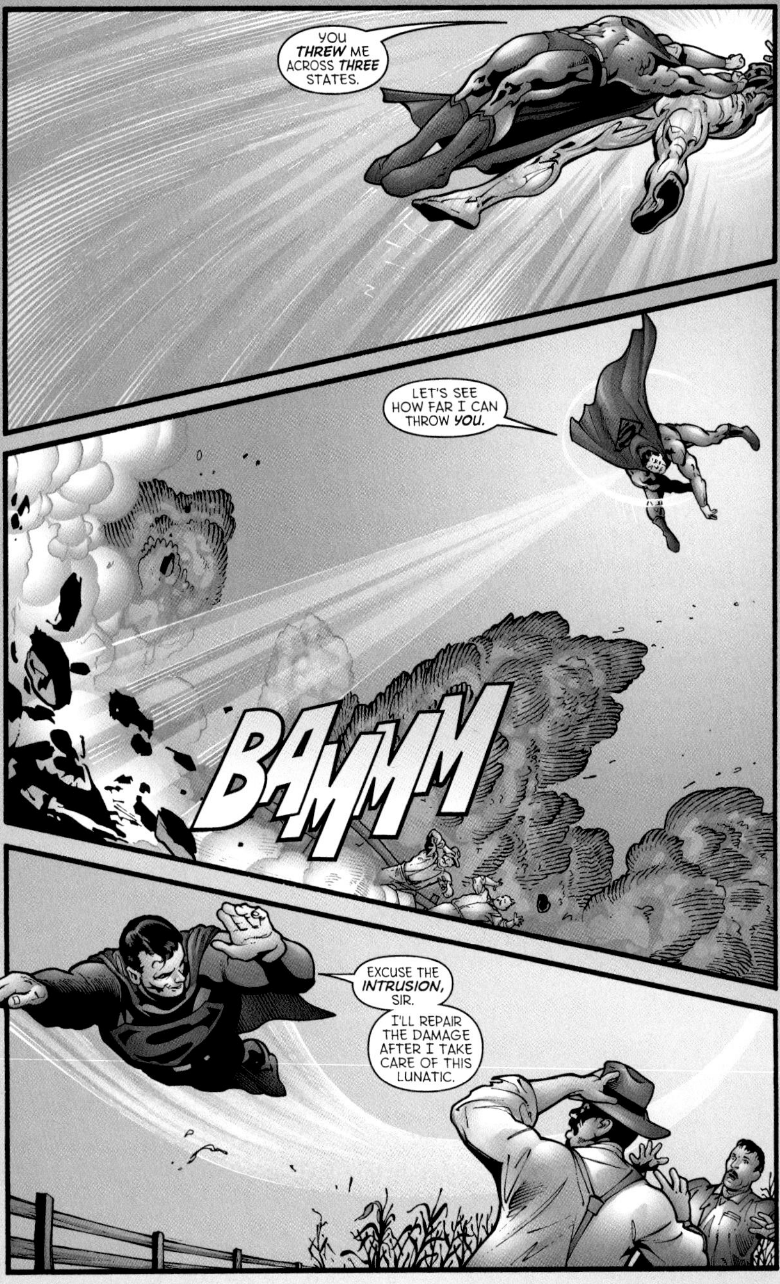
YOU THREW ME ACROSS THREE STATES.
LET'S SEE HOW FAR I CAN THROW YOU.
BAMMM
EXCUSE THE INTRUSION, SIR.
I'LL REPAIR THE DAMAGE AFTER I TAKE CARE OF THIS LUNATIC.

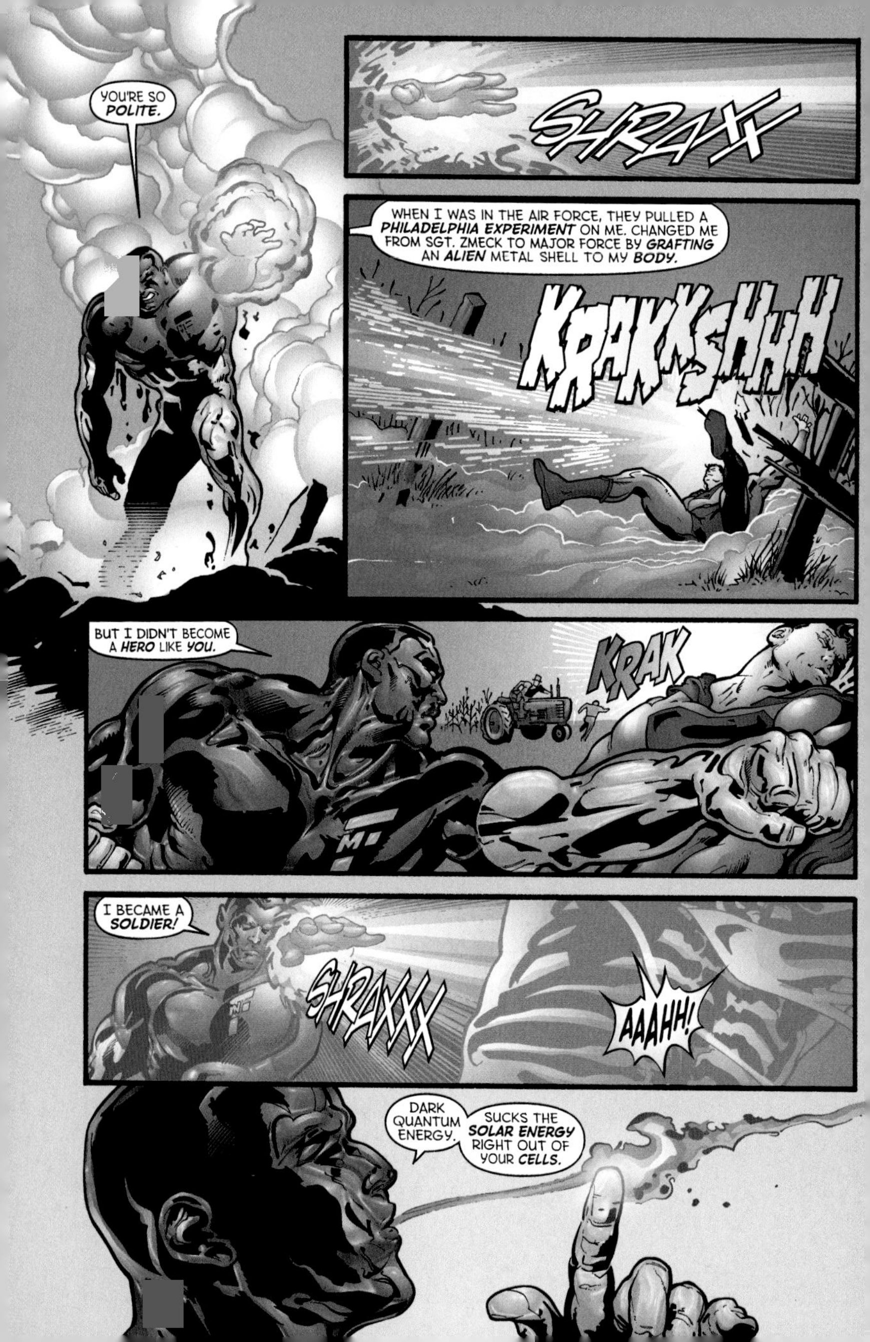

YOU'RE SO POLITE.
SHRAXX
WHEN I WAS IN THE AIR FORCE, THEY PULLED A PHILADELPHIA EXPERIMENT ON ME. CHANGED ME FROM SGT. ZMECK TO MAJOR FORCE BY GRAFTING AN ALIEN METAL SHELL TO MY BODY.
KRAKKSHHH
BUT I DIDN'T BECOME A HERO LIKE YOU.
KRAK
I BECAME A SOLDIER!
SHRAXXX
AAAHH!
DARK QUANTUM ENERGY.
SUCKS THE SOLAR ENERGY RIGHT OUT OF YOUR CELLS.

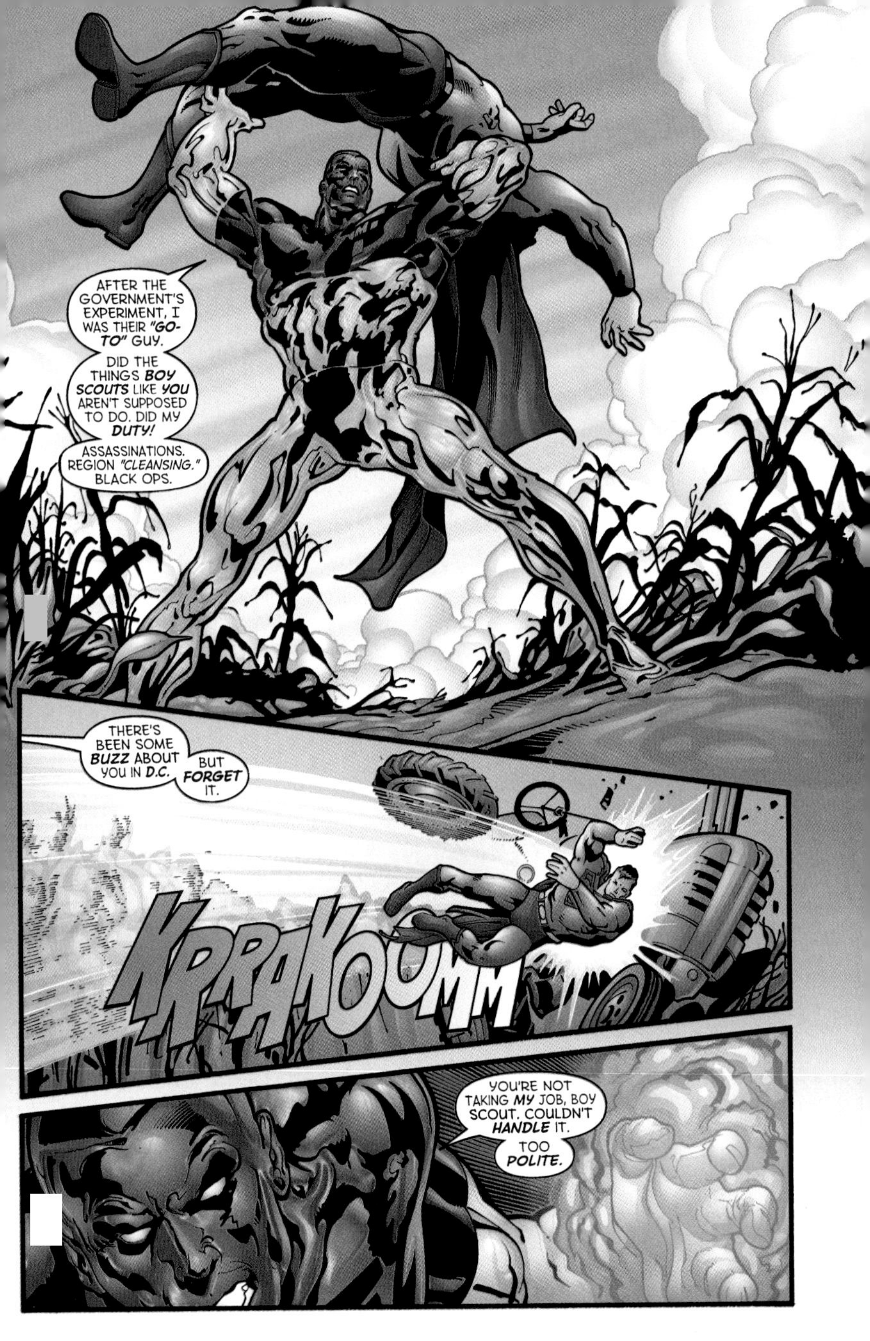
AFTER THE GOVERNMENT'S EXPERIMENT, I WAS THEIR "GO-TO" GUY.
DID THE THINGS BOY SCOUTS LIKE YOU AREN'T SUPPOSED TO DO. DID MY DUTY!
ASSASSINATIONS. REGION "CLEANSING." BLACK OPS.
THERE'S BEEN SOME BUZZ ABOUT YOU IN D.C.
BUT FORGET IT.
KRRAKOOMM
YOU'RE NOT TAKING MY JOB, BOY SCOUT. COULDN'T HANDLE IT.
TOO POLITE.

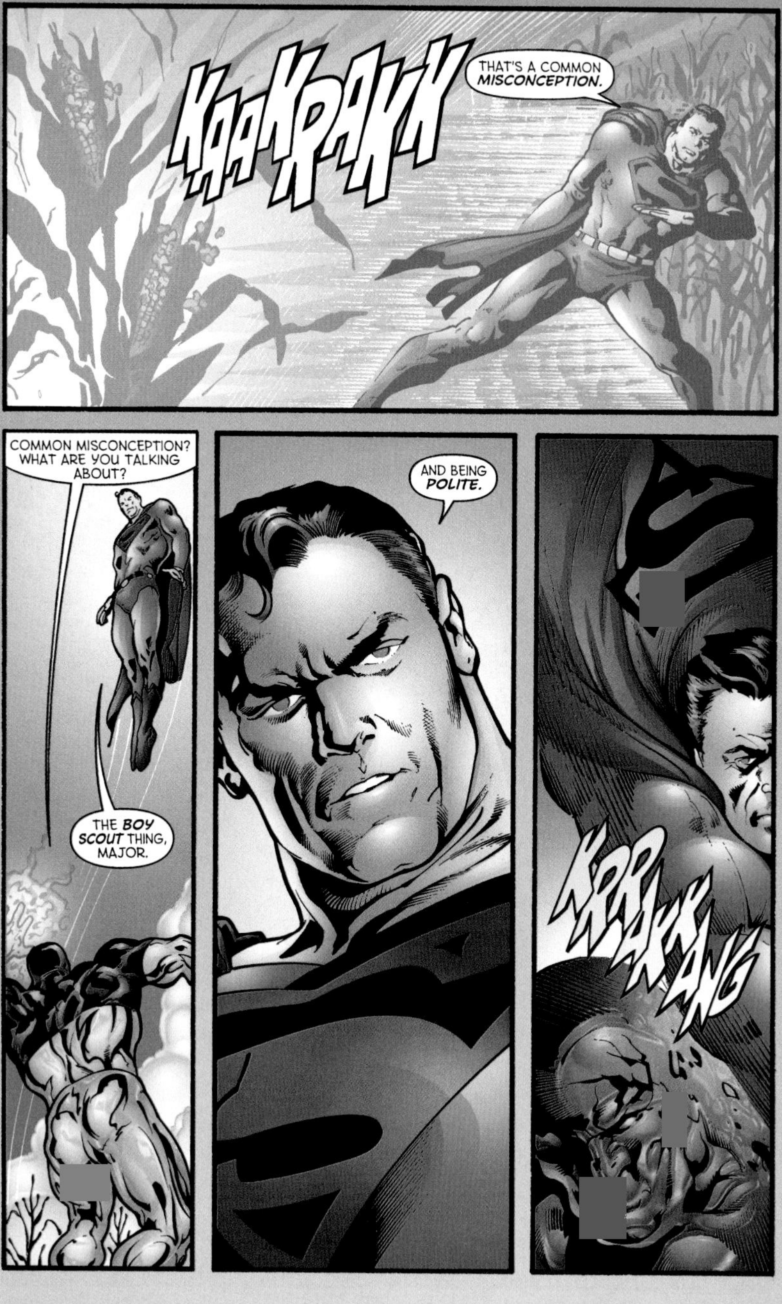
KAAKRAKK
THAT'S A COMMON *MISCONCEPTION.*
COMMON MISCONCEPTION? WHAT ARE YOU TALKING ABOUT?
THE *BOY SCOUT* THING, MAJOR.
AND BEING *POLITE.*
KRRAKKANG

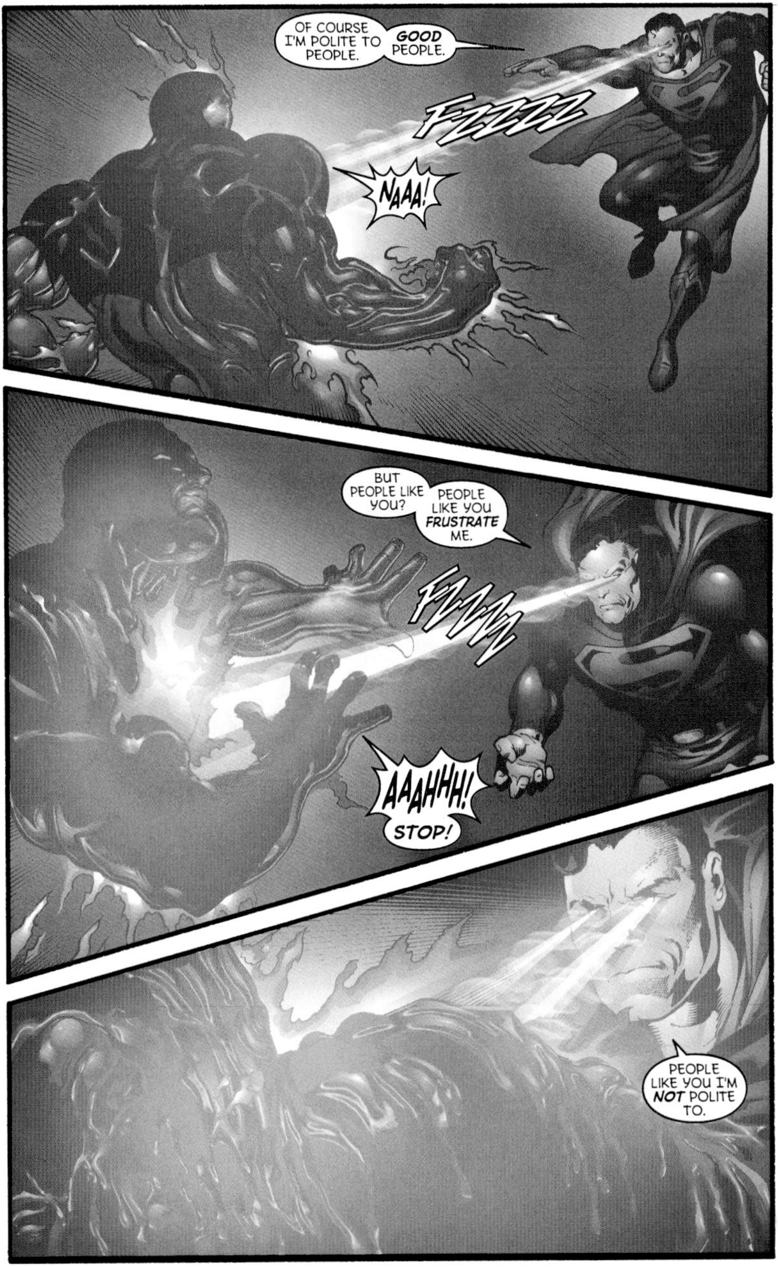
OF COURSE I'M POLITE TO PEOPLE.
GOOD PEOPLE.
FZZZZ
NAAA!
BUT PEOPLE LIKE YOU?
PEOPLE LIKE YOU FRUSTRATE ME.
FZZM
AAAHHH!
STOP!
PEOPLE LIKE YOU I'M NOT POLITE TO.

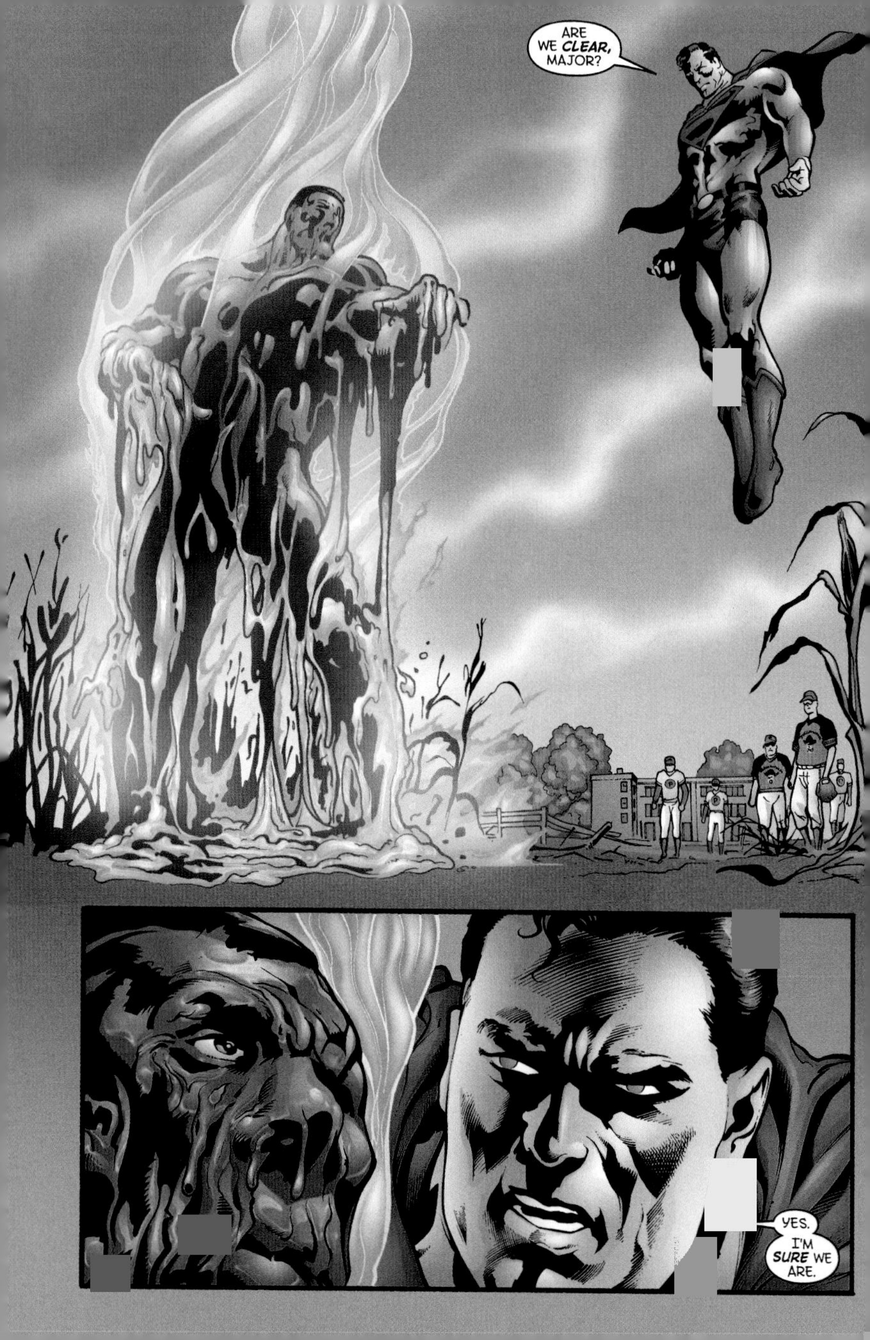
ARE WE CLEAR, MAJOR?
YES. I'M SURE WE ARE.

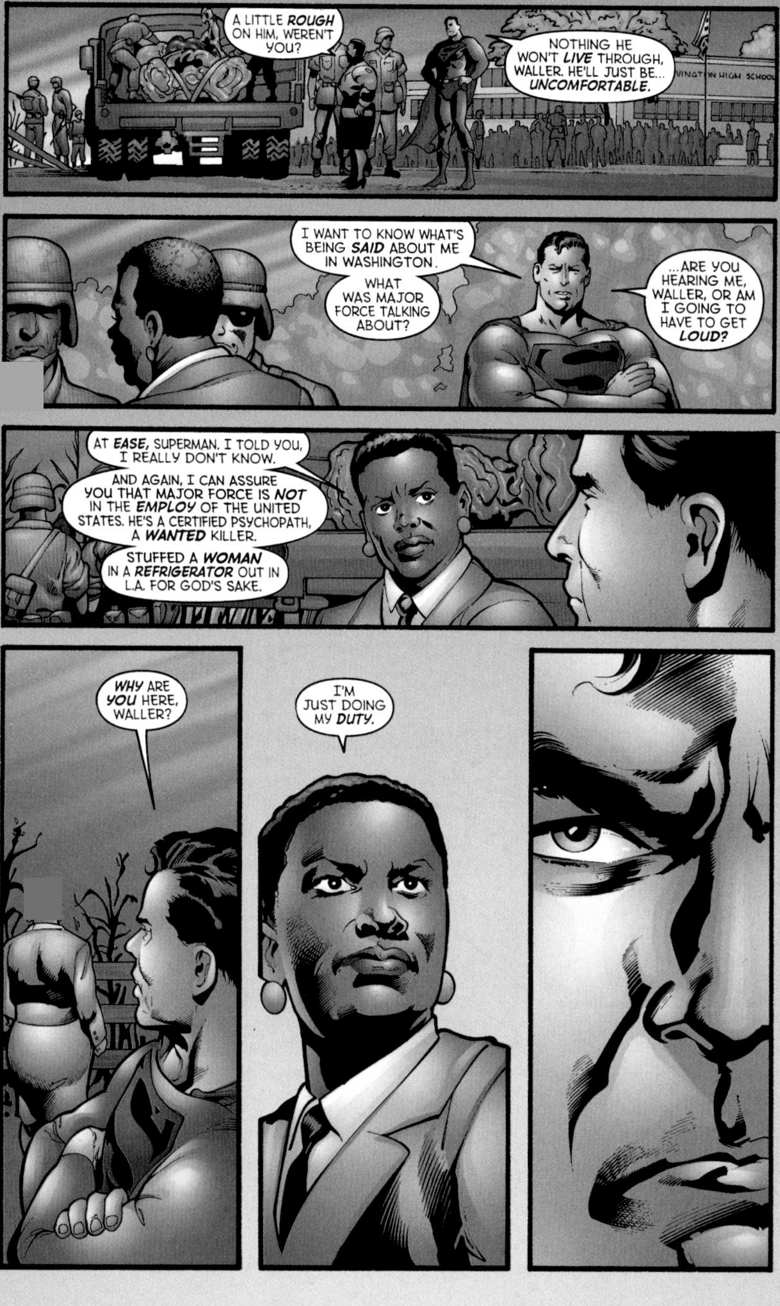

A LITTLE ROUGH ON HIM, WEREN'T YOU?
NOTHING HE WON'T LIVE THROUGH, WALLER. HE'LL JUST BE... UNCOMFORTABLE.
I WANT TO KNOW WHAT'S BEING SAID ABOUT ME IN WASHINGTON.
WHAT WAS MAJOR FORCE TALKING ABOUT?
...ARE YOU HEARING ME, WALLER, OR AM I GOING TO HAVE TO GET LOUD?
AT EASE, SUPERMAN. I TOLD YOU, I REALLY DON'T KNOW.
AND AGAIN, I CAN ASSURE YOU THAT MAJOR FORCE IS NOT IN THE EMPLOY OF THE UNITED STATES. HE'S A CERTIFIED PSYCHOPATH, A WANTED KILLER.
STUFFED A WOMAN IN A REFRIGERATOR OUT IN L.A. FOR GOD'S SAKE.
WHY ARE YOU HERE, WALLER?
I'M JUST DOING MY DUTY.

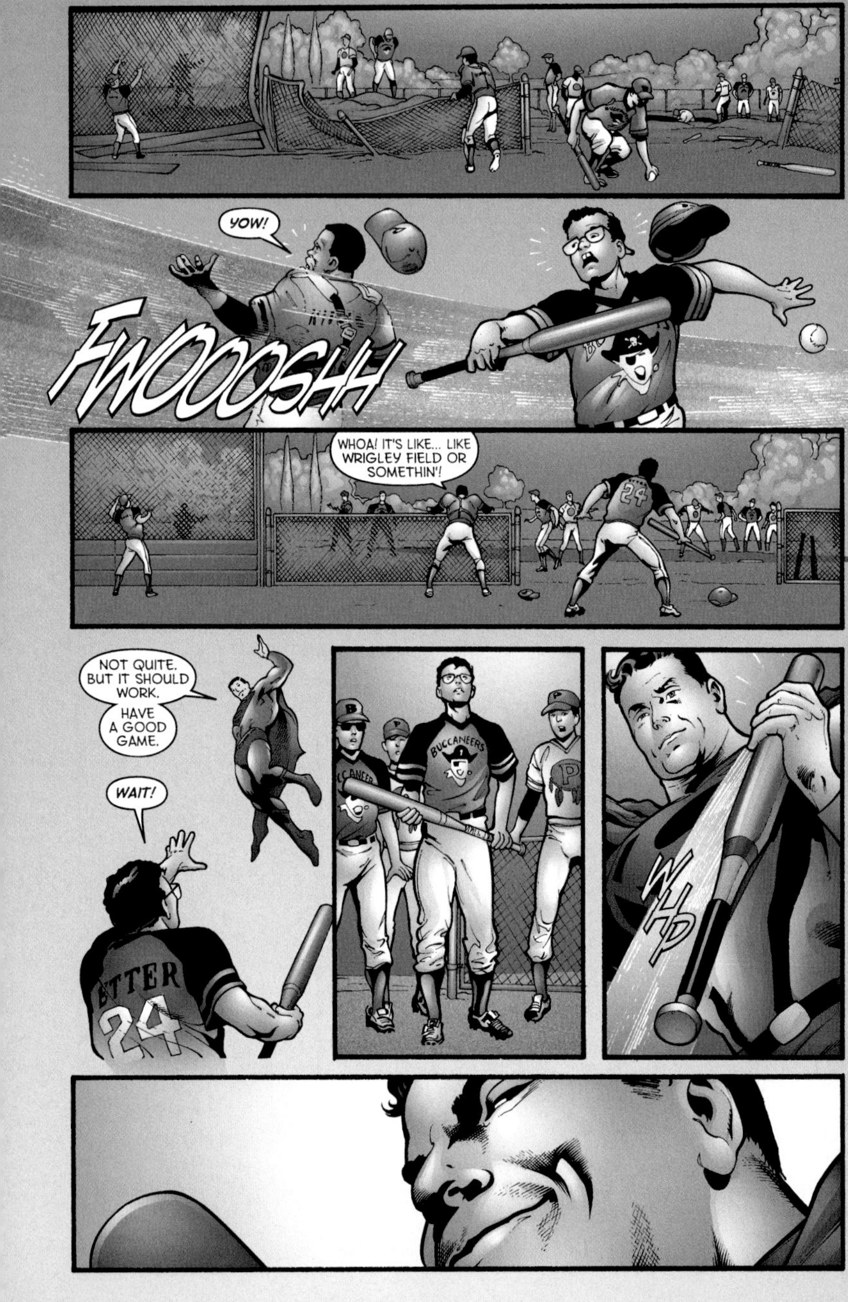
YOW!
FWOOOSHH
WHOA! IT'S LIKE... LIKE WRIGLEY FIELD OR SOMETHIN'!
NOT QUITE. BUT IT SHOULD WORK.
HAVE A GOOD GAME.
WAIT!
BUCCANEERS
WHP

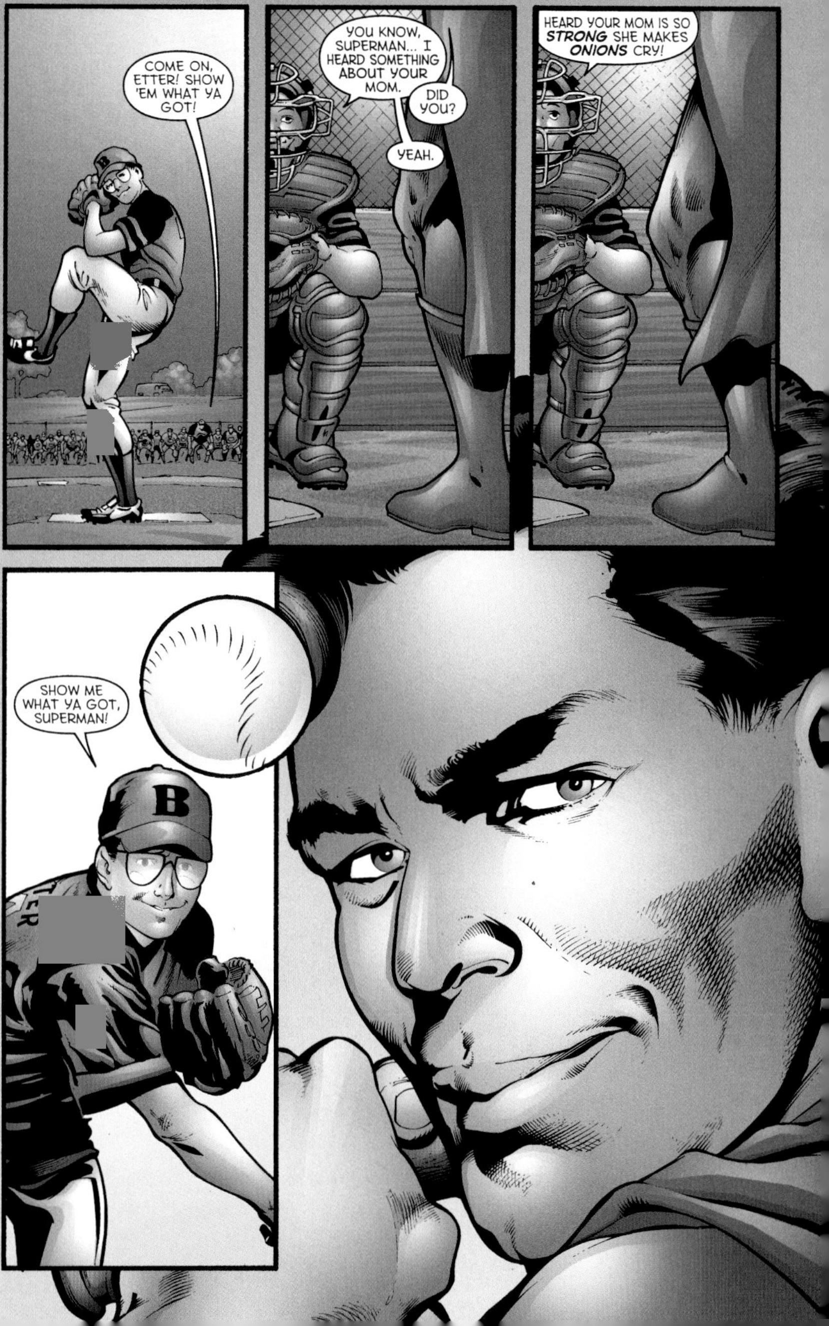
COME ON, ETTER! SHOW 'EM WHAT YA GOT!
YOU KNOW, SUPERMAN... I HEARD SOMETHING ABOUT YOUR MOM.
DID YOU?
YEAH.
HEARD YOUR MOM IS SO STRONG SHE MAKES ONIONS CRY!
SHOW ME WHAT YA GOT, SUPERMAN!

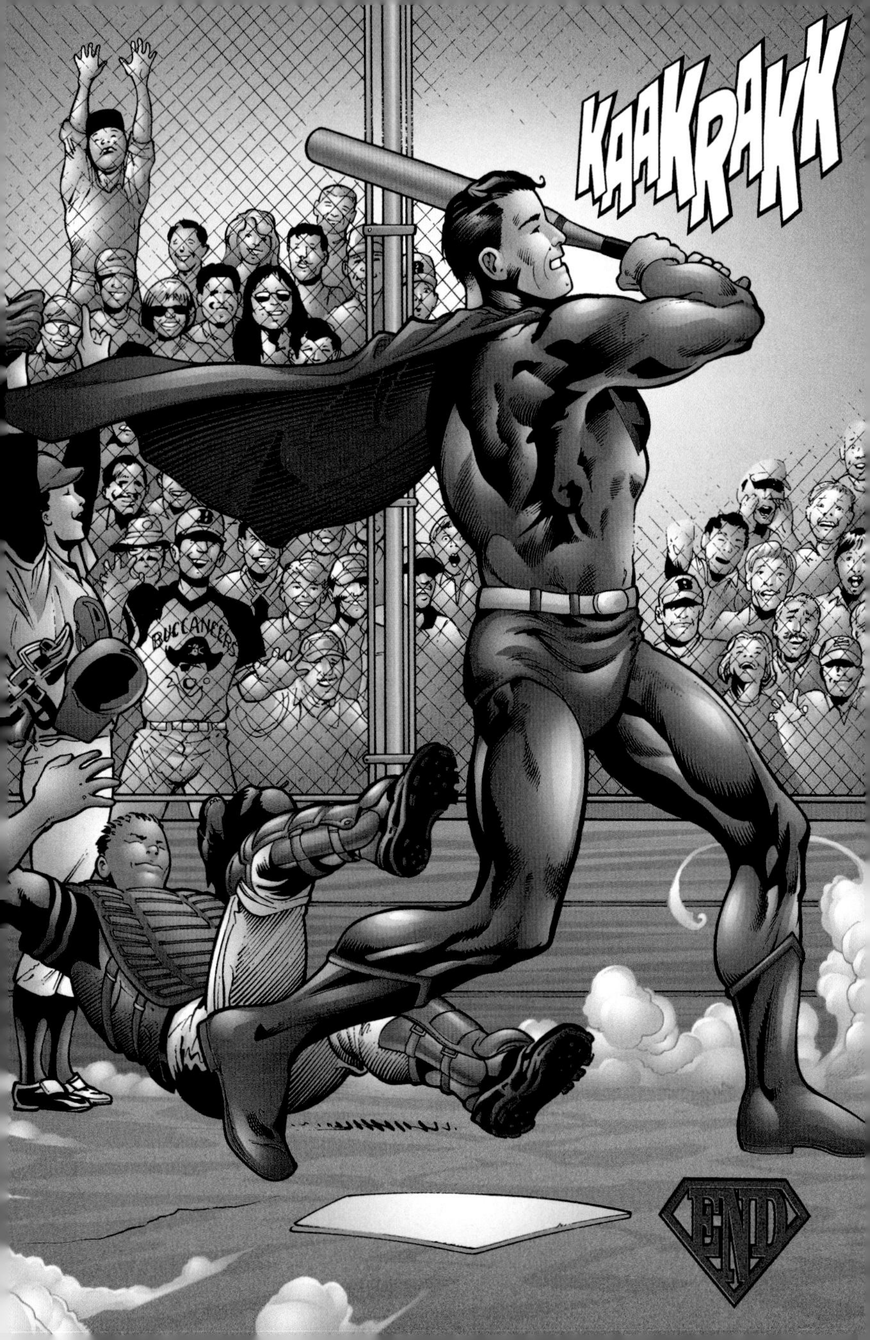
KAAKRAKK
BUCCANEERS
END

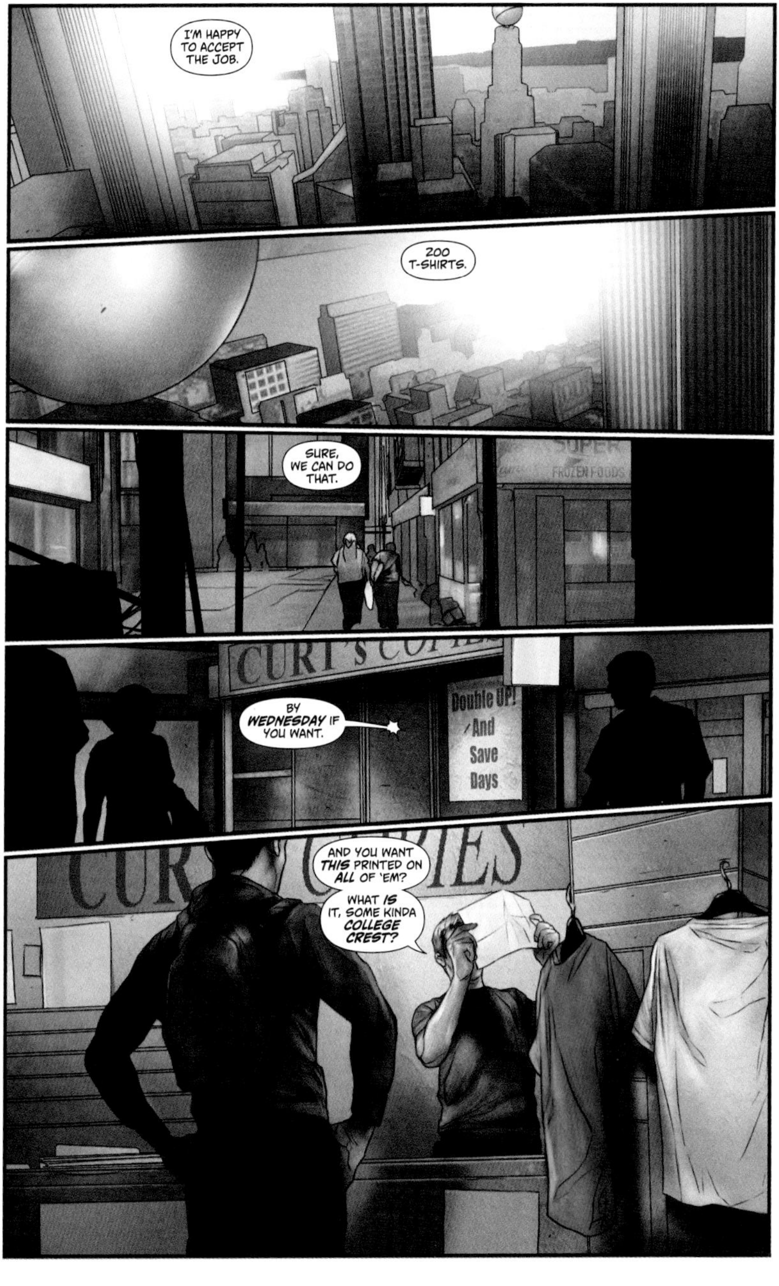
I'M HAPPY TO ACCEPT THE JOB.
200 T-SHIRTS.
SUPER
FROZEN FOODS
SURE, WE CAN DO THAT.
BY WEDNESDAY IF YOU WANT.
Double UP! And Save Days
AND YOU WANT THIS PRINTED ON ALL OF 'EM?
WHAT IS IT, SOME KINDA COLLEGE CREST?

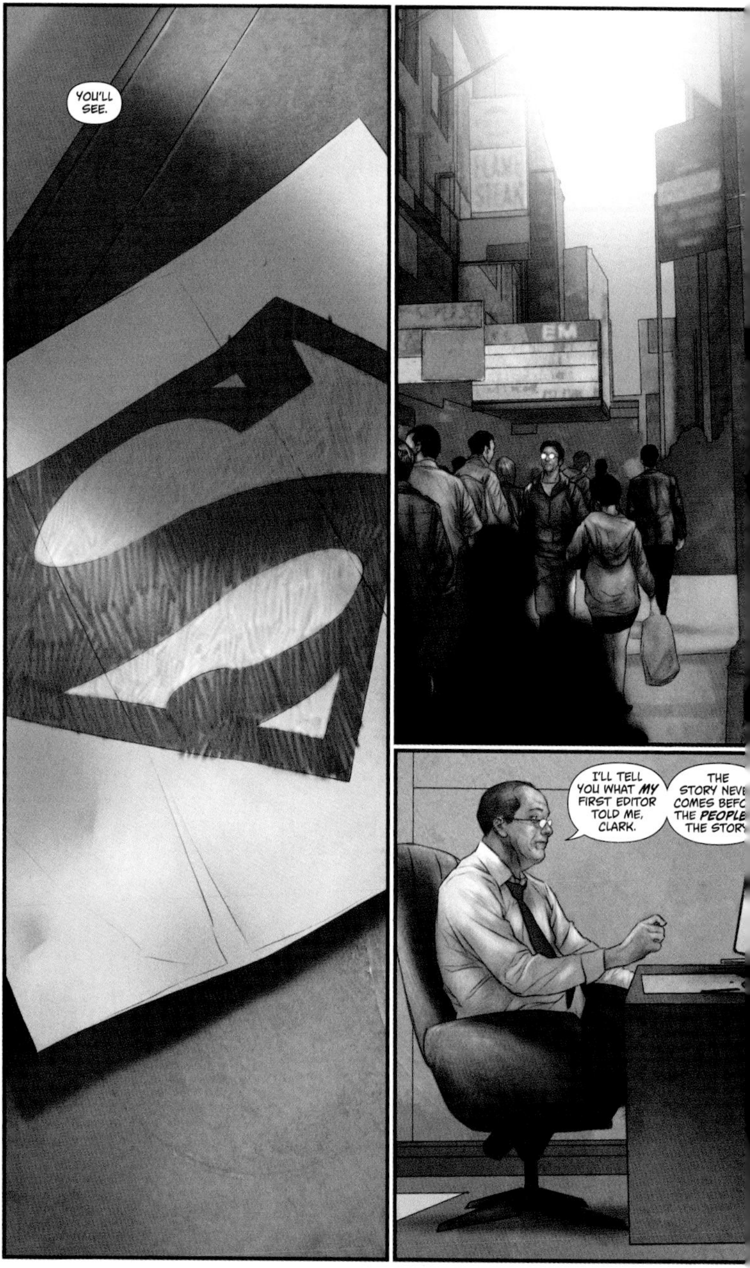
YOU'LL SEE.
I'LL TELL YOU WHAT MY FIRST EDITOR TOLD ME, CLARK.
THE STORY NEVE COMES BEFO THE PEOPLE THE STORY

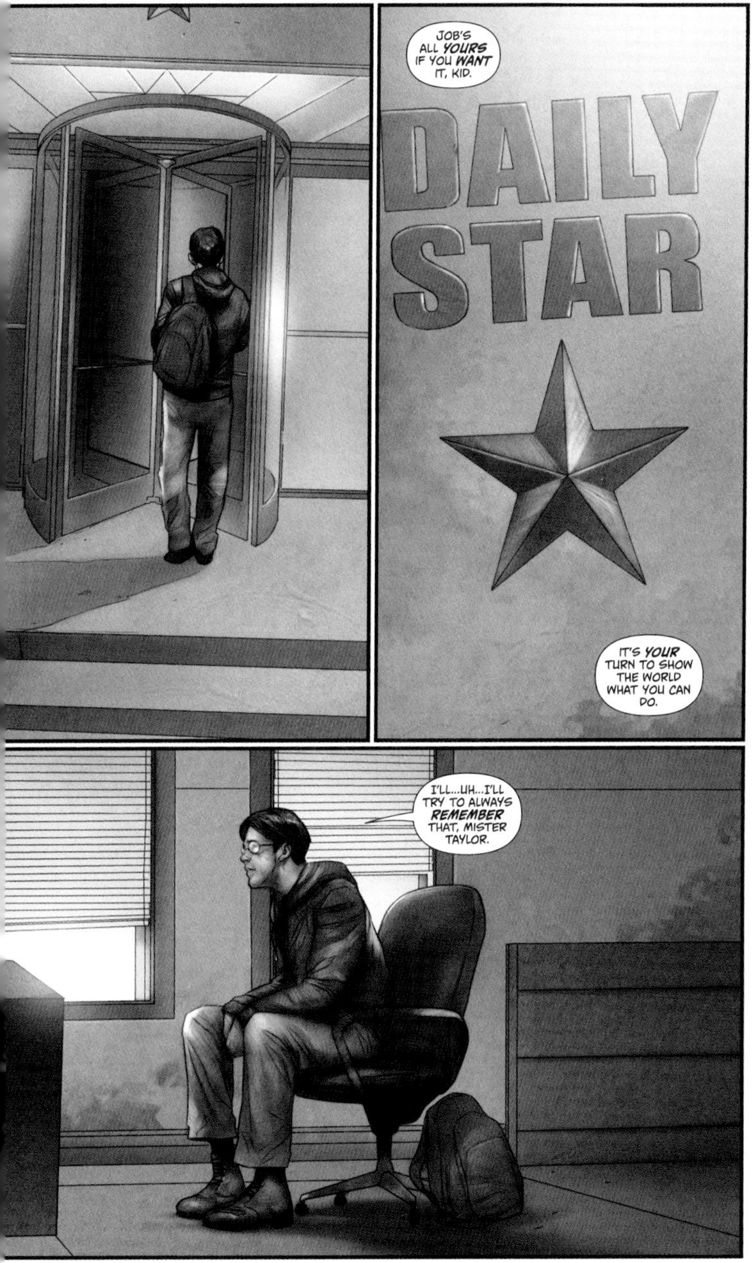
JOB'S ALL YOURS IF YOU WANT IT, KID.
DAILY STAR
IT'S YOUR TURN TO SHOW THE WORLD WHAT YOU CAN DO.
I'LL...UH...I'LL TRY TO ALWAYS REMEMBER THAT, MISTER TAYLOR.

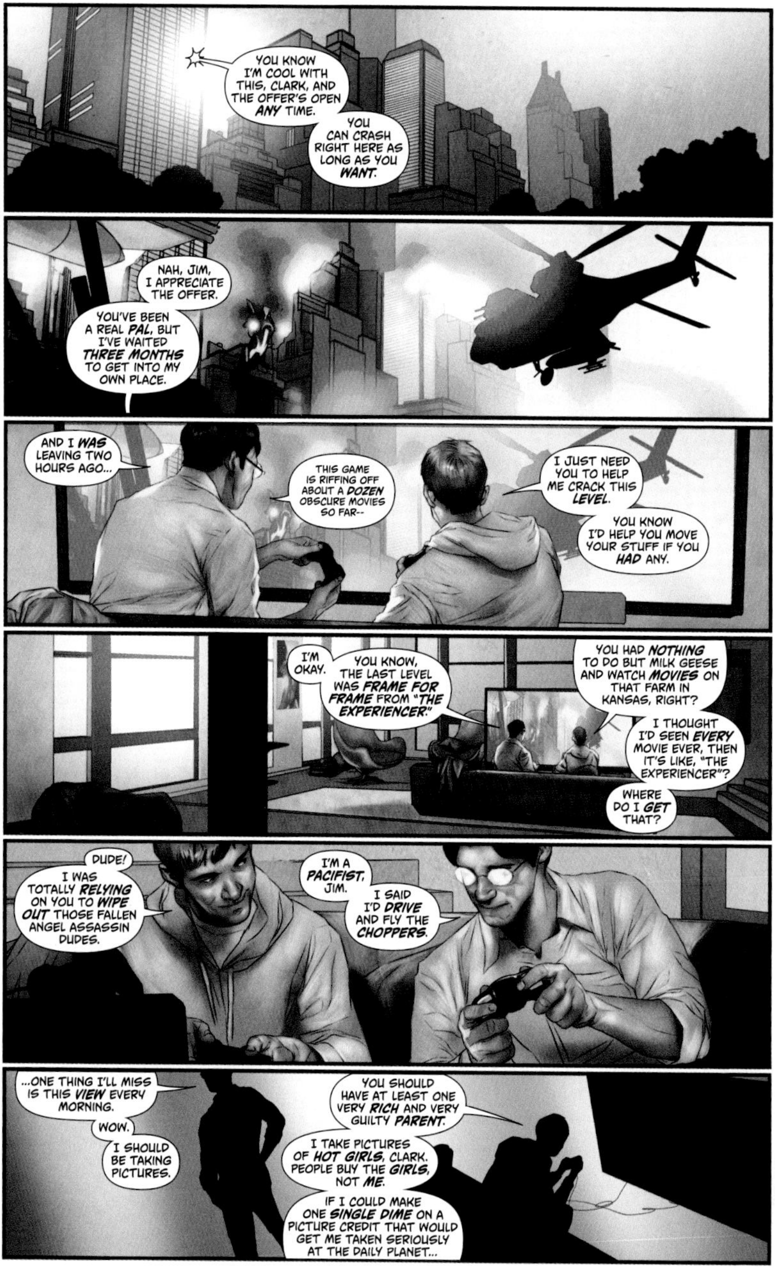
YOU KNOW I'M COOL WITH THIS, CLARK, AND THE OFFER'S OPEN ANY TIME.
YOU CAN CRASH RIGHT HERE AS LONG AS YOU WANT.
NAH, JIM, I APPRECIATE THE OFFER.
YOU'VE BEEN A REAL PAL, BUT I'VE WAITED THREE MONTHS TO GET INTO MY OWN PLACE.
AND I WAS LEAVING TWO HOURS AGO...
THIS GAME IS RIFFING OFF ABOUT A DOZEN OBSCURE MOVIES SO FAR--
I JUST NEED YOU TO HELP ME CRACK THIS LEVEL.
YOU KNOW I'D HELP YOU MOVE YOUR STUFF IF YOU HAD ANY.
I'M OKAY.
YOU KNOW, THE LAST LEVEL WAS FRAME FOR FRAME FROM "THE EXPERIENCER."
YOU HAD NOTHING TO DO BUT MILK GEESE AND WATCH MOVIES ON THAT FARM IN KANSAS, RIGHT?
I THOUGHT I'D SEEN EVERY MOVIE EVER, THEN IT'S LIKE, "THE EXPERIENCER"?
WHERE DO I GET THAT?
DUDE!
I WAS TOTALLY RELYING ON YOU TO WIPE OUT THOSE FALLEN ANGEL ASSASSIN DUDES.
I'M A PACIFIST, JIM.
I SAID I'D DRIVE AND FLY THE CHOPPERS.
...ONE THING I'LL MISS IS THIS VIEW EVERY MORNING.
WOW.
I SHOULD BE TAKING PICTURES.
YOU SHOULD HAVE AT LEAST ONE VERY RICH AND VERY GUILTY PARENT.
I TAKE PICTURES OF HOT GIRLS, CLARK. PEOPLE BUY THE GIRLS, NOT ME.
IF I COULD MAKE ONE SINGLE DIME ON A PICTURE CREDIT THAT WOULD GET ME TAKEN SERIOUSLY AT THE DAILY PLANET...

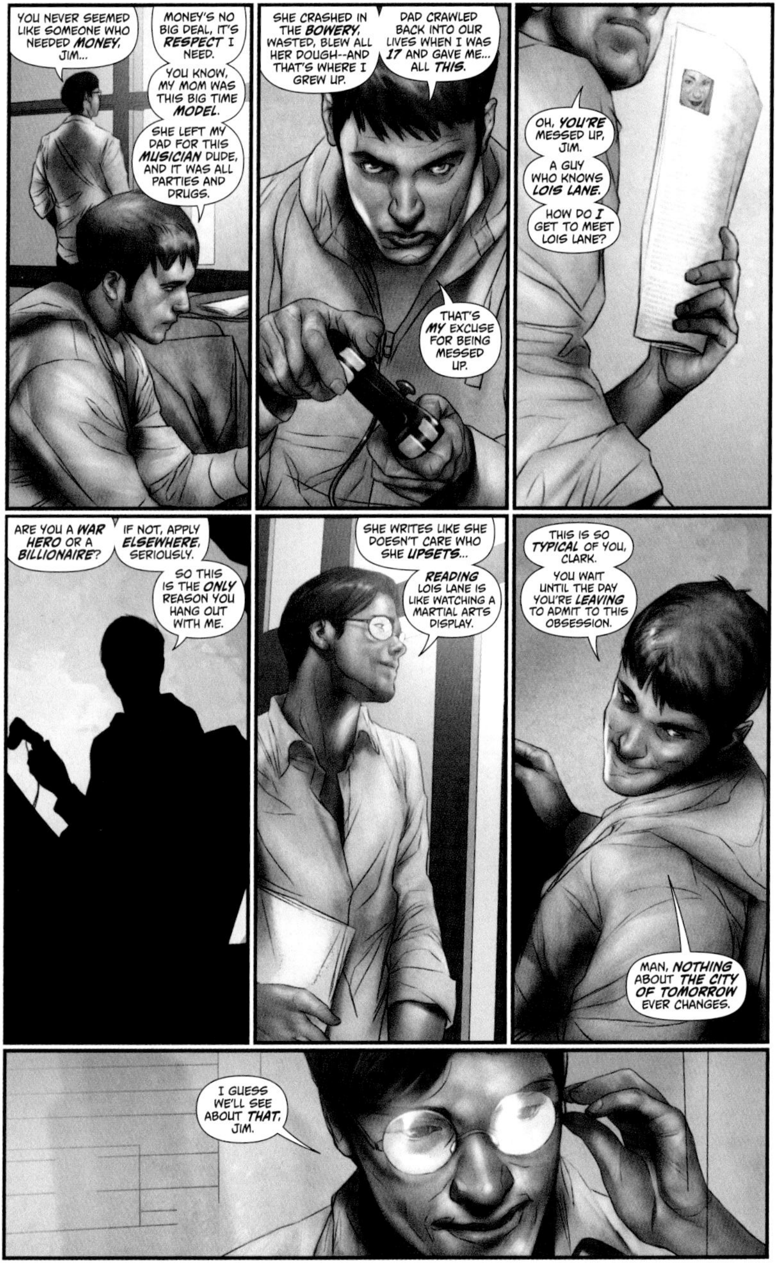
YOU NEVER SEEMED LIKE SOMEONE WHO NEEDED MONEY, JIM...
MONEY'S NO BIG DEAL, IT'S RESPECT I NEED.
YOU KNOW, MY MOM WAS THIS BIG TIME MODEL.
SHE LEFT MY DAD FOR THIS MUSICIAN DUDE, AND IT WAS ALL PARTIES AND DRUGS.
SHE CRASHED IN THE BOWERY, WASTED, BLEW ALL HER DOUGH--AND THAT'S WHERE I GREW UP.
DAD CRAWLED BACK INTO OUR LIVES WHEN I WAS 17 AND GAVE ME... ALL THIS.
THAT'S MY EXCUSE FOR BEING MESSED UP.
OH, YOU'RE MESSED UP, JIM.
A GUY WHO KNOWS LOIS LANE.
HOW DO I GET TO MEET LOIS LANE?
ARE YOU A WAR HERO OR A BILLIONAIRE?
IF NOT, APPLY ELSEWHERE, SERIOUSLY.
SO THIS IS THE ONLY REASON YOU HANG OUT WITH ME.
SHE WRITES LIKE SHE DOESN'T CARE WHO SHE UPSETS...
READING LOIS LANE IS LIKE WATCHING A MARTIAL ARTS DISPLAY.
THIS IS SO TYPICAL OF YOU, CLARK.
YOU WAIT UNTIL THE DAY YOU'RE LEAVING TO ADMIT TO THIS OBSESSION.
MAN, NOTHING ABOUT THE CITY OF TOMORROW EVER CHANGES.
I GUESS WE'LL SEE ABOUT THAT, JIM.

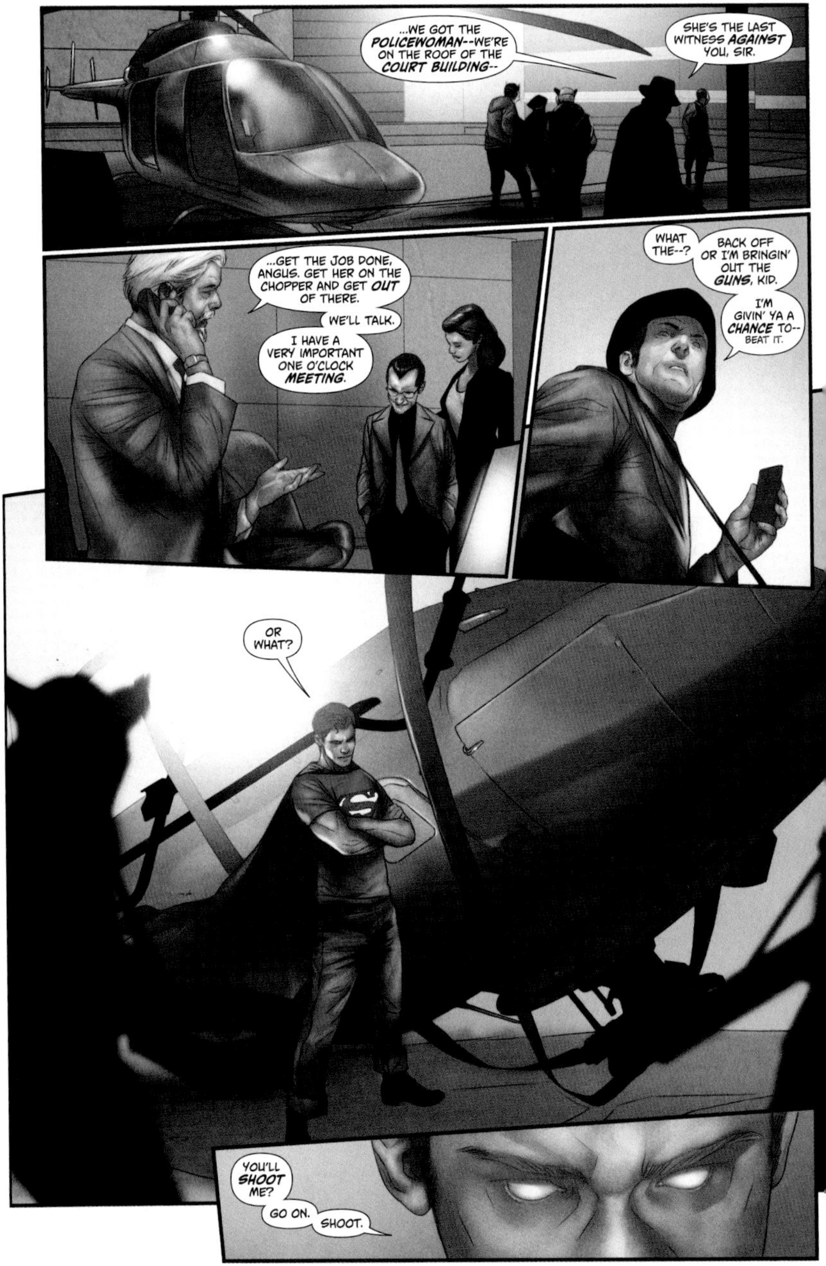
...WE GOT THE POLICEWOMAN--WE'RE ON THE ROOF OF THE COURT BUILDING--
SHE'S THE LAST WITNESS AGAINST YOU, SIR.
...GET THE JOB DONE, ANGUS. GET HER ON THE CHOPPER AND GET OUT OF THERE.
WE'LL TALK.
I HAVE A VERY IMPORTANT ONE O'CLOCK MEETING.
WHAT THE--?
BACK OFF OR I'M BRINGIN' OUT THE GUNS, KID.
I'M GIVIN' YA A CHANCE TO-- BEAT IT.
OR WHAT?
YOU'LL SHOOT ME?
GO ON.
SHOOT.

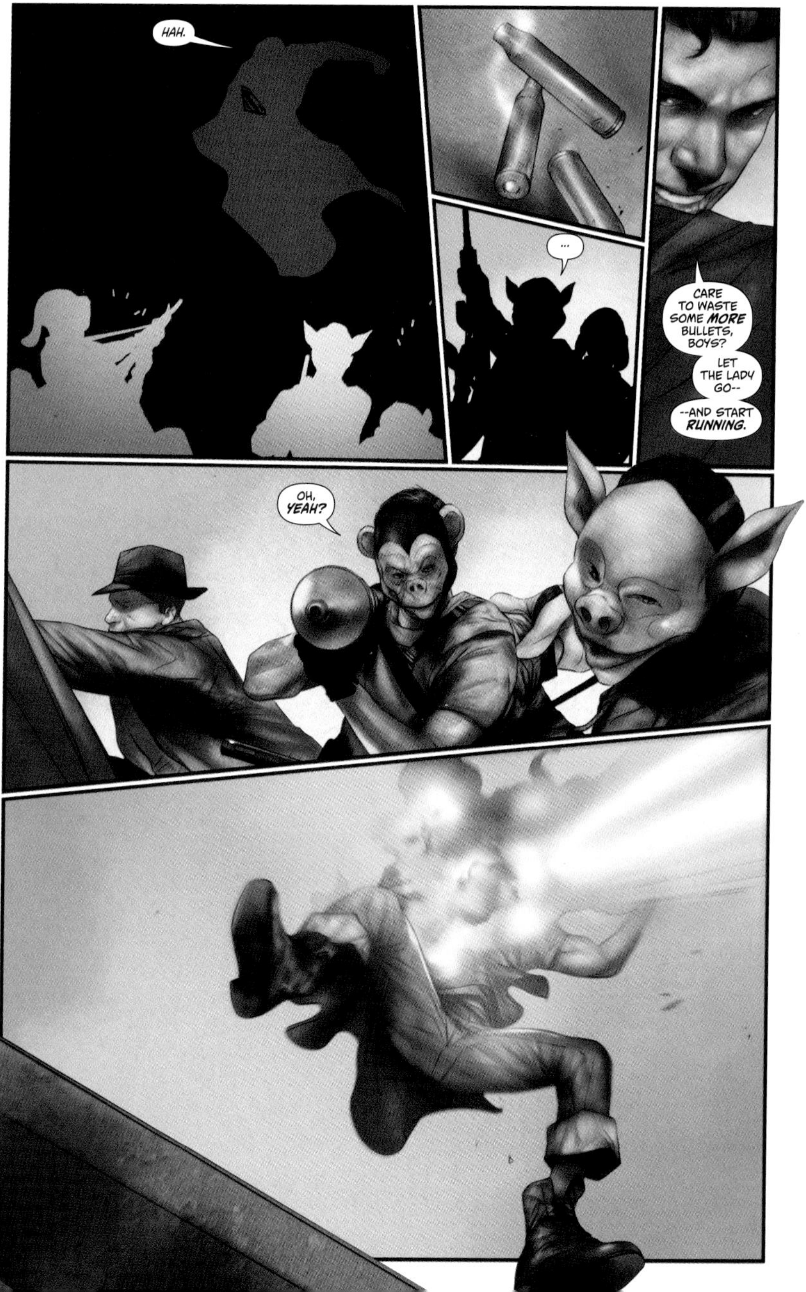
HAH.
...
CARE TO WASTE SOME MORE BULLETS, BOYS?
LET THE LADY GO--
--AND START RUNNING.
OH, YEAH?

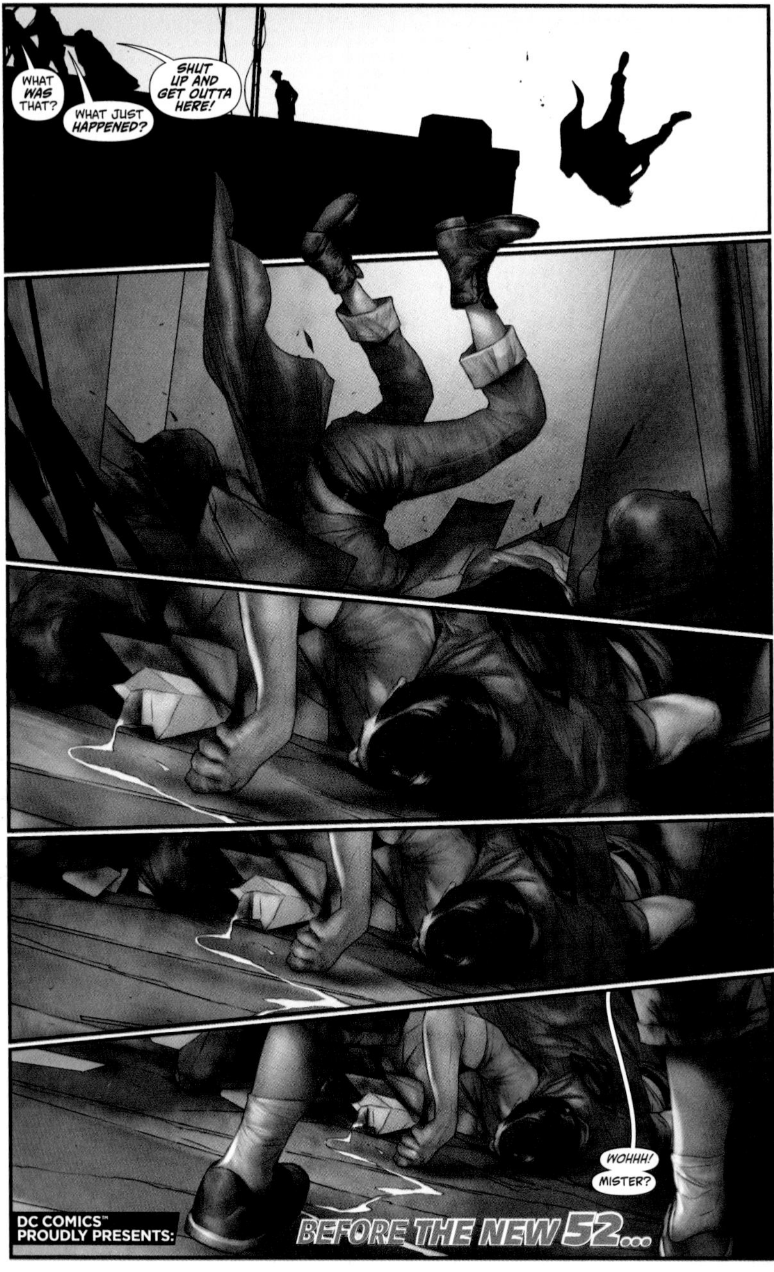
WHAT WAS THAT?
WHAT JUST HAPPENED?
SHUT UP AND GET OUTTA HERE!
WOHHH!
MISTER?
DC COMICS™ PROUDLY PRESENTS:
BEFORE THE NEW 52...

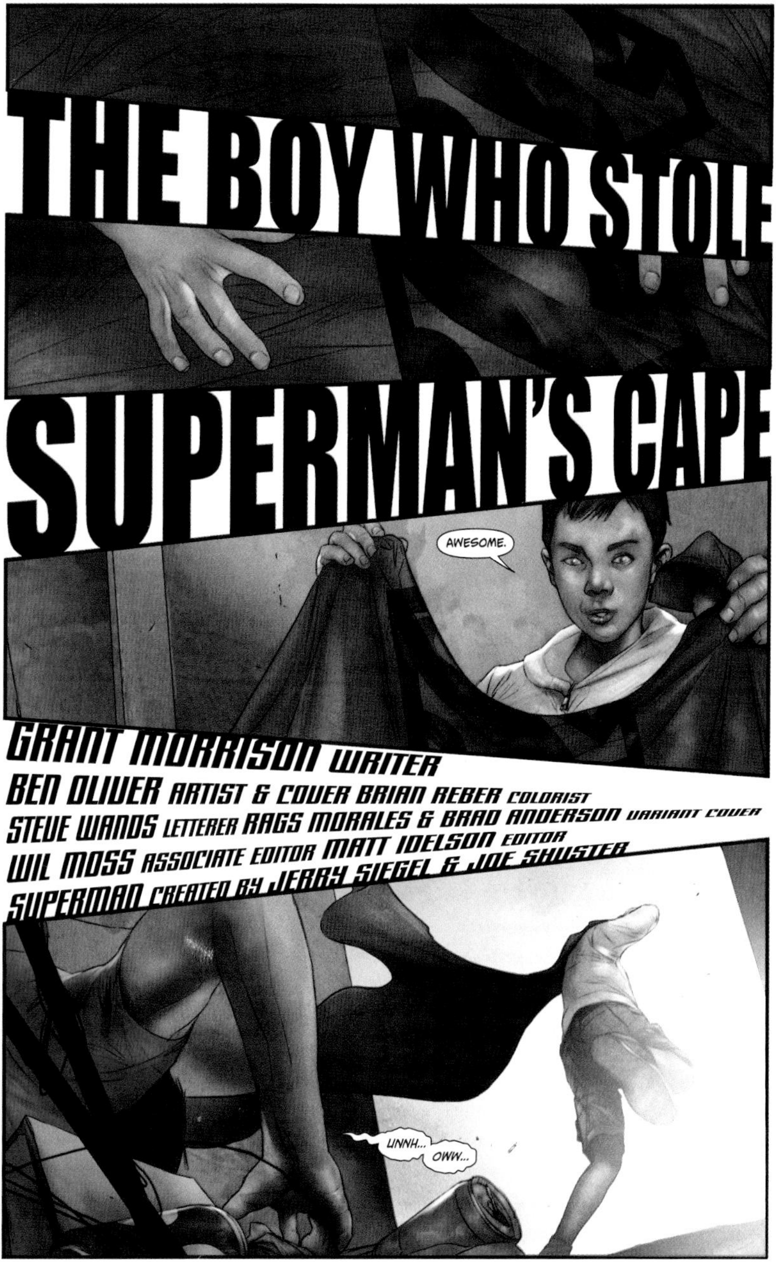
THE BOY WHO STOLE
SUPERMAN'S CAPE
AWESOME.
GRANT MORRISON WRITER
BEN OLIVER ARTIST & COVER BRIAN REBER COLORIST
STEVE WANDS LETTERER RAGS MORALES & BRAD ANDERSON VARIANT COVER
WIL MOSS ASSOCIATE EDITOR MATT IDELSON EDITOR
SUPERMAN CREATED BY JERRY SIEGEL & JOE SHUSTER
UNNH... OWW...

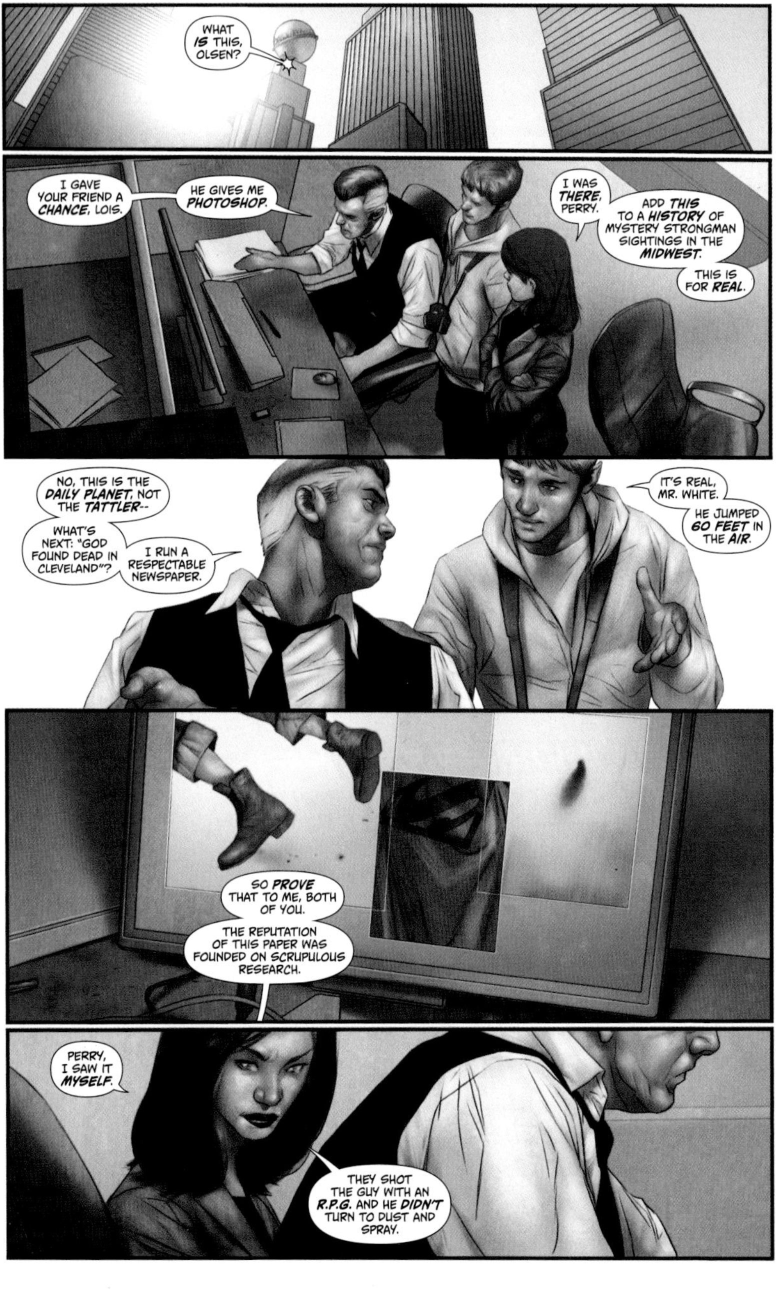
WHAT IS THIS, OLSEN?
I GAVE YOUR FRIEND A CHANCE, LOIS.
HE GIVES ME PHOTOSHOP.
I WAS THERE, PERRY.
ADD THIS TO A HISTORY OF MYSTERY STRONGMAN SIGHTINGS IN THE MIDWEST.
THIS IS FOR REAL.
NO, THIS IS THE DAILY PLANET, NOT THE TATTLER--
WHAT'S NEXT: "GOD FOUND DEAD IN CLEVELAND"?
I RUN A RESPECTABLE NEWSPAPER.
IT'S REAL, MR. WHITE.
HE JUMPED 60 FEET IN THE AIR.
SO PROVE THAT TO ME, BOTH OF YOU.
THE REPUTATION OF THIS PAPER WAS FOUNDED ON SCRUPULOUS RESEARCH.
PERRY, I SAW IT MYSELF.
THEY SHOT THE GUY WITH AN R.P.G. AND HE DIDN'T TURN TO DUST AND SPRAY.

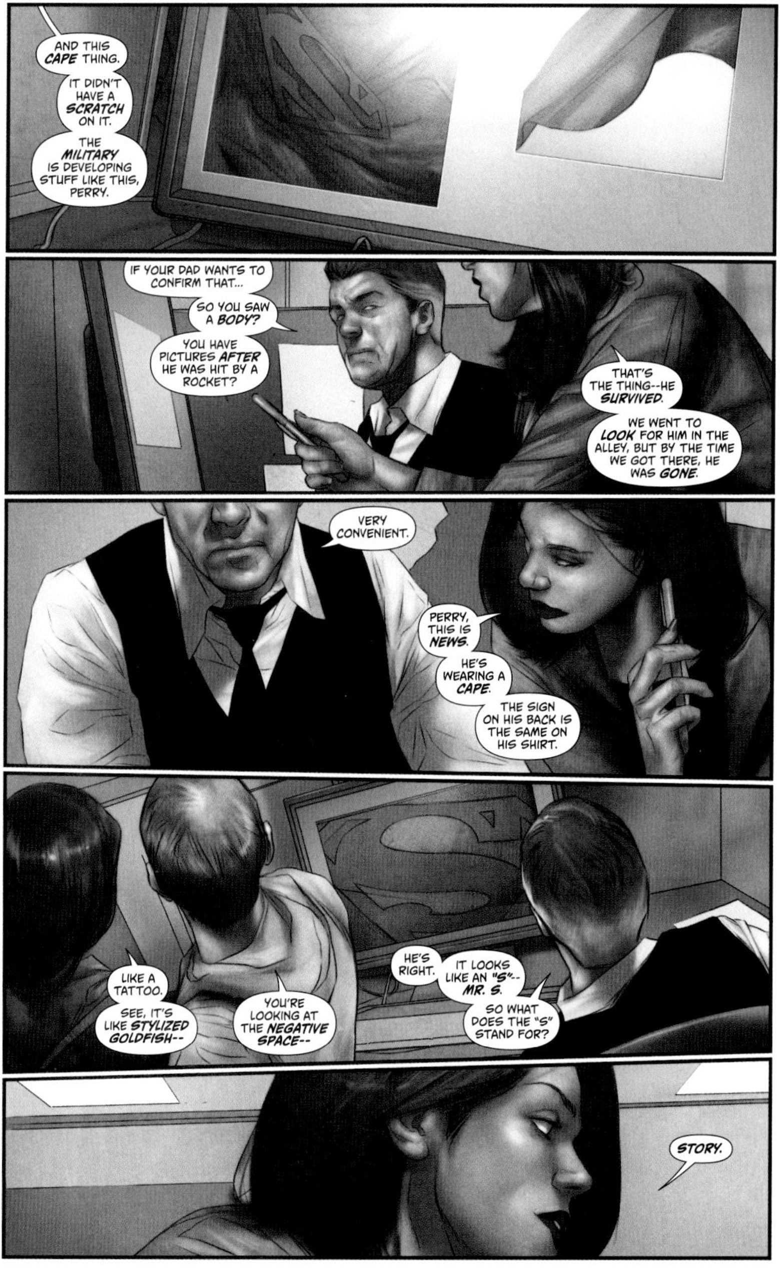
AND THIS CAPE THING.
IT DIDN'T HAVE A SCRATCH ON IT.
THE MILITARY IS DEVELOPING STUFF LIKE THIS, PERRY.
IF YOUR DAD WANTS TO CONFIRM THAT...
SO YOU SAW A BODY?
YOU HAVE PICTURES AFTER HE WAS HIT BY A ROCKET?
THAT'S THE THING--HE SURVIVED.
WE WENT TO LOOK FOR HIM IN THE ALLEY, BUT BY THE TIME WE GOT THERE, HE WAS GONE.
VERY CONVENIENT.
PERRY, THIS IS NEWS.
HE'S WEARING A CAPE.
THE SIGN ON HIS BACK IS THE SAME ON HIS SHIRT.
LIKE A TATTOO.
SEE, IT'S LIKE STYLIZED GOLDFISH--
YOU'RE LOOKING AT THE NEGATIVE SPACE--
HE'S RIGHT.
IT LOOKS LIKE AN "S"-- MR. S.
SO WHAT DOES THE "S" STAND FOR?
STORY.

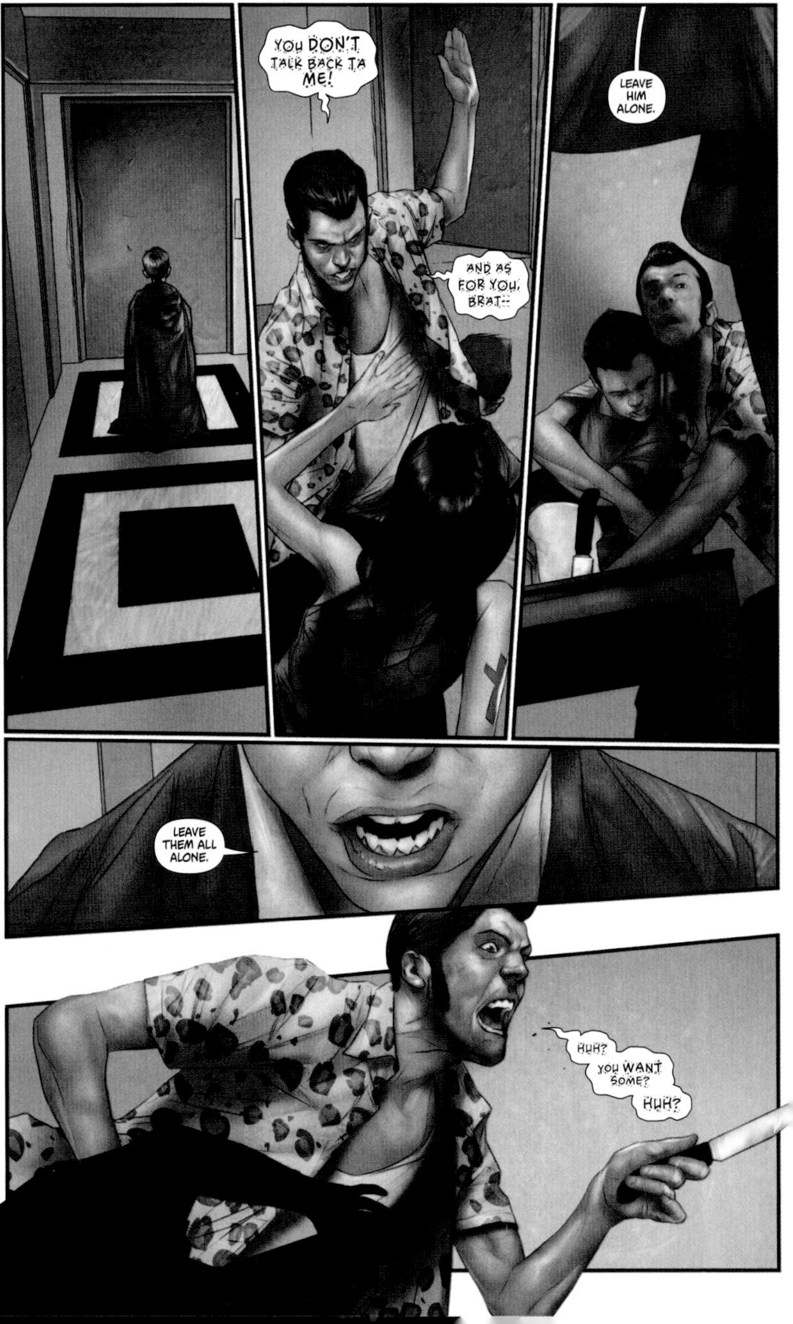
YOU DON'T TALK BACK TA ME!
AND AS FOR YOU, BRAT--
LEAVE HIM ALONE.
LEAVE THEM ALL ALONE.
HUH?
YOU WANT SOME?
HUH?

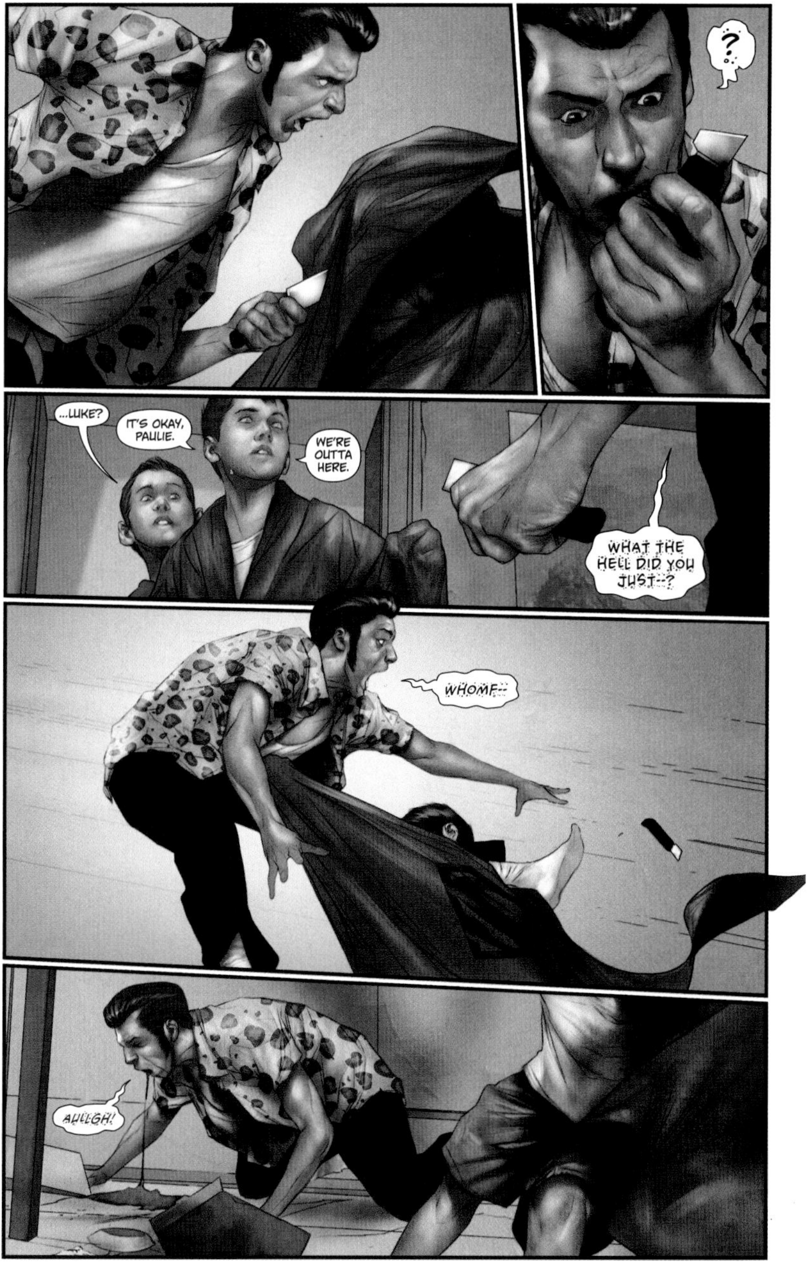
?
...LUKE?
IT'S OKAY, PAULIE.
WE'RE OUTTA HERE.
WHAT THE HELL DID YOU JUST--?
WHOMF--
AULLGH!

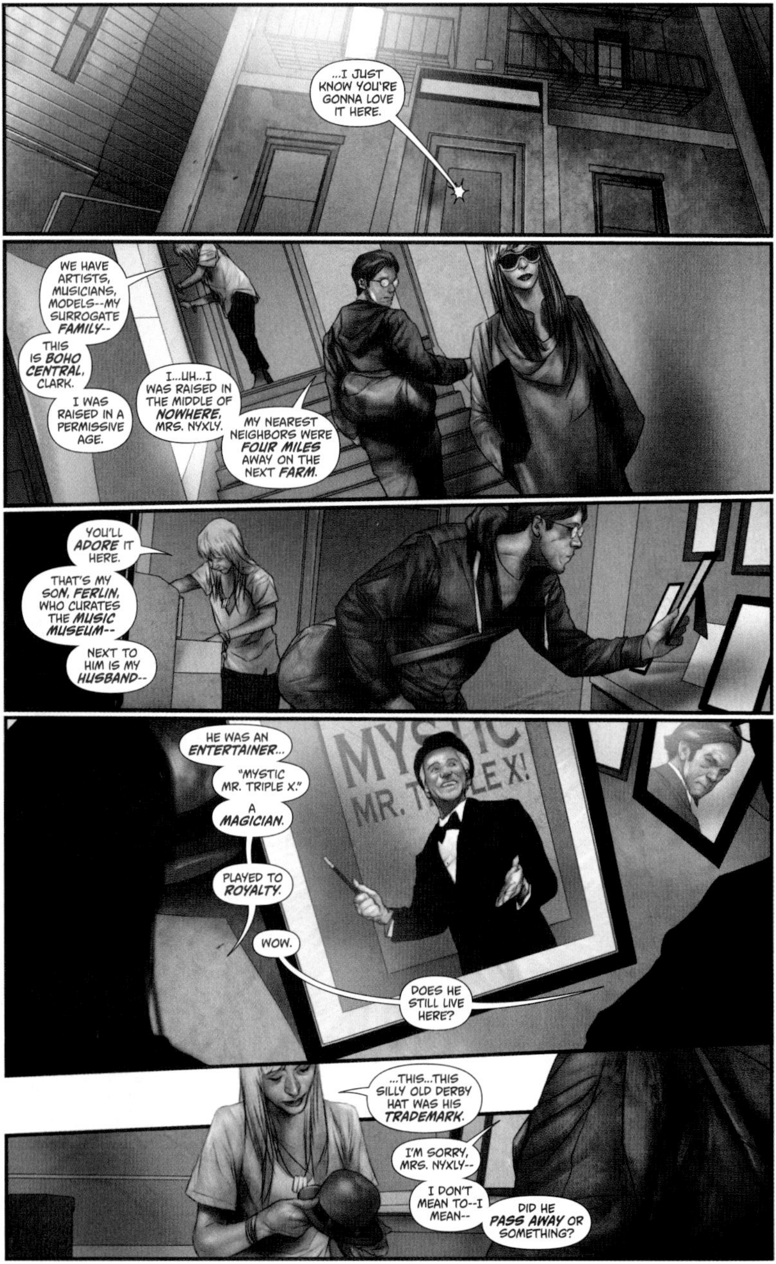

...I JUST KNOW YOU'RE GONNA LOVE IT HERE.
WE HAVE ARTISTS, MUSICIANS, MODELS--MY SURROGATE ***FAMILY***--
THIS IS ***BOHO CENTRAL***, CLARK.
I WAS RAISED IN A PERMISSIVE AGE.
I...UH...I WAS RAISED IN THE MIDDLE OF ***NOWHERE***, MRS. NYXLY.
MY NEAREST NEIGHBORS WERE ***FOUR MILES*** AWAY ON THE NEXT ***FARM***.
YOU'LL ***ADORE*** IT HERE.
THAT'S MY ***SON, FERLIN***, WHO CURATES THE ***MUSIC MUSEUM***--
NEXT TO HIM IS MY ***HUSBAND***--
HE WAS AN ***ENTERTAINER***...
"MYSTIC MR. TRIPLE X."
A ***MAGICIAN***.
PLAYED TO ***ROYALTY***.
WOW.
DOES HE STILL LIVE HERE?
...THIS...THIS SILLY OLD DERBY HAT WAS HIS ***TRADEMARK***.
I'M SORRY, MRS. NYXLY--
I DON'T MEAN TO--I MEAN--
DID HE ***PASS AWAY*** OR SOMETHING?

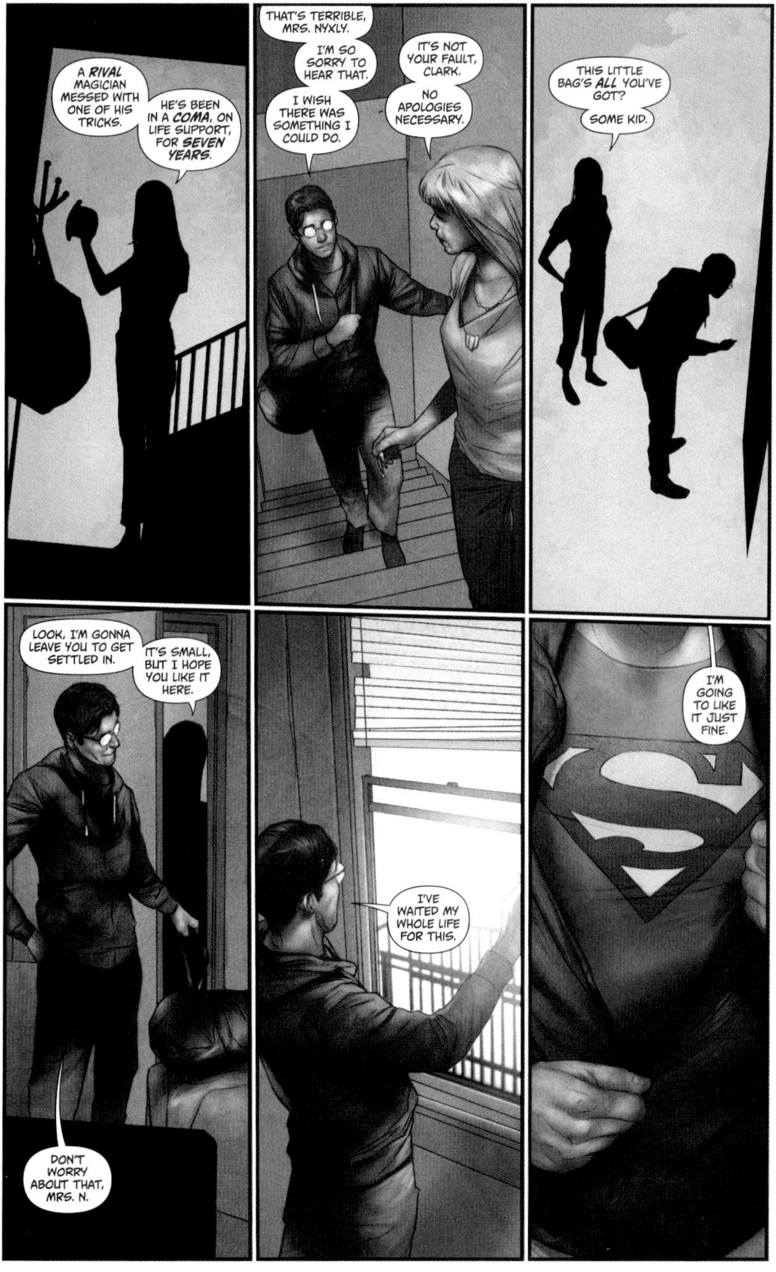
A RIVAL MAGICIAN MESSED WITH ONE OF HIS TRICKS.
HE'S BEEN IN A COMA, ON LIFE SUPPORT, FOR SEVEN YEARS.
THAT'S TERRIBLE, MRS. NYXLY.
I'M SO SORRY TO HEAR THAT.
I WISH THERE WAS SOMETHING I COULD DO.
IT'S NOT YOUR FAULT, CLARK.
NO APOLOGIES NECESSARY.
THIS LITTLE BAG'S ALL YOU'VE GOT?
SOME KID.
LOOK, I'M GONNA LEAVE YOU TO GET SETTLED IN.
IT'S SMALL, BUT I HOPE YOU LIKE IT HERE.
DON'T WORRY ABOUT THAT, MRS. N.
I'VE WAITED MY WHOLE LIFE FOR THIS.
I'M GOING TO LIKE IT JUST FINE.

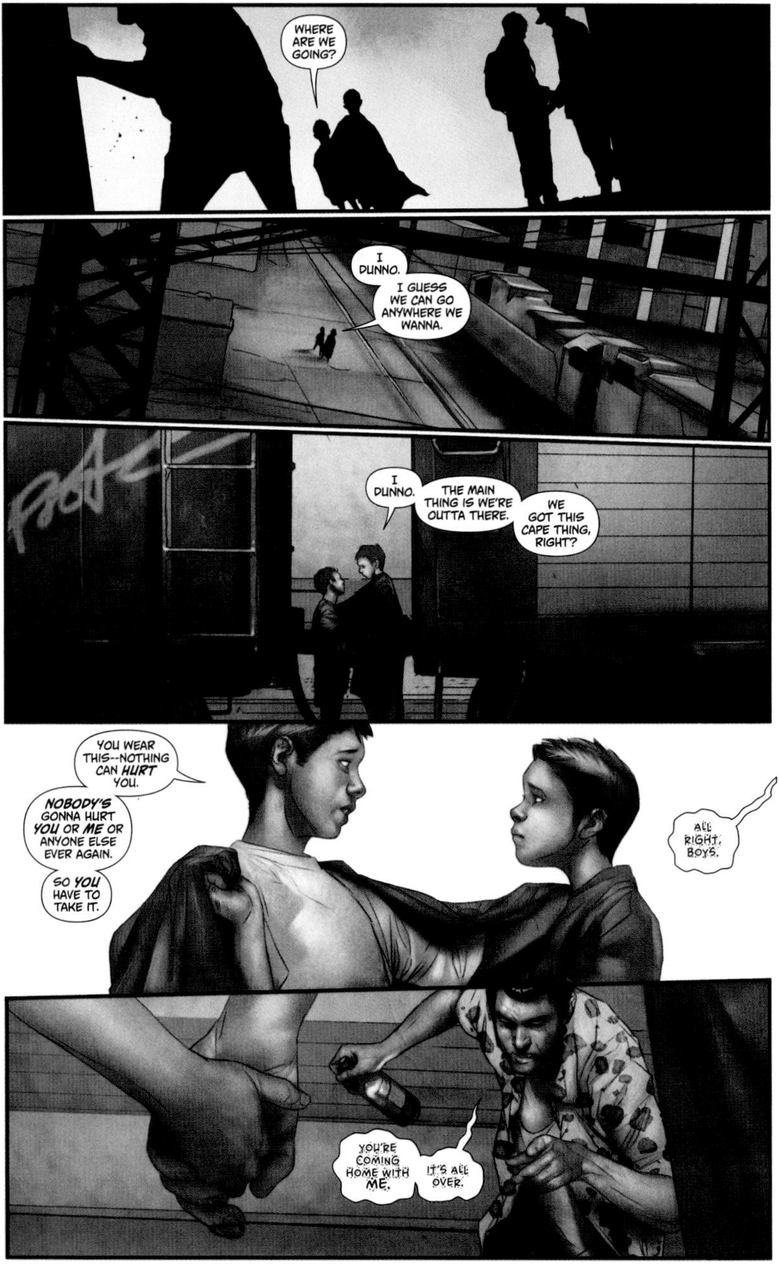
WHERE ARE WE GOING?
I DUNNO.
I GUESS WE CAN GO ANYWHERE WE WANNA.
I DUNNO.
THE MAIN THING IS WE'RE OUTTA THERE.
WE GOT THIS CAPE THING, RIGHT?
YOU WEAR THIS--NOTHING CAN HURT YOU.
NOBODY'S GONNA HURT YOU OR ME OR ANYONE ELSE EVER AGAIN.
SO YOU HAVE TO TAKE IT.
ALL RIGHT, BOYS.
YOU'RE COMING HOME WITH ME.
IT'S ALL OVER.

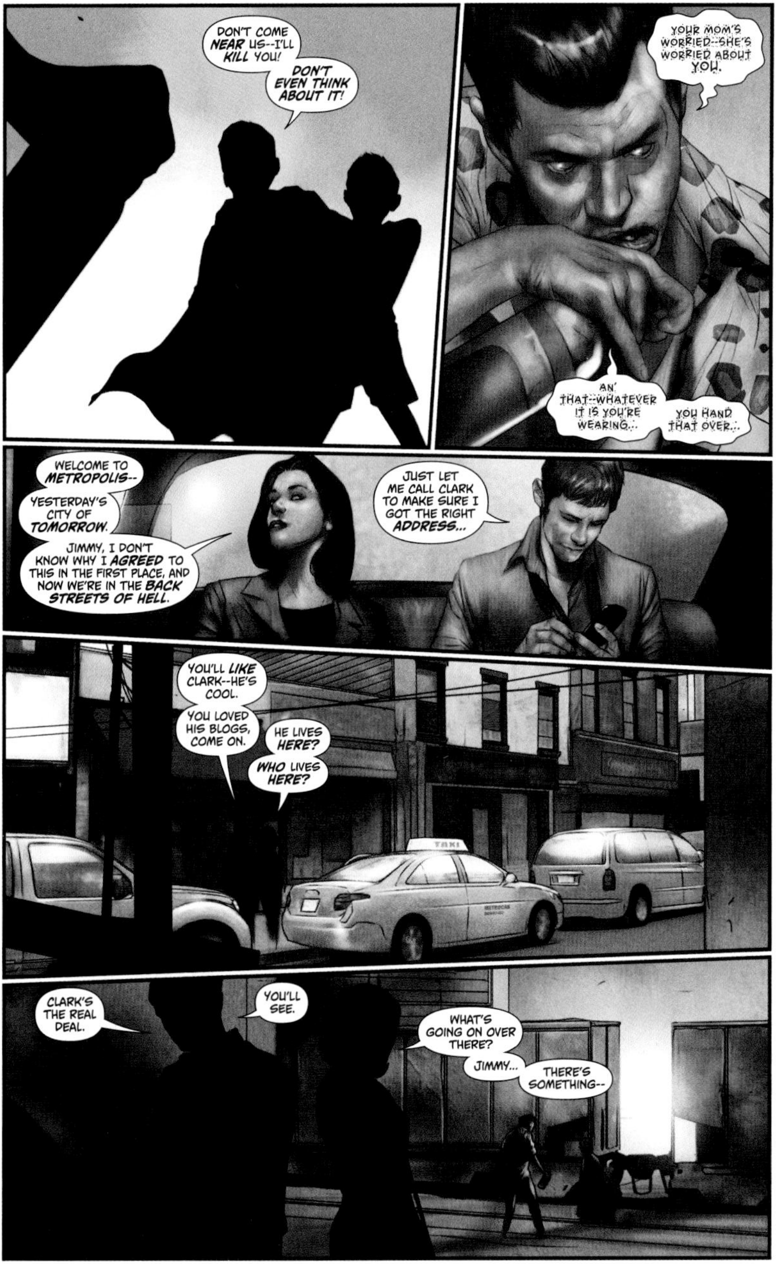
DON'T COME NEAR US--I'LL KILL YOU!
DON'T EVEN THINK ABOUT IT!
YOUR MOM'S WORRIED--SHE'S WORRIED ABOUT YOU.
AN' THAT--WHATEVER IT IS YOU'RE WEARING...
YOU HAND THAT OVER...
WELCOME TO METROPOLIS--
YESTERDAY'S CITY OF TOMORROW.
JIMMY, I DON'T KNOW WHY I AGREED TO THIS IN THE FIRST PLACE, AND NOW WE'RE IN THE BACK STREETS OF HELL.
JUST LET ME CALL CLARK TO MAKE SURE I GOT THE RIGHT ADDRESS...
YOU'LL LIKE CLARK--HE'S COOL.
YOU LOVED HIS BLOGS, COME ON.
HE LIVES HERE?
WHO LIVES HERE?
TAXI
CLARK'S THE REAL DEAL.
YOU'LL SEE.
WHAT'S GOING ON OVER THERE?
JIMMY...
THERE'S SOMETHING--

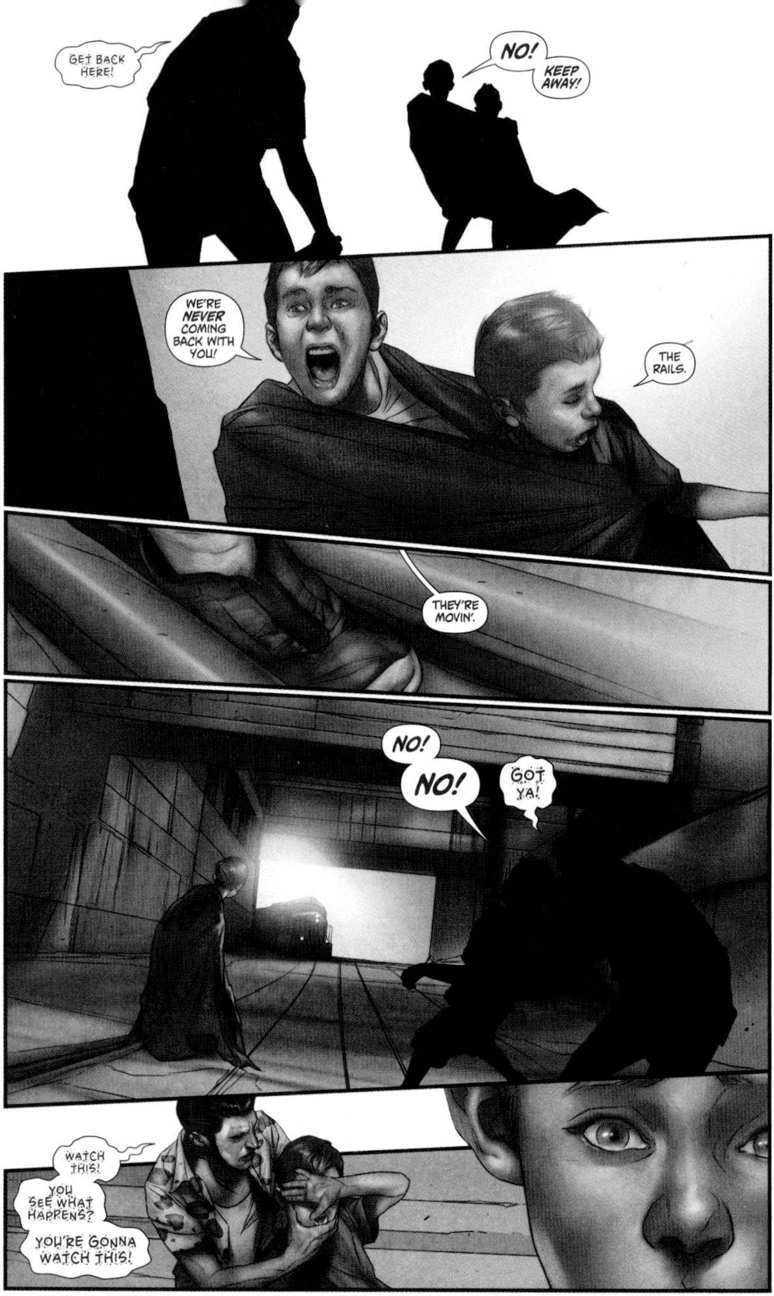
GET BACK HERE!
NO!
KEEP AWAY!
WE'RE NEVER COMING BACK WITH YOU!
THE RAILS.
THEY'RE MOVIN'.
NO!
NO!
GOT YA!
WATCH THIS!
YOU SEE WHAT HAPPENS?
YOU'RE GONNA WATCH THIS!

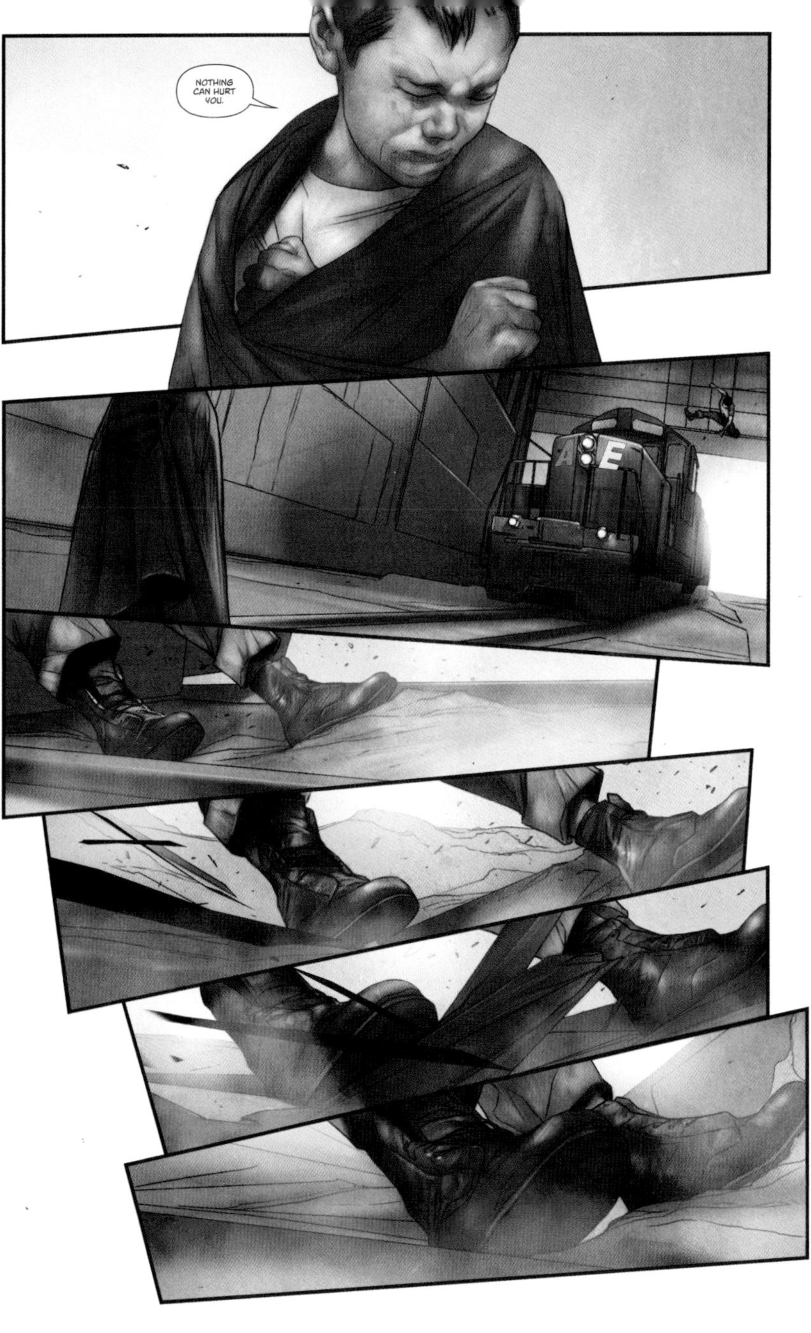
NOTHING CAN HURT YOU.

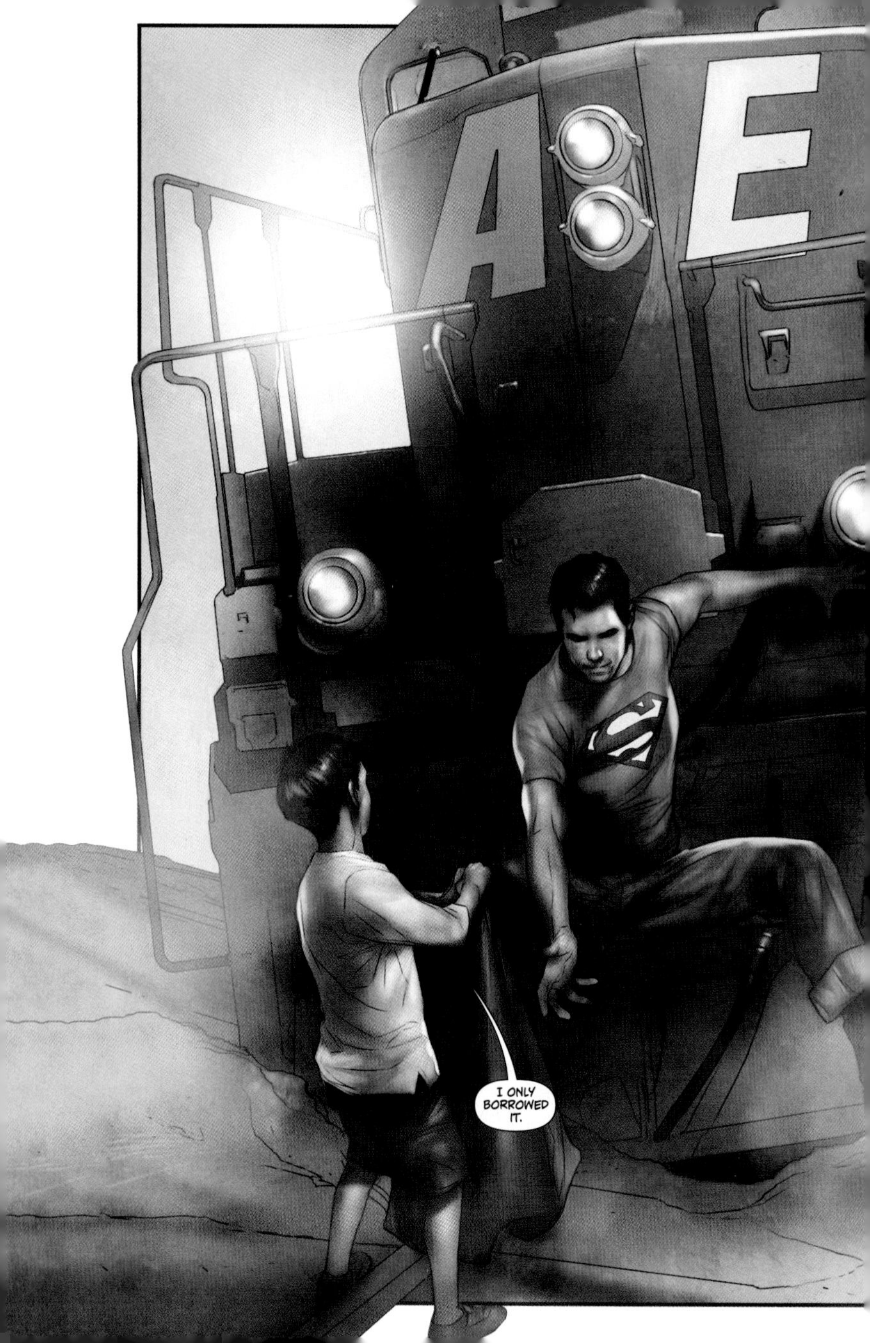
I ONLY BORROWED IT.

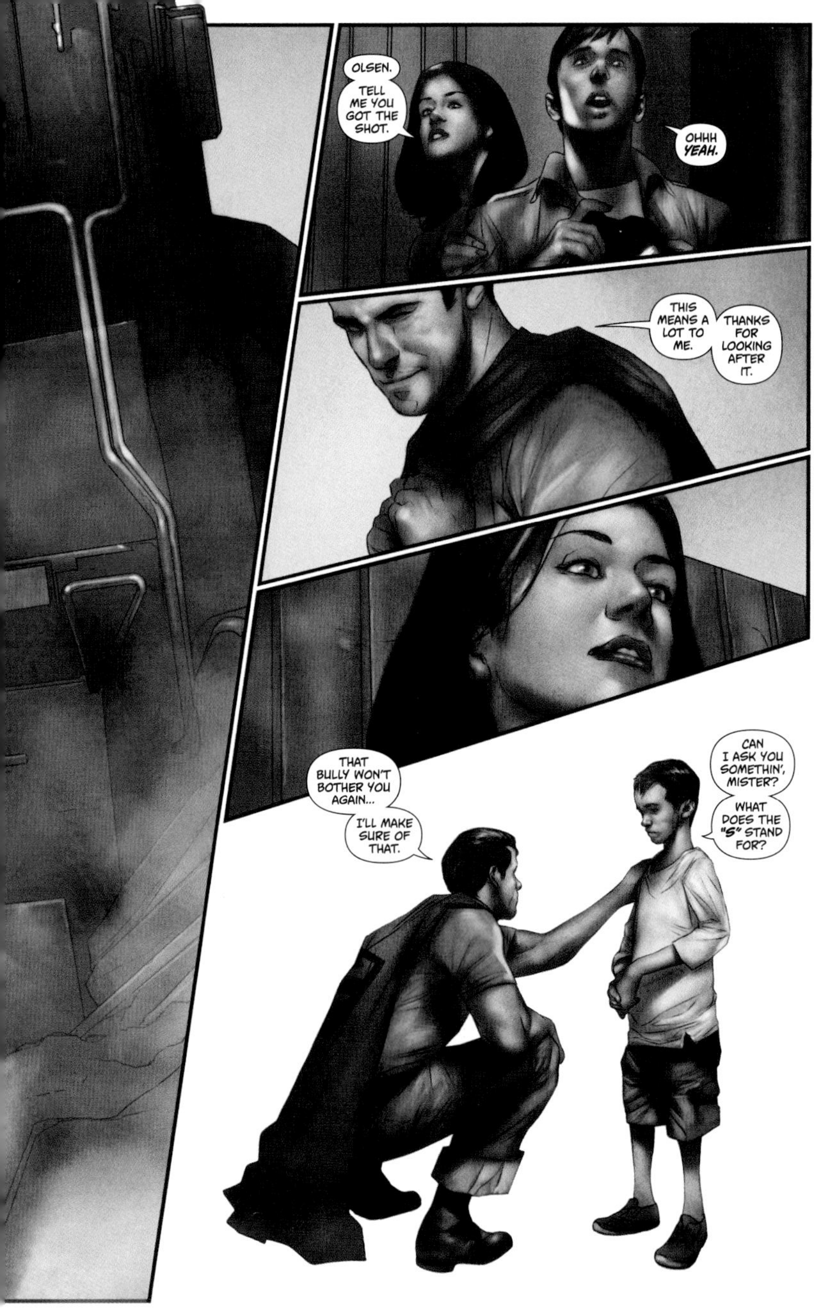
OLSEN.
TELL ME YOU GOT THE SHOT.
OHHH *YEAH.*
THIS MEANS A LOT TO ME.
THANKS FOR LOOKING AFTER IT.
THAT BULLY WON'T BOTHER YOU AGAIN...
I'LL MAKE SURE OF THAT.
CAN I ASK YOU SOMETHIN', MISTER?
WHAT DOES THE "*S*" STAND FOR?

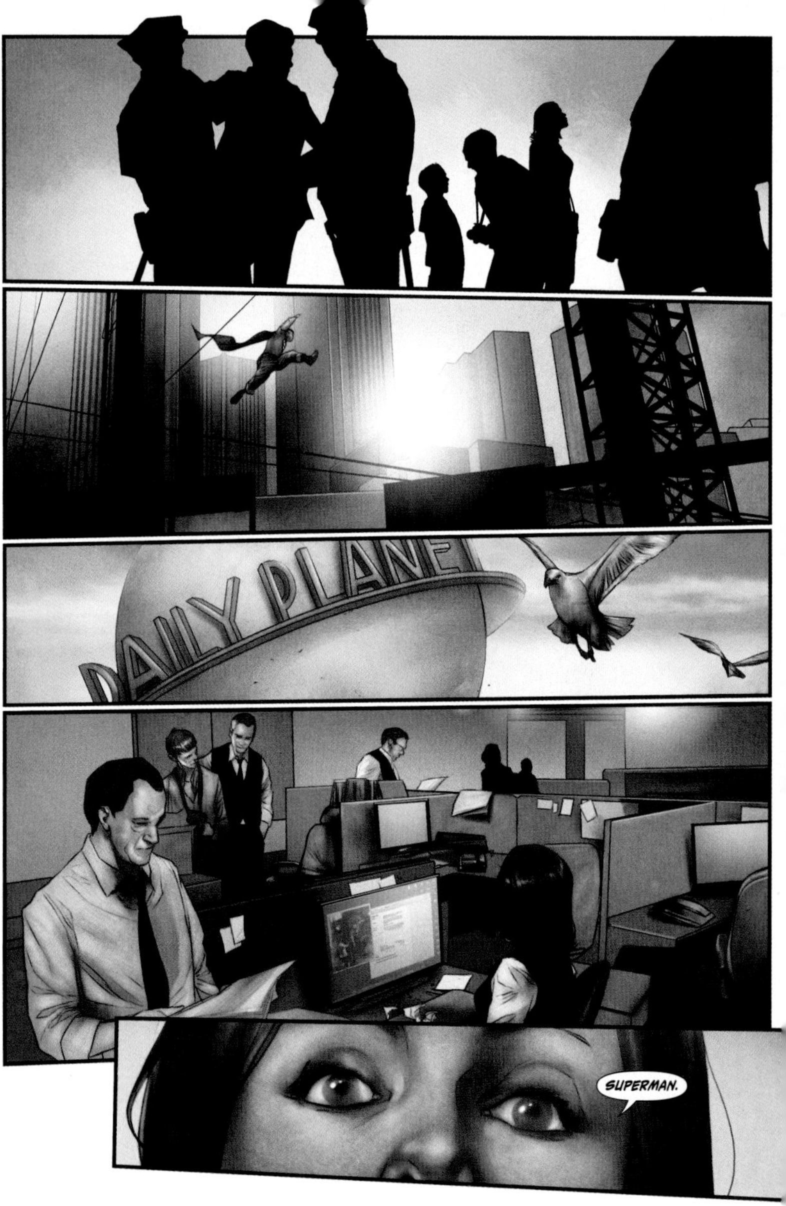
DAILY PLANET
SUPERMAN.

DC COMICS • THE NEW 52
JUSTICE LEAGUE ACTION FIGURES

KATANA & WONDER WOMAN 2-PACK	MARTIAN MANHUNTER	GREEN LANTERN SIMON BAZ	THE FLASH & VIBE 2-PACK
AUGUST 2013	JUNE 2013	IN STORES NOW	JULY 2013

DC COLLECTIBLES™

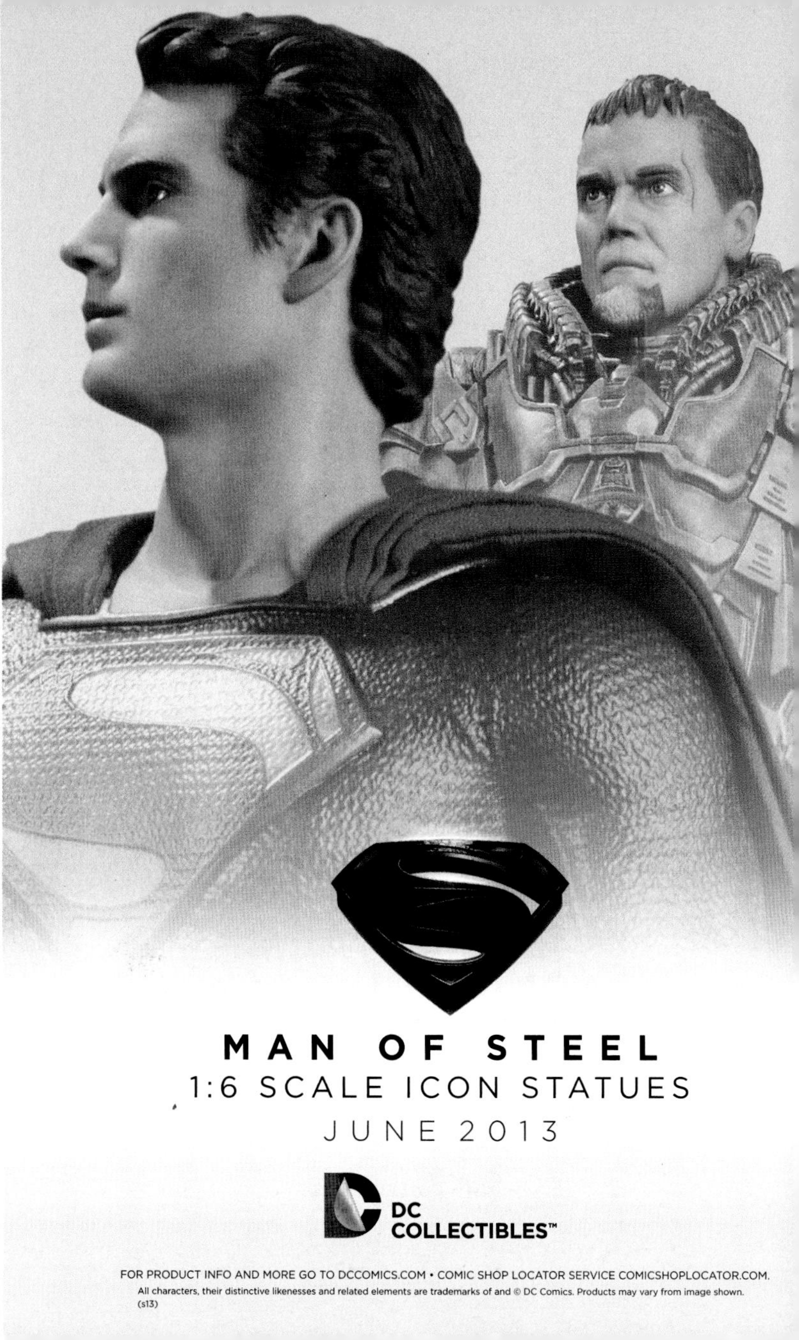

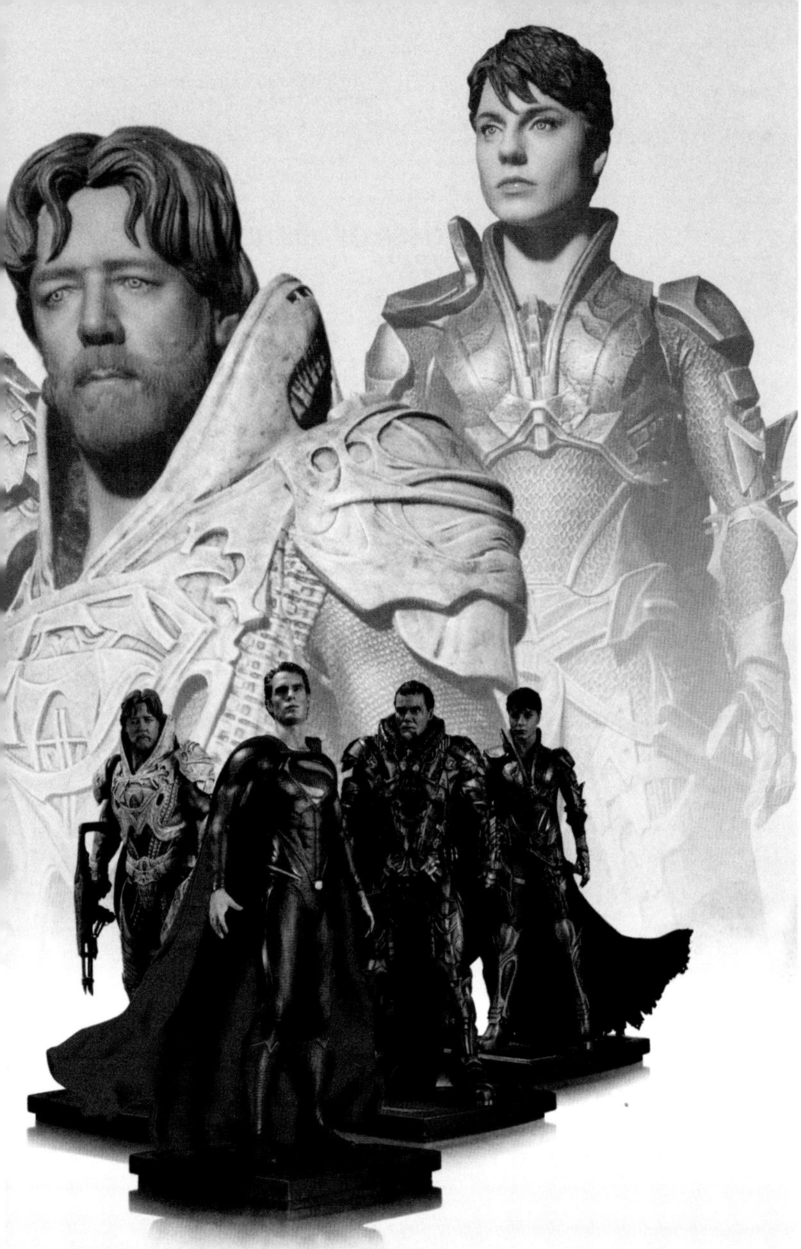

JOR EL SUPERMAN ZOD FAORA

FROM THE WRITER OF *JUSTICE LEAGUE* & *GREEN LANTERN*

GEOFF JOHNS
SUPERMAN: SECRET ORIGIN
with GARY FRANK

SUPERMAN: LAST SON

with RICHARD DONNER & ADAM KUBERT

SUPERMAN & THE LEGION OF SUPER-HEROES

with GARY FRANK

SUPERMAN: BRAINIAC

with GARY FRANK

START AT THE BEGINNING!

SUPERMAN: ACTION COMICS VOLUME 1: SUPERMAN AND THE MEN OF STEEL

SUPERMAN VOLUME 1: WHAT PRICE TOMORROW?

SUPERGIRL VOLUME 1: THE LAST DAUGHTER OF KRYPTON

SUPERBOY VOLUME 1: INCUBATION

GRANT MORRISON RAGS MORALES ANDY KUBERT